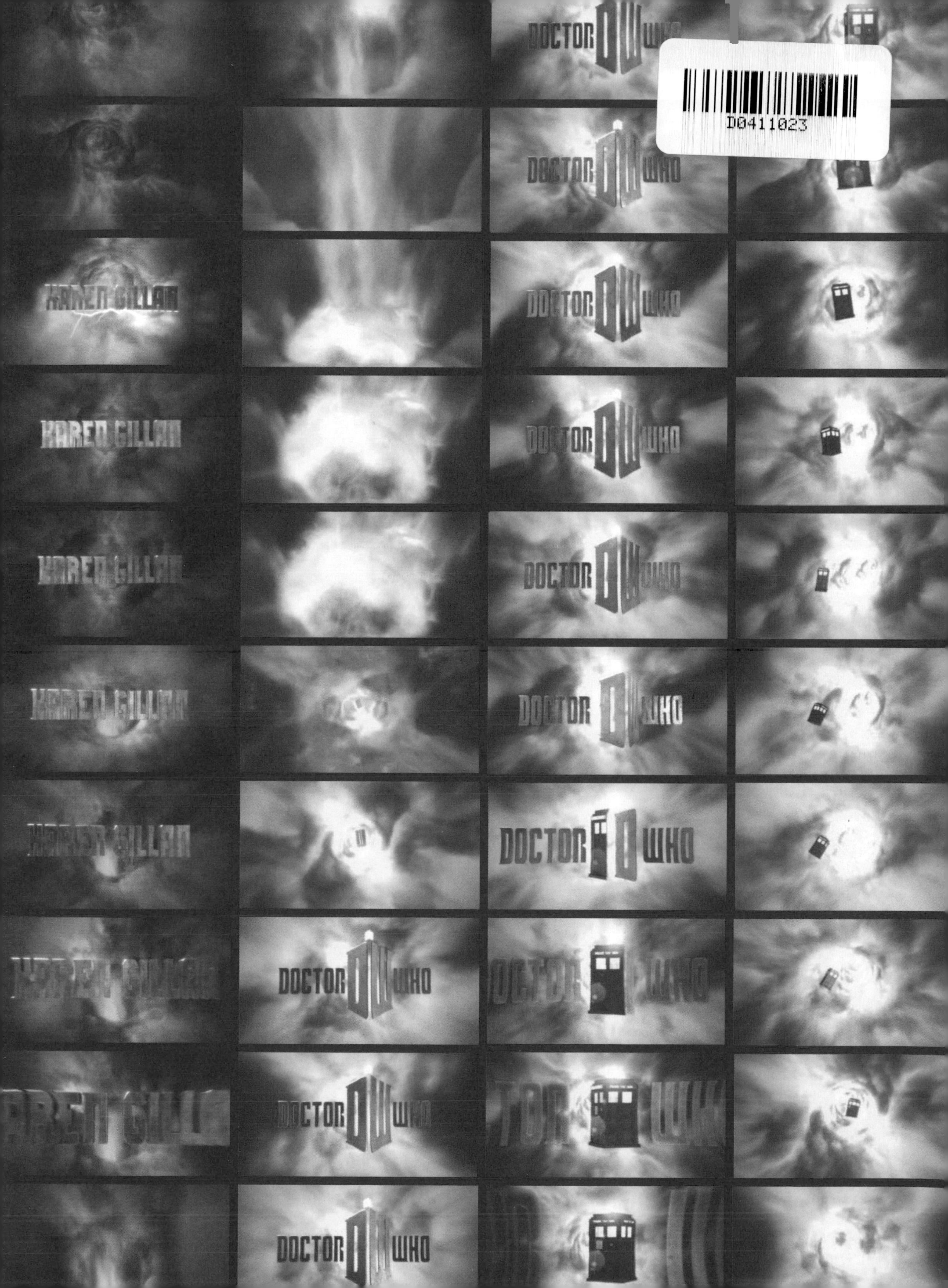
KAREN GILLAN
DOCTOR WHO

THE BRILLIANT BOOK 2011

EDITED BY **CLAYTON HICKMAN**
DESIGNED BY **PAUL LANG**

BBC BOOKS

THE BRILLIANT BOOK

CONTENTS

WELCOME TO **THE BRILLIANT BOOK OF DOCTOR WHO**

HE steps from the battered blue police box, this strange young man in the tweed jacket and bow tie, wild hair blowing in the alien breeze, his eyes bright and alert – he is the Doctor, the mysterious traveller in time and space, setting off on another adventure...

The Doctor looks young – but he is in fact over nine hundred years old. The last of his kind, he travels in the TARDIS – the initials stand for Time And Relative Dimension In Space – a fantastic machine, vastly bigger inside than out, which can take him anywhere and anywhen in the history of the universe. He claims he just wants a simple life, but somehow the TARDIS always seems to land him and his companions right in the middle of trouble. And a simple life wouldn't suit him – he's been exploring and adventuring for so long now, perhaps even he has forgotten why.

The Doctor is never still, never bored, never cruel or cowardly. He's not a man with a mission – he answers to no one, and simply tries to do what's best because it seems like the right thing to do. Despite his long, long life and experience, he never has a plan; he may seem disorganised and chaotic, even petulant or silly at times, but it would be a foolish enemy that underestimated him.

When the Doctor arrives, nothing stays the same. And then, just as suddenly as he arrived, he's gone. He can never remain in one place – there's always another adventure around the corner...

LITTLE Amelia Pond was only 7 years old when she met the Doctor, on the most magical – and terrifying – night of her young life. He promised to return for her five minutes later.

But it actually took him twelve years. Twelve long years in which Amy never quite gave up hope that the incredible stranger in the blue box might return to take her away in his mysterious box. And then one day it happened – the Doctor was suddenly back in the quiet English village of Leadworth, bringing excitement and terrible danger into Amy's life once more.

Two years later he returned again – on the night before Amy's wedding to Rory Williams, a young nurse at Leadworth Hospital. Amy gladly accepted the Doctor's offer to join him on his travels, and so began an incredible series of adventures. Perhaps because the Doctor has been such a large – if generally absent – presence in her life, Amy often refuses to show that she's impressed by him. But she'll plunge headlong straight into danger, because at heart she has an unshakeable faith in her childhood hero.

Rory was to join the crew of the TARDIS a little later – and at first sight he doesn't seem quite as fitted to a life of constant peril. But Rory loves Amy – and it took the Doctor to show Amy how much she loves Rory, too. Eventually, by the most circuitous route imaginable, the Doctor returned them both to Leadworth for their wedding. The first thing 'Mr and Mrs Pond' did was get back in the TARDIS – and trust the Doctor to take them off for even more amazing journeys...

WITHIN these pages, you'll find the whole story of the Doctor's adventures – from Churchill's bunker to the Wreck of the *Byzantium*, from a subterranean city of lizard people to a call centre in Colchester. *The Brilliant Book of Doctor Who* is your indispensable guide to the many worlds the TARDIS has visited. More than that, you can read about the wonders that never made it onto your TV screens. Read Churchill's secret diaries, discover the true nature of the New Dalek Paradigm, uncover the Doctor's previous history with Vampires and discover more about the Legend of the Constant Warrior. *The Brilliant Book* also takes you behind the scenes, to meet the actors, writers, producers, directors and musicians who bring the Doctor's world to life each Saturday evening. And they might, perhaps, let you know a few secrets about travels yet to come.

SO, what are you waiting for? The TARDIS doors are wide open and a whole universe of adventure is waiting for you inside...

"I want to visit the BOTTOM OF THE SEA"

Matt Smith, the man who *is* the Eleventh Doctor, shares his thoughts on wearing a fez, the Lost City of Atlantis, and keeping a tiger in the Pandorica...

THE Eleventh Doctor, he of the bow tie, waggling fingers and unruly hair, burst onto the nation's screens on New Year's Day 2010. He's had a busy year of it, what with crashing his TARDIS, turning up fourteen years late to pick up his new companion, accidentally helping to create a new Dalek Paradigm, battling Weeping Angels, meeting Van Gogh, working in a call centre and having to undo the total destruction of the universe by sacrificing his own life. There's never a dull moment.

It's been much the same for Matt Smith, the 27-year-old actor who is the latest in a long line to bring the Doctor to life. Though for Matt there have been fewer tussles with headless Cybermen beneath Stonehenge and more frantic line-learning in a Winnebego in Cardiff. In the last year Matt has been catapulted into the public eye, and with a schedule as jam-packed as his, we're lucky he's made time to talk to *The Brilliant Book of Doctor Who*. Even though he's late for our interview. Because he went shopping.

After all, even one of the most in-demand actors in the land has got to have some time to pick out the look everyone's going to be copying shortly. Because his Doctor certainly has a flair for fashion. And Matt himself is no different. Interviews with Matt Smith always start and end with a big manly hug, but we're not letting him off the hook that easily. We want to know what he's got in his shopping bags...

Matt, you slave to fashion!
Well, I was having a big shop this afternoon. Sorry about that, I just lost track of time. I got a sort of long smoking jacket. It's really, really cool. It was half price because it was in the sale, so I thought 'hurrah' and I went for it.

You pretty much shaped the Eleventh Doctor's look yourself – how does it feel to now have people stealing your style?
It's one of the things I really like. I think, 'Yay! People dress up as Doctor Who!' I take some sort of weird pleasure in that, to be honest.

You made bow ties cool – is there anything else you want to make cool?
If I made bow ties cool, that's cool. Yeah, bow ties and... ooh, what else? I quite like my brown boots, I'm quite into them. What else do I want to make cool? Nothing springs to mind immediately. There's talk maybe of a hat, a different jacket for the next series perhaps? I don't know, we're going to have to wait and see...

You could go back down the fez route...
The fez *was* cool! Listen, I'm open to anything. My palate is completely open on all fronts concerning hats and jackets. Any excuse to go shopping. As you've already found out!

Have you been inspired by any of your co-stars' fashions?
River Song's shoes from Episode 4! They are *amazing*, aren't they, those shoes? Really amazing. And what was so funny on set was the girls, Karen [Gillan] and Alex [Kingston], going 'Oh my god you've got *this* brand of shoe' – let's say they were Manolo Blahnik's or whatever – and I looked blank. I had no idea what they were, and they were both *appalled* that I didn't know. I was there sheepishly mumblng, 'Oh, is that what they're called...?'

Shoes aside, what's been your favourite moment of this last series?
I think perhaps Episode 12, when the Doctor's dragged into the Pandorica. I think that's a real highlight for me. Also, the first meeting with Amy Pond, the fish fingers and custard, I love that. And I liked showing Van Gogh the art, I think that's rather wonderful. And there's a scene in Episode 6 with Rosanna where the Doctor says, 'I'm a Time Lord, you're a big fish' – that whole scene I really liked. I really love it when the Doctor talks to little Amelia in Episode 13, when he goes back and she's sleeping. I think that's really brilliant writing and it was a joy to play.

And what most impressed you?
I think the production values on Episodes 12 and 13. I'm really proud of them – and actually throughout the series – but you know when you open the doors to the Pandorica chamber and they're these huge, massive doors... I think things like that help to sell it as a top quality show. Oh, and I think Karen's really brilliant in the scene when Rory dies. She really steps up. I just thought, 'Good on you, Kaz'. Looking back at the year as a whole, I'm just so pleased that we all did it and we all got on so well. That's probably my most impressive moment – the whole year!

From impressive to funny – what made you laugh most?
Karen was generally very funny in make-up. I had a great time with Vincent van Gogh, hanging out in the TARDIS waiting to come out for a take. Tony Curran was always very funny and would make rude jokes, which is marvellous. I loved going over to Croatia, too. I guess generally one of my favourite moments is when I first get a script, be it from from Steven [Moffat] or one of the other writers. The first read and you just go 'Wow!'.

Have you had an 'oh my God' moment?
Yeah, New York. When we did the screening for Episode 1 in New York. It was like 'whoah', because the crowds were insane and they were camping out and that was pretty mad. I think me, Karen and Steven were just like, 'Whoa, this is mental'.

What would you like to happen in the next series, or who would you like to see join the show?
I'd quite like to go to Atlantis. And who would I like to have in... Ian McKellen [best known as Gandalf in *Lord of the Rings*] would be quite fun, I think. [Footballer-turned-actor] Eric Cantona I'd quite like. Paddy Considine [star of *The Bourne Ultimatum*] is a wonderful actor. I'd love Lindsay Duncan [who played Adelaide Brooke in *The Waters of Mars*] to come back, I know that's quite hard, but isn't she a *dream*? I'd like Van Gogh to come back, too.

So if you had a TARDIS...
...I'd go to Atlantis, to the bottom of the ocean and to see the dinosaurs. I think it's the mythology of the sea for me, really, which is amazing. And it's water. I like the idea that it's all underwater, it has a magic to it. I like the idea of taking the TARDIS down into the ocean. Think where the TARDIS could get to! But the

"STEVEN MOFFAT CHANGES THE WAY YOU SEE THE WORLD A LITTLE BIT, AS GREAT WRITERS DO"

reality of it is that it would cost loads of money to make.

Will things change now there's a married couple in the TARDIS?
Well, I don't know. It's a first, isn't it? I think the Doctor will sort of always rule the roost and I think that Amy will always rule the roost with Rory. I think it will be very interesting, the shift in the balance of power. I don't think the fact they're married will make a huge amount of difference.

Is the Doctor going to be a gooseberry?
I think he's always a bit of a gooseberry. But I think he'll get on with it as he does. He's far more interested in the structure of stars than he is in girls.

After this series, do you look at cracks differently?
Yes, I do, actually. I think that's the beauty of Steven Moffat. He changes the way you see the world a little bit, which is what great writers do.

If you had a Pandorica, what would you keep in it?
Oh, that's a good question. Are you keeping something in there that you've got to stop getting out, or can you use it as a little storage room?

It's up to you! Karen said she'd put herself in it so she could live for ever.
Wow, that'd be pretty lonely. Maybe I'd put Karen in it so she could live for ever! Because then her wish would come true and my wish would come true – she'd be immortal. So Karen maybe... What else is there? A tiger, perhaps, so they don't become extinct, but I'd want to make sure that he was fed and watered. And a TV or something so he could watch David Attenborough. Also, I'd have to jazz it up for whoever was going to be in there.

Amelia was scared of cracks as a child – what scared you?
Spiders and the dark.

Do they still scare you?
Not the dark as much, but spiders still do. Even though I'm completely fascinated by them at the same time.

You know there was a *Doctor Who* story in the 1970s with giant spiders...
I know, that sounds amazing. Maybe I'll moot it to Herr Moffatt.

You've mentioned often that you enjoyed the classic story *The Tomb of the Cybermen*. Have there been other original stories that you watched...
...And really sort of loved? Yeah, that one with Tom Baker in Paris, *City of Death*, that's a cool one.

The First Doctor, William Hartnell, claimed that in his head he knew what all the TARDIS controls did. Do you?
Yeah, absolutely, I absolutely know what every button does *[lists a lot of very technical terms]*. I really do! There's a manual!

What's on your MP3 player now?
Ooh, that's a good question. Led Zeppelin, *Going To California*.

Finally, there have been lots of crazy *Doctor Who* rumours recently. Will you help *The Brilliant Book* start a new one?
Yes! Let's start a crazy rumour! Steven Moffatt wears coloured underpants. That's just me being mean to poor Steven, isn't it?

Well he's been mean about you...
He's very mean isn't he? Hm. A *Doctor Who* rumour... I know! River Song's going to turn into a wombat! That's a mad one!

FAQ

FULL NAME
Matthew Robert Smith
DATE OF BIRTH
28 October 1982
HOME TOWN
Northampton
FIRST WHO APPEARANCE
The End of Time, Part Two, 1 January 2010
WHO FACT
Matt planned to be a professional football player, but took up acting after he suffered a serious back injury

EPISODE 1

The Eleventh Hour

BY STEVEN MOFFAT

THE STORY

The TARDIS crash lands in Amelia Pond's garden – and the newly regenerated Doctor is just in time to check out the mysterious crack in her bedroom wall. But a quick spin in the TARDIS ends up taking twelve years, and the grown-up Amy isn't exactly over the moon to see her Raggedy Doctor back.

Never mind that, though – the TARDIS is out of action, the sonic screwdriver is burnt to a crisp, and the Doctor's regeneration isn't quite complete. And now, the alien Atraxi are getting ready to incinerate planet Earth, unless they can recapture the escaped Prisoner Zero.

Twenty minutes to save the world – and only one man's up to the job...

MAGIC MOMENT

The Doctor is tossing Amy something. She catches it. And she stares and stares at – the apple. The one she gave the Doctor, with the smiling face freshly cut into it.

THE DOCTOR: I'm the Doctor. I'm a time traveller. Everything I told you twelve years ago is true. I'm real. What's happening in the sky is real! And if you don't let me go right now, everything you've ever known is over.
AMY: I don't believe you.
THE DOCTOR: Twenty minutes. Just believe me for twenty minutes.

He grabs her wrist. The apple is still in her hand – he holds it up to her face.

THE DOCTOR: Look at it. Fresh as the day you gave it to me. And you know it's the same one.

On Amy and the Doctor – and it's like the world around them has gone away.

THE DOCTOR: Amy. Believe for twenty minutes.

On Amy: fighting everything inside her. Then:
She raises the keys, unlocks the car. The Doctor is freed.

AMY: What do we do?
THE DOCTOR: Follow that nurse!

FAMILIAR FACES

ANNETTE CROSBIE

Mrs Angelo

Annette was the long-suffering Margaret, wife of Victor Meldrew, in BBC sitcom *One Foot in the Grave*.

OLIVIA COLMAN

Coma patient/ Prisoner Zero

Olivia has appeared in comedy shows such as *Peep Show*, *Green Wing* and *Look Around You*.

WHERE IN THE WORLD?

The leafy Cardiff district of Llandaff and the Welsh village of Rhymney stood in for sleepy little Leadworth.

SPOT THE CRACK

Right there on Amelia's bedroom wall – but also take a close look at the TARDIS monitor near the end of the story...

NUMBER CRUNCHING

12 The number of years between Amy's first and second meeting with the Doctor.

4 *The number of psychiatrists Amy saw in that time.*

FANTASTIC FACTS

» It's not unusual for the Doctor to suffer from a spot of 'post-regenerative trauma'. In fact, the last time he changed faces – in *The Christmas Invasion* (2005) – he had to spend hours and hours in bed to recover! » Back in *The Invasion of Time* (1978), we saw the TARDIS's swimming pool in all its glory – but no library. In The TV Movie (1996), the Doctor seems to have fitted some huge bookshelves to the walls of his new control room. Maybe that was part of the library? All TARDISes are fitted with architectural configuration technology (as seen in *Castrovalva*, 1982), with which the interior rooms can be shuffled around, redecorated or even deleted – this explains the new-look control room here. » The TARDIS's cloister bell rings whenever the ship is in grave danger. Here, it rings when the TARDIS's engines start phasing. We first heard it in *Logopolis* (1981), signalling dire events in the Fourth Doctor's future. Other causes have included the TARDIS careering towards the explosion that created the universe (*Castrovalva*) and the Master turning the Doctor's ship into a Paradox Machine (*The Sound of Drums*, 2007). » Young Amelia 'doesn't have a mum and dad' and, years later, she seems a little vague on the layout of her own home. All of this – along with the fleeting shadow we glimpse as Amelia's waiting outside for the Doctor – is explained in *The Big Bang*. » Perception filters, such as the one disguising the 'extra' room in Amy's house, were first mentioned in *Human Nature* (2007). The fob watch containing the Doctor's memories was disguised with one, so he could hide from the Family of Blood. » This isn't the first time the sonic screwdriver has been blown to smithereens: see also *The Visitation* (1982) and *Smith and Jones* (2007). » The Doctor mentions another of the Shadow Proclamation's articles – just like he did back in *Rose* (2005). The Shadow Proclamation are intergalactic lawmakers, and we meet them in *The Stolen Earth* (2008). » During the Doctor's confrontation with the Atraxi, we all of his previous incarnations: William Hartnell (1963–1966), Patrick Troughton (1966–1969), Jon Pertwee (1970–1974), Tom Baker (1974–1981), Peter Davison (1982–1984), Colin Baker (1984–1986), Sylvester McCoy (1987–1989, 1996), Paul McGann (1996), Christopher Eccleston (2005) and David Tennant (2005–2010).

BEHIND THE SCENES

STEVEN MOFFAT

Writer

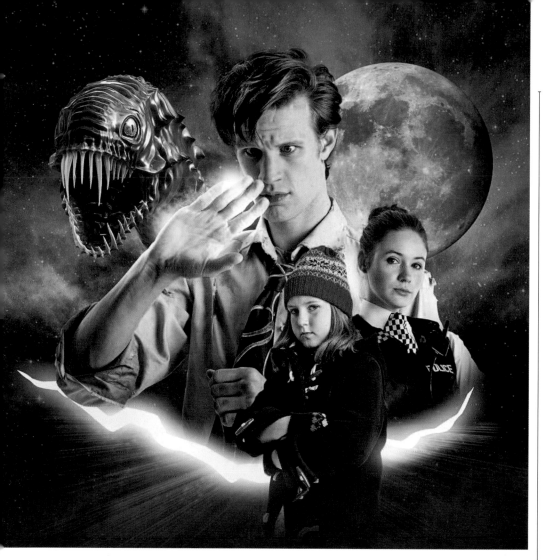

Where did you get the idea for the cracks in the universe?
The wall above my son's bed! I came up with the whole idea for *The Eleventh Hour* before I'd actually accepted the job as Russell's successor, but this was the most difficult script I've had to write because it had to do so much in such a short space of time.

Was it difficult establishing a new Doctor when there's nobody in this story he's ever met before to react to this new incarnation?
It just means that the Doctor has to shine – to be so completely Doctor-y from the first second that everyone he meets is completely mesmerised by this man. Never mind who he used to be, Matt Smith's Doctor becomes Amelia's whole world within a few minutes. And I've seen Matt manage that with rooms full of grown journalists, so it wasn't a big ask really...

Did you have the series' whole story planned in your head from the start? Or did you leave yourself some 'wiggle room'?
Oh, tons of wiggle room. But with fixed points. A bit like time travel, really.

DELETED!

THE DOCTOR: *(Exploring the new TARDIS's console)* Oh that's how you do it! Now I get it! This would have saved a lot of trouble.
AMY: What is it?
THE DOCTOR: The steering wheel! Nine hundred years, I should've read the manual. Wonder how it works?

VILLAGE PROFILE

This is Leadworth

Leadworth! A unique and special village in the heart of beautiful Gloucestershire, and all just thirty minutes' drive from the hustle and bustle of Gloucester...

THE 17th-century poet Sir Thomas Mapplethorpe once wrote, *Leadworth, o Leadworth! Place of enchanted soil and healthful air*, and nothing has changed since then.

Leadworth is home to the Royal Leadworth Hospital. Founded in 1904, the Royal Leadworth serves the local community and many neighbouring towns and villages, and contains the largest coma ward in the whole of Gloucestershire.

Visit our beautiful 13th-century Parish church, rebuilt in the 14th, 15th and 16th centuries following fires, but still standing!

Take it easy on our traditional village green surrounded by shops and a café. Here, in July, you'll find the Tudor market and, in August, the village fête. Or rest your legs and take advantage of our many benches with their delightful views of Leadworth, including our scenic 19th-century duck pond.

DID YOU KNOW...
The name Leadworth comes from the nearby River Leadon, and the old English word 'worth', meaning an enclosure or homestead

DID YOU KNOW...
Harry Potter author J.K. Rowling grew up in Tutshill, just forty miles from Leadworth

Around the village

Feeling peckish? The village café serves a delicious selection of hot and cold home-cooked meals. *(Closed all day Sunday, all day Tuesday, and from 2pm Wednesday.)*

Fancy yourself as the next Will Young? Friday night is Karaoke Night at the Wig And Cravat, Leadworth's leading nightspot!

Two fat ladies, eighty-eight! It's bingo night at Leadworth Community Centre, every other Wednesday! *(Contact Portia Davis at Leadworth Community Centre for details.)*

Feeling adventurous? No visit to Leadworth would be complete without a trip along the Leadworth Trail to Upper Leadworth! Explore the ruins, or play on the swings! It doesn't matter whether you're 8 or 80 – the fun never ends in Upper Leadworth!

So whether you want to sit back and chillax, enjoy the finest food and hospitality this side of the Cotswolds, or urgently send that postcard to your nearest and dearest, Leadworth is the place to be!

16 AROUND GLOUCESTERSHIRE

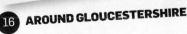

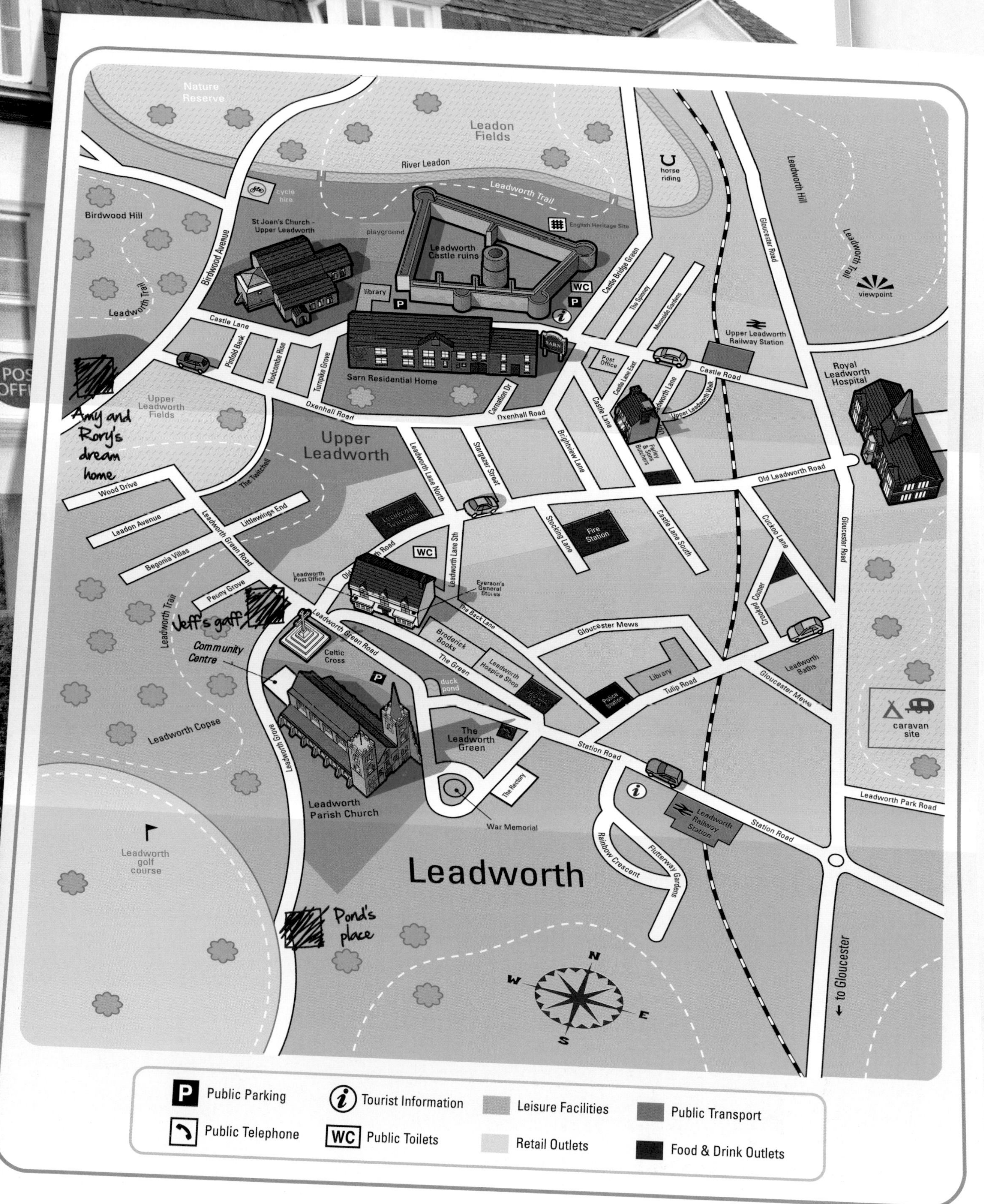

Nature Reserve
Leadon Fields
River Leadon
horse riding
Leadworth Hill
cycle hire
Leadworth Trail
Birdwood Hill
St Joan's Church - Upper Leadworth
playground
Leadworth Castle ruins
English Heritage Site
Gloucester Road
Birdwood Avenue
library
Castle Bridge Green
The Spinney
Moonside Gardens
viewpoint
Castle Lane
Pinfold Bank
Hodcombe Rise
Turnpike Grove
Sarn Residential Home
Upper Leadworth Railway Station
Post Office
Castle Road
Royal Leadworth Hospital
Upper Leadworth Fields
Oxenhall Road
Carnation Dr
Castle Lane
Brightview Lane
Amy and Rory's dream home
Upper Leadworth
Leadworth Lane North
Stargazer Street
Old Leadworth Road
Wood Drive
The Twitchell
Leadon Avenue
Littlewings End
Leadworth Green Road
Stocking Lane
Fire Station
Castle Lane South
Cuckoo Lane
Begonia Villas
Leadworth Lane Sth
Peony Grove
Leadworth Post Office
Everson's General Stores
The Back Lane
Crooked Corner
Jeff's gaff
Leadworth Trail
Community Centre
Celtic Cross
Leadworth Green Road
Broderick Books
Gloucester Mews
Leadworth Hospice Shop
The Green
duck pond
Library
Tulip Road
Police Station
Leadworth Baths
caravan site
Leadworth Copse
The Leadworth Green
Station Road
Leadworth Grove
The Rectory
Leadworth Parish Church
War Memorial
Leadworth Railway Station
Leadworth Park Road
Leadworth golf course
Rainbow Crescent
Flutterway Gardens
Leadworth
Pond's place
N
W
E
S
← to Gloucester
Public Parking
Tourist Information
Leisure Facilities
Public Transport
Public Telephone
Public Toilets
Retail Outlets
Food & Drink Outlets

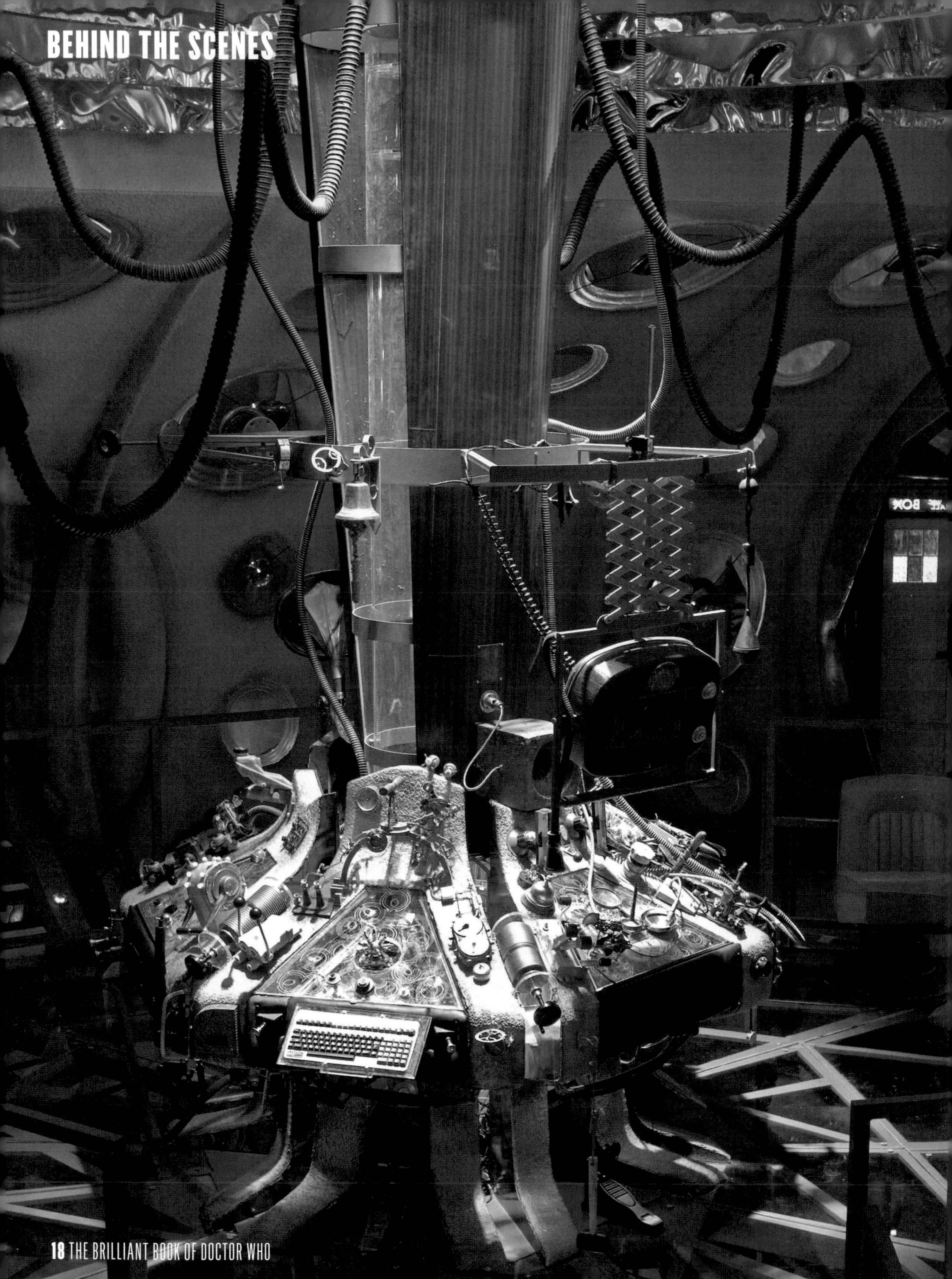

DOCTOR WHO | ART DEPARTMENT

THE TARDIS

MOST TV production designers dream of reimagining the Doctor's preferred mode of transport through time and space, the TARDIS. Edward Thomas has been lucky enough to do it twice. In 2004, the quietly-spoken Welshman pulled together a bunch of creatives including renowned comic-book artist Bryan Hitch, with the brief of creating a TARDIS for the new millennium.

'It was a real team effort,' recalls Edward now. 'We worked out of a tiny office at BBC Wales in Llandaff, Cardiff. I headed up the team, with supervising art director Stephen Nicholas and a core group of concept artists and draftsmen.'

That 2004 design represented a combination of the different designers' specialities and disciplines. 'The TARDIS interior had to suggest a very technical machine, so you want a very technical designer,' says Edward. 'Our man Dan Walker came from an automotive background, so he made sure the TARDIS really felt as though it could be a flying machine and that the switches actually did something. But then something like that could easily seem *too* technical and start looking like a vehicle. So then you need a designer with more of a free flow. We brought in Colin Richmond, who's a theatre designer with the Royal Shakespeare Company among others. He had a much more organic, loose feel to things, so all of a sudden the structure became much looser. Then you've got Bryan Hitch with his early concept drawings and Matt Savage filling in little details like the roundels. So when you amalgamated

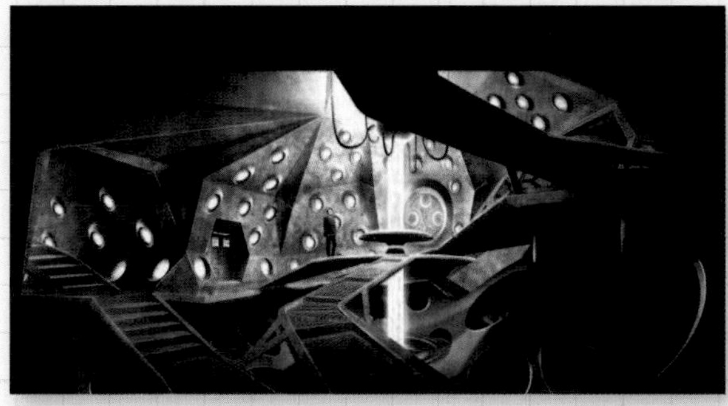

everything, the TARDIS design became very successful.'

Five years later, when it came to redesigning the TARDIS inside and out, Edward 'pulled together as many of the original team as possible. Dan, Matthew and Ben were joined by series concept artist Shaun Williams, along with set decorator Julian Luxton, my associate designer James North and right-hand man Stephen Nicholas. It was a first-class team, ready to rethink the whole concept of this now hugely successful show.'

Being a man who exudes Zen calm, Edward took the oncoming TARDIS interior/exterior change in his stride.

'We always knew the executive producers Steven Moffat, Piers Wenger and Beth Willis wanted to put their own stamp on the look of the TARDIS. Steven had some firm

ideas on what he wanted: "I want it bigger!" I'll admit there were mixed emotions. Following the success of the first series, the TARDIS police box and the interior set had become very close to our hearts: something we were all really proud of. But studio space is very limited, so it was out with the old and in with the new, and this one was going to be bigger than anything we had previously built in our Upper Boat Studio.'

As the TARDIS exterior is such an iconic piece of British design, Edward concedes 'it is a huge challenge in knowing when to stop. That's the key to doing what I call a "Mini Cooper": it's not what you *do* change, it's more about what you *don't*. I put the TARDIS box in the same league as the Daleks and Cybermen in terms of iconography, so we kept to the same formula of "If it ain't broke then don't fix it". We referenced the old boxes and reverted back to white window frames and the St John Ambulance logo, as per Steven's request. All the key measurements remained identical to the 2005 box, and we went for smoked glass in the windows in order to reflect the environment the TARDIS was in.

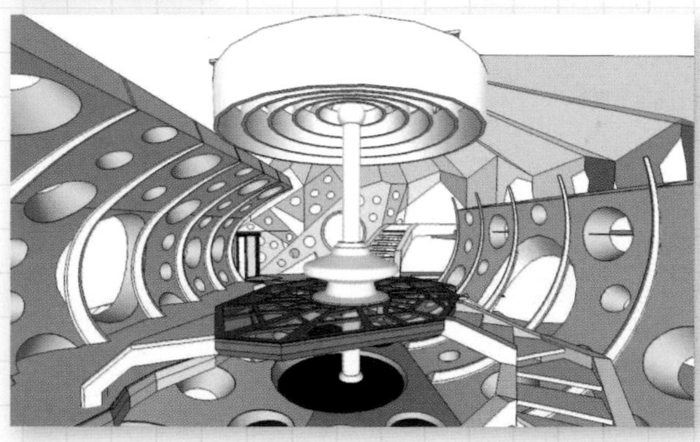

The windows then have flat light sources behind them so we can light them up in night scenes, to show her off in all her glory!'

EDWARD found a curious kind of inspiration for the new interior's design, while on holiday in Mauritius. 'I took a photograph of some rainwater falling from a tin roof against the night sky,' he says. 'This abstract image of water droplets frozen in time [reproduced above] became instrumental in our thought process. It was our key reference that we reverted to, time after time. Each droplet represented a room of the TARDIS – each one falling into alignment whenever it was called upon.'

Edward and James North spent several days scouring through various images from books and the internet.

'We pinned the water droplet image up on the wall,' says Edward, 'along with thousands of other references. Each day, we'd refocus our thought process and pull images down and put new ones up. Over the next week or so, with the help of Dan and Matthew, the wall of reference was gradually replaced with sketches and concepts of the potential new space, until we finally arrived at a concept we could start structurally working with.'

The new TARDIS interior was a triumph against a tight schedule and budget. 'The brief of "bigger" gave us all kinds of problems,' says Edward. 'We ran the set to the extremities of the studio, building around the steel frame left behind by the old Torchwood Hub to save costs. The Hub had been a major build, but since the *Torchwood* series had finished filming, the structure had been reused as various reincarnations, including the Mars base in the *Doctor Who* special *The Waters of Mars*. We stripped all of the cladding back and began sketching away, using a digital 3D model of the framework as our guide. I was always keen to make the console the Doctor's altar within our cathedral of time and space, and the huge glass platform, with the time rotor piercing through it, gave a true sense that the world revolved around the control room and its abilities.'

Edward hails Ben Austin as 'my key set designer. Ben took the 3D model of the steel work and began working in all the elements from our concepts. With my construction manager Mathew Hywel-Davies champing at the bit, we were desperate to sign things off with the execs. We threw together a huge card model with all hands on deck. With the glue still tacky we presented our new creation to Steven, Beth and Piers!'

Having gained a welcome thumbs-up, Edward and his team spent the next fortnight 'fine tuning and designing the console in more detail. Shaun Williams worked closely with my decorator Julian Luxton on the console's concept. Each day, more and more fantastic items came through the door.'

The result, as you'll have seen, was more than worthy of Amy Pond's delighted astonishment at the end of *The Eleventh Hour*. The new Doctor has a time machine to be proud of.

FROZEN IN TIME

The Doctor's TARDIS interior has changed several times since the show began in 1963. Yet certain design elements remain constant...

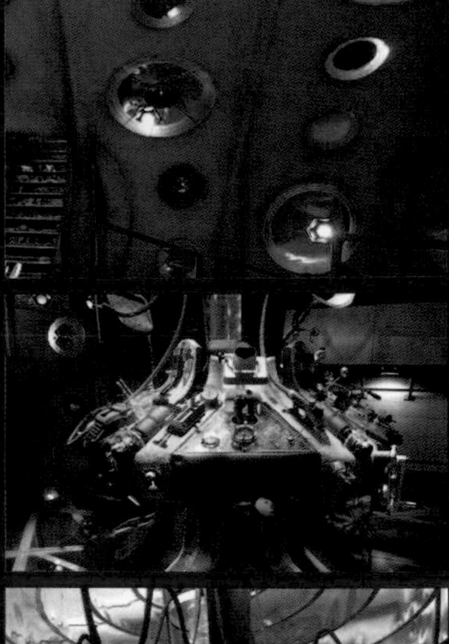

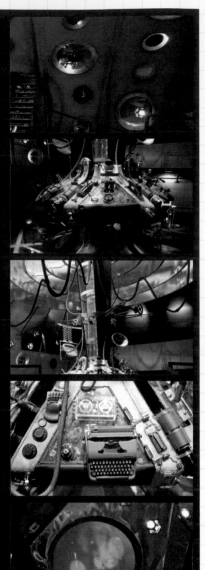

ROUNDELS

Circular shapes, embedded in the walls. Occasionally removed to reveal vital components. Those moments aside, the roundels' primary function is to look nice!

HEXAGONAL CONSOLE

This same basic shape has stayed consistent for almost 50 years. In 2008's episode *Journey's End*, the multi-sided format was finally explained: the TARDIS was originally intended to be flown by six operators.

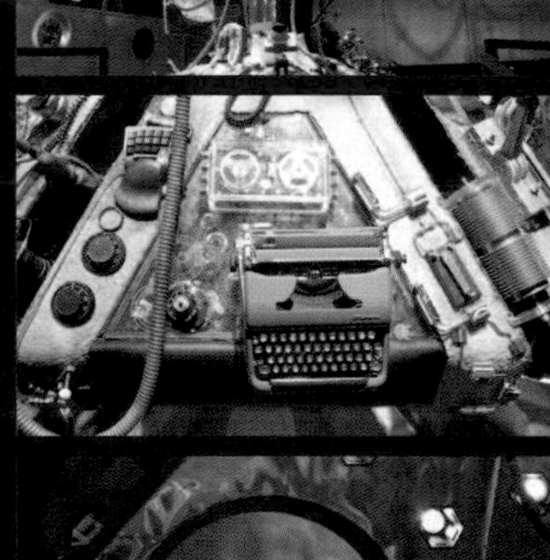

TIME ROTOR

Largely transparent column, sometimes called the 'time column'. The internal motion of the time rotor signifies that the TARDIS is moving.

RETRO TECHNOLOGY

Despite being probably *the* most iconic sci-fi ship ever, the TARDIS console rarely looks entirely futuristic. Low-tech and/or eccentric items are never too far away, such as the old-fashioned typewriter in the current design.

SCANNER SCREEN

Wall-mounted device (although from 2005–10 it was attached to the console) allowing the Doctor and his companion(s) to see outside and judge whether they fancy leaving the TARDIS. They generally do!

THE
DOCTOR
BOX

EPISODE 2

The Beast Below

BY STEVEN MOFFAT

THE STORY

Amy gets a crash course in time travel when the Doctor takes her to the far future, to see the destiny of the British people. Crowded aboard Starship UK, the Brits are drifting through the galaxy on a spaceship that just shouldn't work. How can a huge starship move without any engines?

But that's not the only mystery. Why are the children of Starship UK so frightened? What secrets are the creepy Smilers guarding? And just why has the gun-toting monarch Liz 10 chosen to forget all about the Beast Below?

The Doctor reckons he has all the answers – but even he is overwhelmed by the horrifying truth. So, thank heavens he's got the quick-thinking Amy Pond at his side...

MAGIC MOMENT

The Doctor, Amy and Mandy duck down – the corridor behind them, grinning Smilers advancing from the shadows...

On Liz. Blam blam blam blam blam blam! The Smilers, crashing to the floor, sparking and exploding. On Liz, relaxing as the last of them falls. Smiles, looks down at the Doctor. (The others are now crouched at her feet – just to avoid the gunfire, but the effect is of grovelling courtiers.)

LIZ: I'm the bloody Queen, mate.

She spins the guns round her fingers, slams them into the holsters.

LIZ: Basically, I rule.

FAMILIAR FACES

SOPHIE OKONEDO

Liz 10

Sophie was nominated for an Oscar for her role as Tatiana in the 2004 movie *Hotel Rwanda*.

TERRENCE HARDIMAN

Hawthorne

From 1996 to 1998, Terrence played the scary villain in the kids' show *The Demon Headmaster*.

WHAT WE LEARN ABOUT THE DOCTOR

We're not really the ones learning about the Doctor this time; but Amy starts to understand a great deal. As exciting and interesting as the adventure is, for Amy it's about trying to figure this man out – and it's always exciting to see someone new make that journey. Plus it's crucial to this story, and how it resolves, that Amy understands the man she's run away with.

UNSEEN ADVENTURES

According to Liz 10, the Doctor took afternoon tea with our current monarch Queen Elizabeth II, hung out with Henry XII, and made a lie of Elizabeth I's nickname. In fact, the Doctor's dalliance with 'The Virgin Queen' was last mentioned at the start of *The End of Time*, Part One – and may explain Elizabeth's furious reaction on seeing him at the end of *The Shakespeare Code* (2007).

NUMBER CRUNCHING

1989 AMY POND IS BORN

1,308 *Amy's age, according to Starship UK's electoral roll.*

3297 THE YEAR IN WHICH THIS STORY IS SET.

» The Earth was ravaged by solar flares in the 29th century, leading to the evacuation of the planet aboard the nation-starships. But four centuries have passed since then (see *Number Crunching*), and these aren't the only humans cluttering up the spaceways in this era. At this time, humanity is spread across the galaxy, hunting for vital natural resources and founding new colonies. In the centuries leading up to Earth's evacuation, humans travel to the Sense Sphere *(The Sensorites,* 1964*)*, found a colony on Delta Magna *(The Power of Kroll,* 1978-1979*)* and establish the Nerva navigational beacon at the limits of the Solar System *(Revenge of the Cybermen,* 1975*)*. And, somewhere among the stars, thremmatologist Professor Sarah Lasky is hoping to make her name with the discovery of a brand new source of food *(Terror of the Vervoids,* 1986*)*... **»** Liz 10 reminds the Doctor of his disastrous run-in with Queen Victoria in *Tooth and Claw* (2006), during which he was 'knighted and exiled... on the same day!'. **»** Is the Doctor a parent? Amy asks him just that, but he seems reluctant to answer. The Doctor told Rose in *Fear Her* (2006) that he 'was a dad once' – but this shouldn't really come as a surprise, considering we met his granddaughter in the very first *Doctor Who* story, *An Unearthly Child* (1963). **»** When Amy asks him about the fate of his people, the Doctor gives a brief précis of the Time War: 'There was a bad day, bad stuff happened.' You need look no further than *The End of Time,* Parts One and Two (2009-2010*)* to find out exactly how bad that day was. **»** Liz 10 describes herself as 'not technically a British subject', so the role of the British monarch hasn't changed much in 1,300 years. Queen Elizabeth II is equally not a British subject – after all, we're her subjects! The Queen isn't considered a British citizen partly because of her elevated position in society, and partly because she's not just the Queen of Britain. Could Liz 10 also be the monarch of Starships Canada, Australia and Jamaica? **»** The work tent Amy investigates stands outside a branch of Magpie Electricals. The ill-fated Mr Magpie's legacy obviously still persists, more than 1,000 years after Doctor met him in *The Idiot's Lantern* (2006). (Incidentally, Captain Jack Harkness, Martha Jones and Wilfred Mott also own Magpie-brand TVs. And so does the Doctor!)

FANTASTIC FACTS

BEHIND THE SCENES
STEVEN MOFFAT
Writer

Would you say this is one of the scarier stories of the series?
To be honest, I never quite know how scary they're going to be. Yes, this one's got its scary moments – but it's also a big, mad, fantasy of an episode. A sort of Roald Dahl episode – lots of humour, quite black, some good twists and turns. And our first chance to see Amy Pond and her Doctor stepping out of the TARDIS and setting the universe to rights!

The Smilers look like they were inspired by those funfair fortune-telling booths...
Oh, very much funfair, yes. There's nothing creepier than something than something that's supposed to look friendly and human, and doesn't manage either. Or something that was once shiny but is starting to crack! Ohh, dolls, they just shouldn't smile...

DELETED!

AMY: What's it like in your brain?
THE DOCTOR: A great big rollercoaster, packed full of geniuses, all going wheeee!

SPOT THE CRACK

As the TARDIS departs, the crooked smile is visible glowing on the hull of Starship UK.

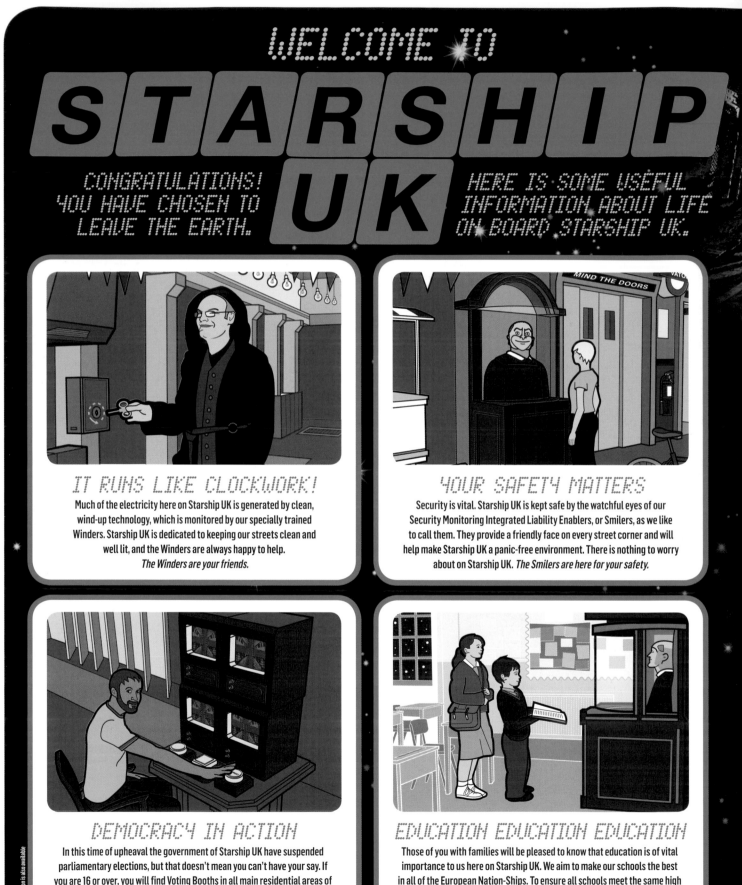

WELCOME TO STARSHIP

CONGRATULATIONS! YOU HAVE CHOSEN TO LEAVE THE EARTH.

HERE IS SOME USEFUL INFORMATION ABOUT LIFE ON BOARD STARSHIP UK.

IT RUNS LIKE CLOCKWORK!

Much of the electricity here on Starship UK is generated by clean, wind-up technology, which is monitored by our specially trained Winders. Starship UK is dedicated to keeping our streets clean and well lit, and the Winders are always happy to help. *The Winders are your friends.*

YOUR SAFETY MATTERS

Security is vital. Starship UK is kept safe by the watchful eyes of our Security Monitoring Integrated Liability Enablers, or Smilers, as we like to call them. They provide a friendly face on every street corner and will help make Starship UK a panic-free environment. There is nothing to worry about on Starship UK. *The Smilers are here for your safety.*

DEMOCRACY IN ACTION

In this time of upheaval the government of Starship UK have suspended parliamentary elections, but that doesn't mean you can't have your say. If you are 16 or over, you will find Voting Booths in all main residential areas of Starship UK. Here you can learn about the important issues facing us as we journey into the stars, and let your voice be heard by choosing to FORGET*.

*A PROTEST option is also available

EDUCATION EDUCATION EDUCATION

Those of you with families will be pleased to know that education is of vital importance to us here on Starship UK. We aim to make our schools the best in all of the European Nation-Ships. To ensure all schools meet the same high standards, classes are taught by specially programmed Smiler units, providing a friendly face for your child every day. *The Smilers are here for your safety.*

SMILES PER HOUR

Getting about on Starship UK couldn't be easier. The Vators provide fast, clean transit around our new home, and all Vators are monitored by Smilers, making your journey that little bit safer. Please note that the lower levels of Starship UK are off limits. These decks house the engine and maintenance facilities and are unsafe for civilians. *Do NOT attempt access to the lower levels.*

NATIONAL TREASURES

Though we may be travelling through the stars, the UK just wouldn't be the same without some of its familiar landmarks. That's why the National Trust has preserved some of our greatest treasures, rebuilding each with a painstaking attention to detail. Stonehenge, Buckingham Palace, the Colossus of Swindon, and many more are all here for you and your family to enjoy.

DOs and DON'Ts

We want your time on Starship UK to be as comfortable and safe as possible, so here are some handy tips on how to make life here more agreeable. For all of us.

We're in this together. Communities build happiness. Everybody needs good neighbours.

Be good. Rules keep us safe. (See separate 600-page document, 'Rules And Regulations For Starship UK' for full details.)

The Smilers are here for your safety. They keep a careful eye on all of us, 24 hours a day, 7 days a week. Don't worry – they don't miss a thing.

The Winders are your friends. They are here to help. But remember they have important work to do – never interrupt a Winder while he is winding.

Keep calm and carry on. It's the British way, after all!

Do not drop litter. Keep Starship UK tidy. Those who drop litter will face on-the-spot penalties.

There is nothing of interest below the habitation decks. Trespassers will face on-the-spot penalties.

Do not approach or touch the Smilers. They are the property of Starship UK. Anyone caught touching or defacing a Smiler unit will face on-the-spot penalties.

Any area designated 'OFF LIMITS' or 'RESTRICTED ACCESS', regardless of location, is for authorised personnel only. Anyone caught in a restricted area will face on-the-spot penalties.

STARSHIP UK – A FUTURE SAFE FOR ALL OF US!

The Vators are provided by Vatorverse, sponsored by McLintock Candy Burgers. *If it's sweet and it's a burger, it must be a McLintock!*

The National Trust is sponsored by Lancashire Sector Tea-Flavoured Hot Drink. *For a cuppa that's worth owt, choose Lancashire Sector.*

Starship UK's schools are sponsored by Junior Derekon, the happiness supplement for those aged 16 and under. *You won't go wrong with Derekon.*

"My secret's out. I LOVE THE BAGPIPES!"

Karen Gillan, who plays the frankly magnificent Amy Pond, shares her innermost thoughts on tears, Scottish music, and being papped in Tesco...

The Brilliant Book of Doctor Who has made its way to a basement studio in London, where Karen Gillan is recording yet more top-secret *Doctor Who* stuff. There's digging going on – we immediately scan the floor for suspicious holes and wonder if we should have dressed for Rio.

We hear Karen before we see her. First her familiar laugh, then that unmistakable Scots lilt, then, in a blaze of red hair and miniskirt, there stands *Doctor Who*'s SexiestTravelling Companion Ever (copyright every newspaper for the past year). She's one of the most famous women in the galaxy now, of course, having wowed audiences as the awesome Amy Pond, the girl who waited 14 years for her imaginary best friend to give her a lift, fell pregnant in a dream world, had her fiancé erased from history, flirted shamelessly with Vincent van Gogh and finally got the fairy-tale wedding every girl dreams of.

So famous is Karen now, we discover, that she can't even buy a sandwich in peace...

Hello Karen. What's happening in this studio today then?

I've been doing ADR *[Additional Dialogue Recording]* for Episode 13, which I watched a bit of and I started crying! Matt made me cry on screen and then Matt walked in and I was like, 'I haven't been crying'. I was just really happy to see him! That's my story anyway.

Talking of crying... the end of Episode 9, when Rory died, was a real tear-jerker.

That was a tough one, actually. It was nice to get to do something like that because Amy really hides her emotions a lot. She's really guarded, so it was nice to do something where she let that guard down completely and her real feelings actually show through.

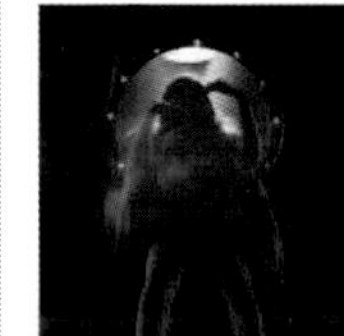

So, first ever married couple in the TARDIS...

Yeah! I'm so excited!

How is that going to work?

I don't know! I think Steven Moffat said that he reckons it's going to be funny. I'll go with that.

Do you think there are going to be domestics? Or kids?

Oh no, not for a long time for Amy. And Amy doesn't indulge in domestic arguments. She just doesn't involve herself at all and therefore sorts of... wins!

Is the Doctor going to be a gooseberry?

No, the Doctor's far too important to Amy. So it'll be interesting to see how it pans out. She's got this one guy, the Doctor, who is everything to her –basically her childhood hero. And then she's got her new husband. But she's got a really different relationship with Rory from the one she has with the Doctor. So I think it's going to be fairly equal, there's not going to be a gooseberry situation. »

If you had a Pandorica what would you put in it?
Oh my God. My most feared thing, I guess, which is... I don't know! Something like a spirit. I don't like spirit things. So the spirit that's haunting me, I'd put that in there.

There's a spirit haunting you?
Well, my mum believes that people are coming back to haunt us, but not in a bad way, in a good way. So even though I don't actually believe it, because my mum's saying it, part of me thinks, 'Are they?'

Is there something you'd want to keep safe in the Pandorica? Because Amy was preserved there for 2,000 years, of course.
Oh yeah, that's true! I'll put myself in there. That's what I'll do. Forget the spirits, I'm putting myself in the Pandorica and then I'm coming out. Oh. Hang on. I don't know how I'm going to get out because you need your own DNA to open the doors. Well, basically, first of all I'm going to have a kid and that'll have my DNA, and then I'll leave it a note saying 'come back' when it's really old and about to die, and then I'll come out and see how things have progressed.

Pushing past your poor, decrepit offspring!
Well, it'll be on its last legs by then, so...

Do you look at cracks differently now?
Yeah, they all look a lot more sinister. Crooked smiles. It's funny because loads of people have been telling me stories about their kids having cracks in their walls and parents have been winding up their kids saying, 'That's an Amy Pond crack,' and they're all scared. Parents can be mean. It's not just me, in my Pandorica!

You're a dedicated follower of fashion – did you pick Amy's wedding dress?
No. We tried on two which I really loved and they were a bit unconventional, so that's quite good for Amy. They were quite vintagey-looking, but you wouldn't necessarily know they were wedding dresses unless you saw it in the situation. What we needed, because you saw it for the first time in Episode 1, was something you knew immediately was a wedding dress, because it's hanging up there for the cliffhanger. So we couldn't go with the first one. so Ray *[Holman, costume designer]* just chose me that one. I quite like it because actually I don't think it's the one that Amy would necessarily choose, so it sort of looks like someone just put her in it. Like the whole wedding is just sort of happening around her.

Can you tell us a secret about the boys?
If this was a visual thing I'd show you how Matt dances. It's like this *[points folded hand towards face]*. It's directly facing you and then it's a wafting motion. I don't know how you'll write that down.

With great difficulty.
Haha! We should come back to that one when I think of something good!

What's been your favourite moment of the entire series?
Filming the wedding scene. It was really emotional, the climax of the whole of Amy's story that's been building throughout the series. By that point I just felt really attached to Amy and I cried. I found myself crying quite a lot, reading the script. I've never done that reading a script in my life. Like, hysterically wailing! And it was a lot easier for me to cry on set without any help of a menthol tear stick or anything. Just because I felt *so* much towards these scenes that she was in. So favourite moment would be filming the wedding in the finale. And also the dancing scene in the wedding, which was hilarious. Half of it got cut out. There was

"I CRIED, READING EPISODE 13. I'VE NEVER DONE THAT WITH A SCRIPT BEFORE IN MY LIFE"

one scene where Matt and I were dancing and I fell over and they just carried on the music. I was on my back and Matt decided to grab my feet and then just started dragging me around. I was like, 'What's happening?' It was really weird. We just carried on while I was getting dragged around by my feet. Elvis was playing.

What's been the funniest moment for you?
I'm terrible for corpsing. At nothing! We were filming this scene at the very end of Episode 13, with me, Rory and the Doctor, and they were making fun of me about something and I tried to defend myself – but it came out as just random noises. I don't know what happened. They started laughing at that and I, for some reason, completely lost the plot and couldn't stop laughing. It was sort of half crying and half laughter. It went on for ages and we were running out of time. The director was actually shouting at me and it just made me laugh even more. So actually that wasn't a funny moment to anyone else but I found it totally hilarious!

FAQ

FULL NAME
Karen Sheila Gillan
DATE OF BIRTH
28 November 1987
HOME TOWN
Inverness, Scotland
FIRST WHO APPEARANCE
Soothsayer, *The Fires of Pompeii*, 2008
WHO FACT
Karen once imitated Beyoncé and dyed her hair pink, inspired by the *Bootylicious* music video!

What's been Amy's biggest fashion disaster?
What's she worn... I reckon the shorts in Episodes 8 and 9.
C'mon, she was dressed for Rio.
She *was* dressed for Rio. Nobody else was. Ha! Trust Amy.
How's life for you now you get papped buying sandwiches?
Well, technically Luke [Karen's PR man] was holding the sandwiches that day! It's weird. How is that even news? Me in Tesco? That was hilarious. It couldn't have been a more un-glam setting. We were in the bargain prices section buying cheese sandwiches. It's really weird, but you know what? They've not been that bad. Some people have them waiting on their doorstep, but I never know that they're there. So it's kind of OK.
What's been the most 'oh my god' moment on *Doctor Who*?
The obvious one is seeing the TARDIS. It was Matt and me going, 'This is *our* TARDIS'. That was, like, Oh Em Gee!
What would you most like to happen in the next series?
I'd like to see Amy carry on in the TARDIS so I've still got a job! I'd like to see her getting even more hilarious stuff to do and I'd like to see her remain the same old Amy and not get all boring with marriage. I don't think being married will make much of a difference to her, to be honest. I'd like to see the relationships explored further, deeper. I wanna see Amy fight some aliens from really far in the future. I want them to go and see how humans have developed really far in the future. We might look physically different, but we'll have amazing technology by then.
What's on your MP3 player right now?
Let me find out... Oh no! *The Great Big Scottish Songbook*. Oh why? That's terrible! I like bagpipe music. Hahaha! Oh god, I wish this hadn't come out.
And finally, we still need some cast secrets!
Matt's got Girls Aloud on his MP3 player. That's not really very good though. Arthur wears ski boots with granny jumpers. Matt wears pearls, but that's not really a secret. Apparently his cleaner was like, 'Matt's got lots of pink pants and pearls.' Ha! Oh, and Arthur never really sleeps. I think he's a vampire or something...

EPISODE 3

Victory of the Daleks

BY MARK GATISS

THE STORY

It's 1941, and Prime Minister Winston Churchill faces his darkest hour. Britain is under nightly bombardment by Nazi aircraft, German forces are advancing towards their borders, and the war hangs in the balance. But Churchill has a secret weapon...

Professor Bracewell's Ironsides seem like the perfect soldiers. Tireless, obedient, and packing some serious heat. With these mechanical miracles under his command, Churchill could turn the tide of war and ensure a victory for the Allied forces.

There's just one problem: his soldiers aren't as perfect as they seem. They're the Daleks. They have a plan. And not even the Doctor is going to beat them this time...

BEHIND THE SCENES

MARK GATISS

Writer

Way back in *The Power of the Daleks* (1966), we saw the Doctor's arch-enemies acting as friends to a human colony. Was this part of the inspiration for *Victory of the Daleks*?
That idea has always appealed to me. They were pretending to be something they weren't, and I thought it was such a good idea it should be done again! I enjoyed the idea of them being sly. I think they're at their most frightening when they're like that – you can sense a sort of crafty intelligence. And obviously, it gives you licence to make them say things they'd never normally say. Given that the Daleks' vocabulary is quite limited, it was brilliant to make them say, 'Would you care for some tea?'!

Following the activation of the Progenitor, the Daleks are 'racially pure' once more...
Again, that's one of the things I wanted to get back to. They can't operate the Progenitor because they're no longer pure enough to be recognised by it. These new Daleks are, as it were, the purest they've been since the very beginning. What that means in the long term, I don't know – that's all to be decided. The real reason behind it was that the Daleks need to be properly *back* – this eternal threat once more. They're not struggling for survival any longer, they're going to win. Hence the title!

DELETED!

THE DOCTOR: You are my enemy! And I am yours! You are everything I despise! The worst thing in all creation. Remember Necros? Spiridon? The Arrows of the Half-Light? I've defeated you! Time and time again, I've defeated you. And now you've crawled out from under your filthy stone one last time. Like a disease. A plague! Manipulating. Scheming. Exterminating! Well, not on my watch. Do you hear me? I sent you back into the Void! I saved the whole of reality from you. I am the DOCTOR! The Oncoming Storm! And you are the DALEKS!

UNSEEN ADVENTURES

In the original script, the Doctor mentions previous run-ins with Churchill, during the PM's time serving with the army in the Sudan and also having 'dodged doodlebugs' with him in 1945. He also attended his funeral in 1965. Read more about their times together on page 32...

SPOT THE CRACK

The crack appears on the wall in Churchill's bunker, just behind the TARDIS as it fades away...

FANTASTIC FACTS

So, Winston Churchill knows the Doctor! We've never seen them meet on screen, though here the Doctor mentions a few other times he ran into the British PM. ›› The Daleks need the Doctor's 'testimony' so they can prove to the Progenitor that they truly are Daleks. The Daleks that pose as Ironsides have an impure genetic code: this is most likely because they are survivors from the Doctor's destruction of the Reality Bomb in *The Stolen Earth/Journey's End* (2008). Those Daleks had been genetically reconstructed from the DNA of their creator Davros, himself not a true Dalek. (It may not be so cut and dried, though. A line excised from the script makes it clear that the Daleks have been 'mixing [their] genes with other races just so [they] could go on and on'. The Daleks in *Bad Wolf/The Parting of the Ways* (2005), for example, had used human DNA to rebuild a new army – so maybe these Daleks hail from that era?) ›› 'They invaded your world, remember?' the Doctor asks Amy of the Daleks. 'Planets in the sky! You don't forget that!' But evidently, she does. The Doctor is talking about the world-shaking events of *The Stolen Earth/Journey's End*, which Amy really should remember. But, because of her unique place in space and time, and the effect of the cracks in the universe (see... well, just about the whole series!), Amy has no memory of these things because, in one way, they never happened. ›› The new Daleks come in five flavours! And they each have a title: red is Drone, orange is Scientist, white is Supreme, blue is Strategist... and the yellow Dalek is the curiously named Eternal. Writer Mark Gatiss admitted on *Doctor Who Confidential* that he doesn't know what that 'Eternal' title might mean – but see page 36 for more...

MAGIC MOMENT

With great difficulty now he's one-handed, BRACEWELL closes the barrel, his face impassive.

CHURCHILL: Bracewell! Put the gun down.
BRACEWELL: My life is a lie and I choose to end it.
AMY: In your own time, Paisley boy! Cos right now, we need your help.

BRACEWELL: But those creatures. My Ironsides. They made me? I... I can remember things. So many things. The last war. The squalor and the mud and the awful, awful misery of it all... What am I? What am I?
CHURCHILL: What you are, sir, is either on our side – or theirs. Now, I don't give a damn if you're a machine, Bracewell. Are you a man?

FAMILIAR FACES

IAN McNIECE

Winston Churchill

Ian played Bert Large in ITV1's *Doc Martin* – and he first played Winston Churchill in the 2008 stage play *Never So Good*.

BILL PATERSON

Professor Bracewell

Bill starred in paranormal drama *Sea of Souls* and appeared with Arthur Darvill in BBC1's *Little Dorrit*.

THE LOST DIARIES

of Winston Spencer Churchill

FOR YOUR EYES ONLY
For the record, these random entries from the diaries of the late Sir Winston Churchill appear to have been excised from the notebooks found amongst his possessions upon his death last year.

It is conceivable that they were sketches for a work of fantastic fiction and, as such, reveal a hitherto unexpected side to the great man. Yet the consistency of their tone gives one pause. Who was this imagined stranger 'The Doctor'?

Some portions of these diaries remain secret. Further enquiries should be forwarded to Colonel Amanda Prince of the Unified Intelligence Taskforce.

Blenheim Palace. 1879

The cracadyle ran off with the sausages. Mr Punch was verry cross. Nanny says his nose is funny. I liked him. The Punch and Judi man was verry nice as well. He was tall with a big long scarfe and had boggle eyes like a clown. He called me Winnie. I liked him. He rann after the cracadyle and smashed it up with a stick becas he said it was not a cracadyle it was called a sibermatt. And then the Punch and Judi box wasn't there any more and the goggle man was gone. Then I went to sleep. It was a good birthdee.

St George's Preparatory School, Ascot, March 18th 1882.

What on Earth is the use of Latin? I am considered such a dunce that they have sent me to a special teacher who is tucked away in a little cubby hole behind Big Hall. He is a very odd little fellow with very deep lines about his mouth which I take to mean he smiles a good deal. Yet he is very wise and has that grand gift of communication. His dress is shambolic and I have seen the other masters look at him a bit askance. In my view, however, it does not matter if one's trousers are a little too short, what matters is character. And this fellow has it in spades. The other morning the conversation ran thus: 'In Latin, Mensa means table', said the Doctor. That is what I must call him, by the way. He has not vouchsafed a surname! 'Then why does mensa also mean "O table",' I asked. The little Doctor cleared his throat an d said 'Ah well. You would use that when you were addressing the table.' At this I laughed but the Doctor frowned and said, 'You never know when it might be very, very important to address a table in Latin.' This made me laugh even more.

I am sorry to say that when I turned up for my extra lessons today, there was no sign of the little man. No-one seems to know where he has got to.

Havana, Cuba. October 26th 1895.

I am twenty one years old today and under fire! This is a very satisfactory thing! A present arrived in the form of a box of finest Cuban cigars. I fear I have entered into a lifelong contract with a dangerous mistress: tobacco! After dinner, and about to enjoy one of the cigars, there came a crash as someone hurled themselves through the French windows d tipped a bucket of water over me! He was a very skinny fellow in spectacles and a brown suit and he muttered something about 'Sontaran grenades' and 'destablising history' before vanishing through the remains of the windows with the soggy remains of my cigar! Then he was back, popping his head around the curtain and grinning like a lunatic. 'Nice to see you again, Winnie!' he piped, and was off again! I caught a curious – and oddly familiar – sound on the warm Cuban air. It was like a water buffalo in distress. For some reason it brought back all manner of childhood memories, though I can't for the life of me think why.

Omdurman. The Sudan. September 3 1898

A stroll by the Nile the evening before last. The heat oppressive but, great heavens, the beauty of the place! On the blue waters, the feluccas are like pocket handkerchiefs nipping and tucking on the evening breeze. After a glass or two, I fell to arguing with a lanky, beak-nosed cove in a ruffled shirt about the best means of defending oneself. This fellow, who said he was some kind of doctor and was very spry for his age, suddenly came at me with a sort of strangulated cry and a whole lot of curious movements of the sort one sees Chinese acrobats doing in music hall entertainments. For myself, I stuck with Queensbury and caught him a good 'un under the chin! After several more glasses we were firm friends and Well, bless me if there wasn't – standing there in the desert – a tall wooden box that seemed oddly familiar. Perhaps it was the headiness of the wine but I suddenly knew that its blue doors were the same blue doors through which I had entered what I took to be the Doctor's little cubby hole back at prep school! rooms within rooms and a wonderful, ridiculous engine with a great bellows-like thing in its centre w called 'Tardis' which travels through time and space! Great Pyramid of Cheops! Then it was no small task to the very last of the Osirians was no more!

LONDON. JANUARY 2ND 1911.

They are asking what right I had to be there! What right? I am the Home Secretary. And if the Home Secretary cannot be present when a gang of dangerous and armed revolutionaries lays siege to a London house, who the devil can? I was called out at an ungodly hour to Sidney Street, a grisly little slum in Stepney which it had previously been my good fortune never to go near! I authorised the Scots Guards to come to the aid of the police. As I awaited their arrival, I took the opportunity to smoke a cigar. There came a grinding racket, like some kind of ill-kept steam engine and suddenly there was the Doctor's blue box in the alleyway! It had appeared out of thin air! I rushed forward in greeting when the box opened up and out came an old man whom I had never seen before. The Doctor, it seems, has a disagreeable habit of changing his face! This newcomer fixed me at once with a penetrating stare. He was dressed for the cold in cloak and astrakhan hat and said it was a very great pleasure to meet me! I told him we had met before at which he looked properly astonished, gripped his lapels and made a funny little clucking noise. 'That,' he said, 'is the trouble with time travel!' a Thrassalian raiding party, afterwards incinerated in the inferno which swept Sidney Street.

Chartwell. May 1931.

At work on The Book. Clemmie came to ask whether I should be joining her for lunch and I was a little short with her, alas. This chapter is proving a most difficult beast. I try to put myself in the mind of my illustrious ancestor Marlborough but today found myself much distracted. Perhaps a growing fear that my best days are behind me and that I stand no chance of matching Marlborough's greatness. Then, as I gazed out over the estate fair-haired and pleasant lad, beaming at me like an idiot. I told him it was too early in the year for cricket, but damn it if this wasn't the Doctor in another of his curious fancy dress outfits! the field of Blenheim itself! The roar of canon was deafening and we threw ourselves under the scant foliage in order to protect ourselves from Marshal Tallard's onslaught. It was a thing of wonder to me to be present on this great battlefield and to see, in the flesh, my noble kinsman I shall never be able to eat celery again.

Chartwell. November 16 1936.

The King has been to see Baldwin and stated that it is his irrevocable decision to marry Mrs Simpson! In this, I should have backed him to the hilt were it not for the fact that the Doctor rang to tell me Mrs Simpson is 'a shape-shifting alien from Verossikon Prime' and that the King has a nasty surprise coming on his wedding night!

Buckingham Palace. May 8 1945

[redacted] the Princesses having quit the room, I found myself alone. Alone to contemplate this extraordinary evening. Victory! Victory at last. And yet the familiar melancholy swept over me. The black dog. What lay ahead for me now? Suddenly, there was a figure at the door and I turned, expecting to see His Majesty. Instead, there stood a rough-looking fellow with wing-nut ears and a leather jacket, whom I assumed had come to take out the royal dustbins. 'Get your coat, Winston. Time for another trip'. Bless me, if it wasn't the Doctor yet again! Come to cheer me up! We found the familiar blue box parked in [redacted] and not merely to Rome where I might have had some words with the shade of Signor Mussolini, but to Ancient Rome! [redacted] there, in the court of the Emperor Tiberius himself, a remarkable meeting with some sort of creature not of this world which had disguised its form as one of the Emperor's reclining benches. [redacted] 'O table!' I said and the Doctor winked at me. 'Told you!' he smiled.

WHITEHALL. OCTOBER 1941.

Much buoyed by the Doctor's recent appearance, altered again and looking very wet behind the ears! The bow tie, though, is a very good choice.

I heartily wish he had left me with Bracewell's blessed Spitfires! It seems the good Professor (or the Paisley Pinocchio as I believe Miss Pond referred to him) had been converting the aeroplanes for some time, using this 'gravity bubble' method which his former masters had devised. I must confess to being a little concerned that this mechanical man is still at large. What if the Dalek creatures were to reassert their control?

Perhaps I might track him down and put him to use with the other boffins. I'm sure he would be jolly useful at Bletchley Park w[redacted] Turing gave a great cry and said[redacted]

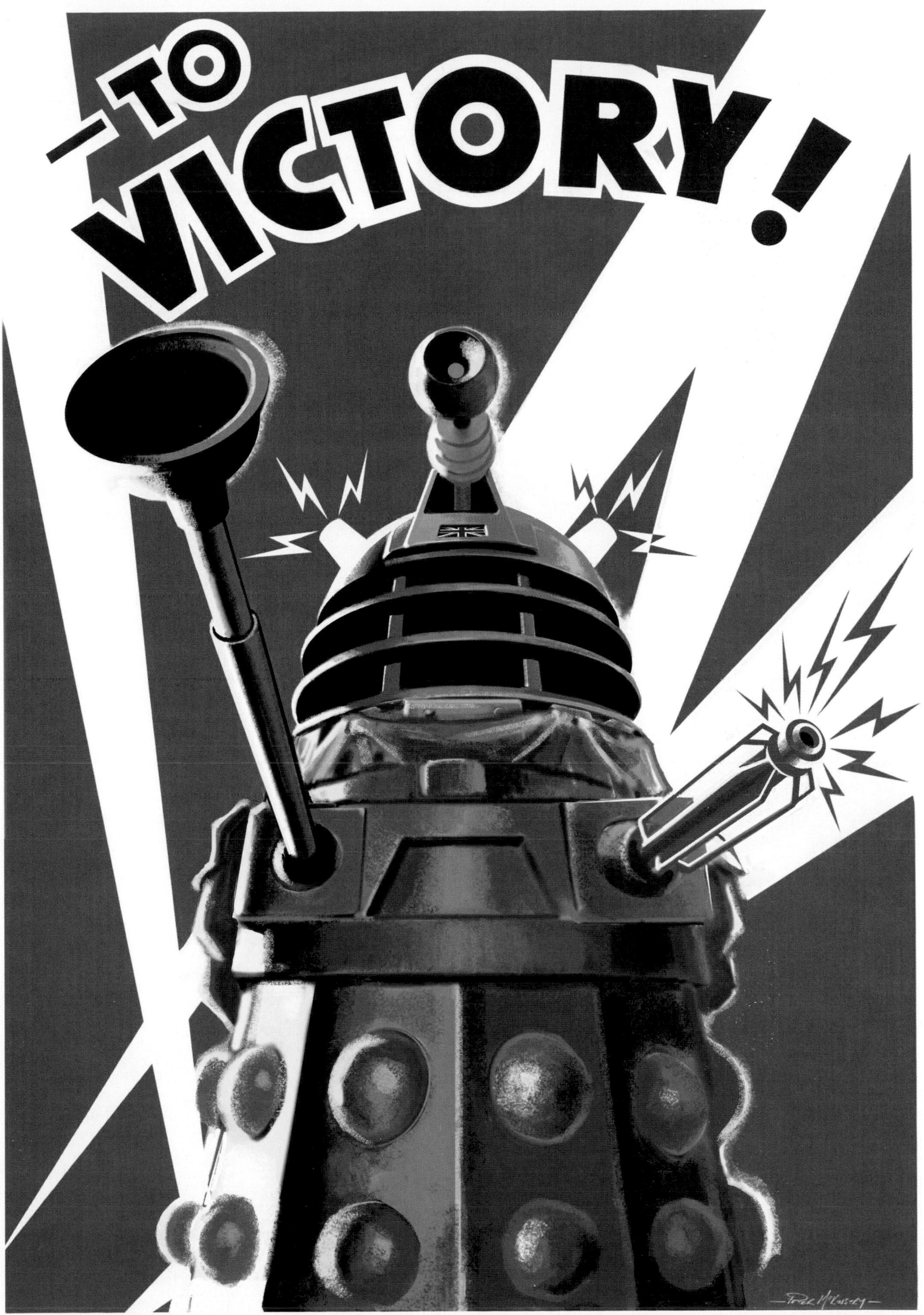

Printed by the MOD Ministry of Defense Room 73,Public Relations Office, Fillongley Warks .Test Print awaiting approval,Not for public display until further notice.
Ref: 20773/04021985

THE NEW DALEK PARADIGM

SUPREME

Engineered to combine the most callous and devious aspects of the race, the Supreme is the unquestioned leader of the dreaded Daleks. All battle information and intelligence is relayed through its colossal brain.

DRONE

The foot soldiers of the Dalek race. Bred for total obedience to the cause of Dalek supremacy. Utterly ruthless, aggressive and lethal.

Know your enemy! Vital information compiled by the ADF – Anti-Dalek Force – concerning the newest race of Daleks. All citizens of this galaxy should be on their guard against this even deadlier threat to all lifekind...

THE NEW Dalek paradigm was created using a device called the Progenitor. Many such devices were created thousands of years ago on the planet Skaro [homeworld of the Daleks – see Dalek VidFile titled *Genesis of the Daleks* for further information on Skaro] as a means of safeguarding the purity of the Dalek race. They were scattered through the universe – like seed pods – but, over time, information on their landing sites was lost.

To the Daleks, the Progenitors became almost a myth. However, following Davros's attempt to explode his Reality Bomb [see Public InfoFile *The Stolen Earth*], one crippled Dalek ship fell back through time and found itself close to planet Earth. There, its crew picked up a trace of one of the Progenitors. They also detected temporal activity around the human being known as ***'winstonspencerchurchill'*** and realised that this was due to his long-running association with an alien known as 'the Doctor' [InfoFile restricted – ADF eyes only]. So the Daleks set a trap...

ETERNAL

The function of this mysterious Dalek has never been ascertained. Its black and yellow livery, however, known all over the Universe as Nature's danger colours, may give some indication of its deadly purpose...

STRATEGIST

These Daleks devise complex schemes of conquest and extermination across thousands of years and millions of galaxies. Expert at assessing the weaknesses of enemy races, the Strategists' schemes achieve almost one hundred percent success – unless they encounter the Doctor.

SCIENTIST

All thinking related to the survival of the Daleks begins with the Scientist caste. In addition to endless experimentation with DNA, the Scientists are also charged with the creation of new weaponry and biological warfare against other races.

MAKING MUSIC

Doctor Who's composer **Murray Gold** gives us an exclusive glimpse into his marvellous musical mind...

OK. You don't know me. Just to get it out of the way, I write the music for *Doctor Who*. I'm sitting on a plane right now. I travel around quite a lot once I've finished a series. That's because *while* I'm working on it I have *no time* for anything, not even gardening. Or swimming. It's pretty full-on. I sit at my desk most of the winter and spring – and a little bit of the summer – and eventually it all gets done and I finally get up from my chair and dust off my creaking bones.

People ask all sorts of questions about the music for *Doctor Who*. Some of the most common are: 'Do you get the episodes early?' (Yes), 'Do you write all the music while watching the episodes?' (Mostly), and 'Can I have your job?' (Yes, if you bring me ice cream). The most difficult question to answer is: 'How do you do it?' The short answer is, I don't really think about it.

And here's the longer answer.

I OFTEN have ideas about the music while I'm reading a script. I'll be asking myself all kinds of questions: *is this a monster who is tiny and lives in a cupboard, or are there two billion of them invading Earth in giant spaceships?* I'll be thinking, *what sort of sound will work best for this monster?* or *what sort of girl is this companion?* Is she funny, or chatty or dreamy or lonely? Is the monster loud and obnoxious, or does it grow in your shoe and up your leg?

Most importantly, I've learned to listen to my feelings as I read the script. Am I excited? Why? Do I want these characters to end up together? Do I sympathise with the Doctor? Why am I worried about Amy?

All these questions are useful because, from experience, I know that if *I* feel these things, then so will many of the viewers. It's a sort of trust – a connection if you like. I will try and focus on these feelings and intensify them with music.

After my initial thoughts I might jot down some ideas at the piano: melodies, rhythms. I'll usually keep a tape recorder or my iPhone close by, so while I'm thumping away I can record it, in case something good comes out. I usually sing while I'm playing. I've sung all my life – mostly in private because I have a very average voice – but from singing hundreds of tunes, I feel my mouth knows the *shape* of a good melody. I always imagine I'm singing to someone I care about and ask myself if the melody has enough atmosphere or drama to draw them in. I sometimes even ask people who happen to be around whether my piece moves them or changes their mood in any way. That's my job. I'm a mood changer.

Doctor Who uses a musical technique called *leitmotif*, which is just a fancy word for *character theme*. A theme is a tune or melody that you associate with a character and helps you to feel you know them better. The themes are often quite simple, but the simpler they are the more variations are possible. Both Rose and the Ninth Doctor had strong themes in the first series and, as the moment of their tragic separation drew nearer, it was like those themes grew in power. What started as a simple melody became associated in *your* minds with strong feelings of friendship and even love and, eventually, a memory of the characters and the good times you had with them. This is one of the reasons I'm very lucky.

The great stories and characters make my music *sound* better.

Writing tunes is all very well but I also have to deal with the budget. Each season there will be some variation in scale from story to story. *The Eleventh Hour* in Series Five was extra length. And *everything* happened. There were invaders from space and a creature that stole shapes; there was time travel, and two important new characters in Matt's Doctor and Amy. In fact, every Doctor in history appeared in the story at one point, and the newest one, Matt, had to choose an outfit for himself. I could easily have spent the whole budget on just that episode! But there were 12 more to come, including a spectacular finale, and it was important we had enough left to make the music for the whole season. Piers Wenger, one of the executive producers, had given me a synopsis for the season finale in September 2009. The final episodes were only just being written, but he knew the overall story. He told me all the Doctor's enemies came back to fight him. He also told me about the other stories: the Angels and the Silurians, the Daleks and Winston Churchill, the Smilers and the Star Whale. Oh, and then one by a famous film and TV writer called Richard Curtis, and another which probably involved two adventures in one, although they might both be dreams. I kept looking for the small episodes but there weren't any. Oh, there might be *one* smaller episode that Gareth Roberts was writing. It was mostly set in a house. But it was important the episode didn't seem small so perhaps that could sound a little bigger than normal...?

I WORKED out we could probably afford three days with the National Orchestra of Wales and perhaps four with a smaller band. All the episodes would somehow have to be recorded in these sessions. Any episodes which missed out on live musicians would have to be done with synthesizers instead.

So much for the budget. Once an episode arrives (by email) I sit and watch it almost immediately. If I laugh and cry and get excited and scared, I know it's going to be easy. If I sit and watch, occasionally looking at the clock, it will be more difficult. But that doesn't happen often. When it does, I see myself as the last line of defence and I have to work extra hard. More often, when I get a great episode in the mail, everything is easy. Every line of the script has a point and moves the story forward; every camera shot faithfully conveys the script; every performance is surprising and natural. And then it's almost as if the music writes itself. Tying it together is like breathing. Everything flows rhythmically.

Most episodes defy easy categorisation. I'm not an expert, but I always thought *Doctor Who* had a different tone to conventional science fiction. Most *Doctor Who* stories are a cross between melodrama, romance and comedy, with thriller and suspense, historical saga and horror thrown in for good measure. Most other science fiction I have seen is quite serious, often even solemn. It has a dark tone and feeds off our uncertainties and superstitions. *Doctor Who* has this, but at its centre there is something that changes everything – the Doctor. He is such a bright, optimistic and dazzling character that he illuminates the world around him. Nothing stays dark for long. He changes the tone of the show with his good humor and quick intelligence. Not only that, but the change from one tone to another is *very* fast. The jokes turn into an escape, an explosion cuts to a political discussion. Horses leap through windows and creatures disappear through cracks and rifts and then, in a wink of an eye, we're taken into a scene of romance and love. The music has to follow these twists and turns, and that can be a challenge.

ON my second viewing of an episode, I'll sit and write directly to the picture with a keyboard. Like an organ player in an old cinema, I just play along. Everything is recorded in Logic (an Apple music program). Sometimes these early sketches are very close to the final versions. But, usually, I go back and 'sculpt' my first attempts until they are hitting the key moments in the dialogue and the action. I try and return to the *leitmotifs* and themes I wrote sitting at the piano and remind myself how many times the piece has been used in previous episodes – in case it's been over-exposed. Wherever possible, I try to add romance and 'mischief' to the music so that it is more than purely descriptive. If something can be 'exciting' that's good, but if it can be exciting *and* romantic *at the same time*, so much the better. The more layers a drama has, the more it rewards the viewer.

When I'm done with my organ-player act, and I've shaped the music into a whole, I send anything that needs orchestrating to Ben Foster. An orchestrator is somebody who writes out all the notes of a piece so that an orchestra can play it. We'll talk about tone and feel, but I know Ben's work so well that I mostly leave him to get on with it and it always comes out sounding great. He makes all sorts of decisions about the instruments and I trust him. That's the best kind of working relationship – when everybody does their job with a minimum of interference. After all, nobody likes being bossed around. I like people to feel happy when we're working together.

Once the orchestra or the small band have been recorded, Jake Jackson mixes it all, gets the levels right, and sends everything back to me. I add all the electronic parts – the synthesizers, weird atmospheres and big drum sounds – and send the finished music to Wales where Tim Ricketts dubs it onto the show – mostly in the right places, although sometimes people move it around while I'm not there and I go crazy! Then we have telephone calls, and reach compromises, and get on with the next episode.

I like to watch the episodes again once I've forgotten what I did on them. I'm my own harshest critic and I try to learn from my mistakes. In the end, even if I've been disappointed with my work, I try and come back with the same exuberance and confidence because, and I hope you won't groan when I say this, *I love this show.* 

UMWELTS FOR HIRE

A *Doctor Who* story by BRIAN ALDISS

Illustrations by MARTIN GERAGHTY

PART ONE

THE railway ran straight for ever. For most of its route it travelled through flat landscape, ground that did not even claim the title of desert. No weeds grew, no animals lived here; only ants survived, busily covering the ground, dominating a land nobody wanted.

Every other day, a train ran along the line, heading north. It consisted of four carriages. A diesel engine was fitted into the front carriage. The other carriages were filled with goods. The doors of the carriages were locked and blind. A roof without features covered the entire train.

The roof was crowded. Men, women and children were stealing a free ride on the train. In the main, all of them lay flat for fear of falling off or being swept off by the bough of a rare tree they were passing. These people were leaving the Republic of Satorn, travelling to Napplekar, hoping for a better life.

They crossed the frontier. There was nothing to mark any difference between the two enemy nations, no barriers, no guards, no change to the barren prospect. Only a post, standing at an angle.

Dino had been hoisted onto the train roof by his father. It had been a hasty manoeuvre, made as the train roared past, just at the point where it slowed for the bend. Only by catching hold of the ankle of someone lying on the roof had Dino managed to haul himself up. Only when he had managed to wriggle into a horizontal position did he dare look back. His father was not to be seen, already lost in dust and heat haze.

He had made an enemy of the man whose ankle he had grasped.

This man was all skin and bone; he was sick of a disease known as aphasia, having lost the power of coherent speech. He sat up and kicked Dino in the stomach. In pain, unguardedly, Dino lost his balance. Arms widespread, he fell from the roof of the train. A woman screamed.

Not greatly hurt but badly shocked, Dino sprawled on the grit. He had to shout at himself to get up. He found he could stand. His right hand and arm were grazed and bleeding. The train was already remote, the noise of its engine fading. He was alone. All around him, the featureless plain stretched to the horizon.

His feelings were mixed. There was a thrilling feeling in being the only intelligence in that awesome space, but with it came anxiety: which way should he go, what could he eat, how cold would it be when night set in?

With that question came a sudden drop in light, as if a great electric bar had failed. Thin cloud trailed across the face of the sun.

Dino was looking anxiously about. In the distance, two round lights appeared. For a moment they appeared static, but no – they were part of a vehicle rushing towards him. He stood helpless with terror.

The vehicle was almost upon him. Dino turned to run, staggered, and then fell senseless to the ground.

In fact he fell, or rather lay, on the couch in the Yumwelt, resting there unconsciously. The re-umwelt operator switched off the Separation Machine. It closed with a fading purr. A nurse came forward and checked the sleeping man's pulse. Of course he slept. The machine had translated himself to himself. She inserted a marginal dose of a synthetic genome into the patient's veins.

This new invention provides revelations. Self-knowledge comes as a shock.

The Doctor and Amy had recently arrived at the Yumwelt, to be warmly greeted by Carmody Jacobs, an old friend of the Doctor's. Ramshackle though the buildings of Yumwelt were, there was a pleasant verandah, facing away from the sun, to which Carmody invited the Doctor and Amy. There coffee and croissants were arrayed before them.

'I can't tell you how grateful I am that you've come. Now we can tackle these crooks in Arpeggio City,' Carmody said. 'They are enemies of knowledge and will close us down if they can.'

The Doctor set his cup down. He beamed at Amy. 'Crooks!'

She smiled back, helped herself to a biscuit.

'So who's the major player there?' the Doctor asked. 'Do you know?'

Carmody gestured as if doubting his own words. 'Well, they say the mayor's behind much of the villainy. She's a woman, Billiant by name. Fay Billiant. But I'd say there was a whole well of wickedness behind her.'

Since the Doctor made no response to this remark, Carmody studied him. 'You're a wonder, Doc! Dressed like a university professor from the old days. Are you going to be safe in Arpeggio?'

Giving an air of being slightly offended by the comparison, the Doctor straightened his

bow tie. Then, with an unexpected smile, he said, 'The jacket's not exactly bullet-proof. But I hope to be safe – and Amy, too.'

Many of the Yumwelt scientists did not dare to enter the pictorial simulacra of their unknown psyches. But they all understood a powerful new tool of understanding had entered the world, struggling itself to be understood. They worked in small underground rooms, in consideration of the high rental costs in Arpeggio, the nearest town.

The Doctor and Amy had been watching the patient in his trance from the next room, through a glass panel.

'Funny way to spend a holiday," Amy remarked. "But if that's the way you want it...'

'He didn't know he wanted it,' said the Doctor. 'He needed it. if I understand what Carmody told us properly, there's more than an element of therapy involved.'

'A good night's sleep might be more use.'

Ignoring the remark, the Doctor said, 'They ran the guy's identity card through the checker thing. There's no such person. So he's come here under an assumed name – Dino Scanlon. He's not who he says he is.'

'Who is he then?' Amy enquired.

'Carmody's' going through dental records now. Could be perfectly innocent. Lots of people change their names in the hope of changing their fate.'

'Or because they get married,' Amy added.

The Doctor didn't answer.

Carmody Jacobs, manager of the Yumwelt, returned to the room, his thin whiskers mingling with blackheads on his plump cheeks. With him came a lean dark-skinned man, hands in pockets. He wore dark glasses and a short robe over his sweater.

'Doctor, we don't want any problems, do we?' said Carmody. 'In the morning, we are summoned before an Arpeggio tribunal for using polysynthia.'

'For using what?' Amy asked.

'It comes from the bacterium Mycoplasma Mycoides,' the Doctor told her. 'The synthetic genome can control how a cell works. But that sort of mild genetic manipulation has just been outlawed here – am I right?'

Carmody nodded. 'Entirely unfair, of course. We use polysynthia to get the body operating properly again when it wakes from the deep sleep. If we can't use polysynthia, we can't let people dream. Or at least, we can't wake them up again safely.' He introduced the other man: 'This is my faithful friend, Shokerandit. He'll go with you.'

'Howdee,' said Shokerandit, without visible animation.

'Come with us?' The Doctor raised his eyebrows.

'As I said, we are summoned.' Carmody opened his hands, a gesture of pleading. 'I am no great speaker or advocate, but we have to make our case.'

'You're asking the Doctor to do it for you?' Amy guessed.

'If he would. I am needed here. The work, the constant monitoring... I cannot leave the patients.'

'You want me to make the case for your Separation Machine.'

'Well, yes.'

'To stand up and defend people's right to dream.'

'Yes.'

'Their right to aspire, to better themselves, to have a vision – an ambition – an aspiration.'

'Absolutely.'

The Doctor's eyes narrowed slightly. 'I'd be delighted,' he decided. He smiled.

Carmody smiled back.

The Doctor moved to shake hands with the newcomer, but the newcomer said what sounded like 'Ronnie mewcome' and slapped the Doctor on his shoulder by way of greeting. The Doctor was momentarily surrounded by mingled scents of nutmeg, cloves and cardamom.

'He's a crack shot. He can hit a postage stamp on the wing at a hundred paces,' Carmody explained.

'We'll watch out for postage stamps,' said Amy.

In Arpeggio City, a drive was on at present to keep crime out of the streets, The Yumwelt had been provisionally cleared by safety regulations; unfortunately, for the transfer of the patient back to normal consciousness, a minimum dose of polysynthia was used, thus making the Separation Machine liable to a new banning order.

The beeper beeped in the little underground ward. The nurse with the patient announced, 'Dino Scanlon is coming round. Do you want me to hold him? I'd have to have a pretext.'

'We can't hold him,' said Carmody Jacobs anxiously. 'I gather we have a record of his fakewelt?'

The nurse agreed they had. She sounded disappointed.

The Doctor, Amy and a lawyer, Felix Deals, were up early next morning to head for the mayor's fortress in the city where the trial was to take place. When Shokerandit joined them, he carried a long-barrelled rifle, slung over his shoulder on a leather strap.

'The great God will bless us,' he told the company. 'He is yet more of a kindness when he sees mine rifle.'

Having made it clear he didn't approve of the weapon, the Doctor asked Shokerandit if he had experienced the umwelt treatment himself.

'This machine it is invented for only those who need it. If I try, then I am lost company with the Great God. I think you suffer the same failing – already lost company with the Great God.'

The Doctor told him, 'Some people do not believe there ever was a God, great or otherwise.'

Shokerandit began nodding his head like an old clockwork doll. 'Such a loss they have expressed, poor sir. How they ever do gain any sanctity such like I enjoy?'

'Well, they just have to do their best...' said the Doctor, trying to conceal a smile.

It was just after sixteen degrees when their hover-beetle rolled from its trap, and strands of daylight had begun to slip between the tall lifestylers. But blackness was as yet the dominant note; street lighting had been demolished – it was reckoned to encourage crime. So said the police. Although crime rates were steadily rising.

Everything appeared quiet in Arpeggio City – a very mortuary – so that Shokerandit switched on the deflector. An image of the vehicle floated above the real thing, to disconcert any villain aiming a weapon at them. Since Mayor Billiant had taken over the city, internecine crime figures had soared. Her stern but beautiful face glowered from autoposters everywhere.

Down a side street the ocean could be glimpsed, still as oil spill. A fire burned on the promenade.

Further down the highway, they turned off and came to the Mayor's stronghold. A tank-like android checked them out and backed the beetle into a parking place. They were then shown into the open air.

Almost in a whisper, Shokerandit told Amy he could feel there was no God in this place.

'Justice hopefully, but you're right – no God,' she agreed. 'I can't honestly say I feel happy here.'

'Without no God, how can you find the precious jewel of justice?'

It was plainly a rhetorical question; she answered it nevertheless. 'With an unbribable jury?'

He said no more.

The yard was framed by immense buildings, mostly in late Twentieth Century Rectangular style, but also by the outline of a recently built elemosque. Although day was creeping in, the sky was tinged a dull red from the jostle of city lights, as the inhabitants switched on their electricity to begin their dealings with another day.

Amy felt a kind of dull pity for the way in which most people were forced to live: did it mean you might make one mistake and become trapped for ever? She at least had the pleasure, the buoyancy, of the Doctor's company.

The Doctor, looking up at the great gaunt buildings, inhaled the scents of claustrophobia.

He saw every reason why the Yumwelt was deemed necessary.

They made their way into the Mayor's fortress. Here in every room, it was easy to surmise, something deplorable had happened – and then, just to make sure, had happened again.

An attendant led them into an overheated side room. Here several moody-looking people, men and women, sat about, awaiting audience or, more likely, conviction. The Doctor stood with Amy and Felix Deals, making a mute conversation of expressions. Shokerandit stood apart, as if not wishing to become contaminated by ordinary humanity.

A small bald man came up and asked first Amy and then the Doctor, rather sheepishly, if they could sign the attendance book. 'You were not on the witness list. I didn't expect to see you here, sir,' he said to the Doctor.

'Nor did I,' the Doctor replied.

Having signed the man's book, the Doctor tore a page from the back and wrote a note he asked to be passed at once to the Mayor, or failing that her secretary:

I can free you from the imprisonment of your own Umwelt.

He did not sign it.

A few minutes after the man with the book had gone, another lackey entered, smiling a dreadful smile of the kind seen otherwise only in dementia wards. With lavish gestures, he showed the Doctor from the stifling room, along a corridor and into an elevator. The elevator glided up to a halt. Immediately, he found himself in a large chamber, one end of which was cluttered with pine trees. From these trees, the Mayor Billant emerged.

She was tall, solid but not fat, holding herself haughtily. Her hair was dyed blonde and she wore a grey uniform.

Making no gesture of welcome, she said, 'Explain what you mean by your impertinent message.'

'If you've already decided my message is impertinent, why are you even asking?' the Doctor said. 'We act out our umwelts, however secret we believe them to be.' He paused, considering her with some scorn. 'I've been reading up on you, you know. In the four years of your rule here as mayor, you've turned what was once a beautiful coastal resort into a kind of civil battlefield. Cromer to the Somme in one easy lesson. You've switched umwelts.'

To this, Billiant responded unexpectedly, 'I'm in a trap. I called you here because I thought perhaps you could help. But I see that no one can help me.' Abruptly she changed her tone. 'Despite a long search, he has gone – possibly to his death.'

'Who's gone? You may well feel you're in a trap. But does that excuse ruining an entire city?'

The question shocked her. 'All right, I cannot take argument.' She buried her face in her hands. 'Go to your trial.'

The Doctor smiled sadly. 'Trial? Oh it won't be a trial, I promise you. It'll be a lecture.'

CONTINUED ON PAGE 100

EPISODE 4

The Time of Angels

BY STEVEN MOFFAT

THE STORY

Doctor River Song is on the run, so it's the Doctor to the rescue. But what was she looking for in the vault of the starship *Byzantium*? And why has she been teamed up with a squadron of military churchmen?

River's arrival makes the Doctor awkward and grumpy, but he's got bigger things to worry about. When the *Byzantium* crashes, the creature hidden in its belly escapes – and now, the Doctor, Amy and River must enter the charmingly named Maze of the Dead to face the might of a rapidly growing army of Weeping Angels.

Don't blink? Blinking is the least of their worries. The Doctor is talking to the dead and Amy has something in her eye...

MAGIC MOMENT

AMY: Aren't you all Mr Grumpy-Face today?
THE DOCTOR: A Weeping Angel, Amy, is the deadliest, most powerful, most malevolent lifeform evolution has ever produced. And right now one of them is trapped inside that wreckage and I'm supposed to climb in after it, with a screwdriver and a torch, and – assuming I survive the radiation long enough, and assuming the whole ship doesn't just blow up in my face – do something incredibly clever which I haven't actually thought of yet. That's my day, that's what I'm up to. Any questions?
AMY: Is River Song your wife? Cos she's someone from your future, yeah? And the way she talks to you, I've never seen anyone do that. She's like, you know, 'Heel, boy!'. She's Mrs Doctor from the future, isn't she? Is she gonna be your wife one day?
THE DOCTOR: Yes. You're right. I am definitely Mr Grumpy-Face today.

UNSEEN ADVENTURES

The Doctor spent time on Alfalfa Metraxis before the fall of the Aplan civilisation, during which period he had dinner with the aliens' chief architect. Like all Aplans, he had two heads – the statues in the maze of the dead had just one...

FAMILIAR FACES

ALEX KINGSTON
River Song
Alex became internationally famous with her role as Dr Elizabeth Corday in the US hospital drama *ER*.

MIKE SKINNER
Josh
The security guard dazed by River's lipstick at the start of the episode is played by the frontman of The Streets.

NUMBER CRUNCHING

2 THE NUMBER OF HEADS ON AN APLAN

1 THE NUMBER OF HEADS ON A WEEPING ANGEL

0 *Probable number of low-level perception filters in the Maze of the Dead*

BEHIND THE SCENES
STEVEN MOFFAT

Writer

Was it difficult to persuade Alex Kingston to return for four full episodes of this series?
No, she loves being River, and it's a thrill every time we get her back.

River made a big impact – on the Doctor and the audience – when she arrived in Series Four. Was the decision to bring her back a no-brainer?
As I wrote *Silence in the Library*, what started as a gimmick began to grow in my head. The story of who she could be, and how, and why. It's a good a story, and there are surprises, so why not tell it? Good mysteries are easy.

Just like River, the Weeping Angels were a big hit. Is it important to keep throwing popular old (even 'new-old') enemies in the Doctor's way?
Probably not actually. I had loads of Angels ideas I never got to use in *Blink* – cos they didn't fit in that sort of cerebral, 'clever' story – so I fancied something more action- and spookiness-based, to see what else they could do. Stand still in different places, as it turned out!

DELETED!

AMY: There's two moons. This isn't Earth. We're on a planet. Doctor, I'm on a planet! This is a planet! Look at it, look, it's all... it's all grey, it's a rubbish planet. Can I breathe here, is it okay to breathe? Course it's okay, I'm breathing. But the sky, is that like our sky? Or is it made of jelly or something? Well, not jelly. But it could be jelly! Is it jelly?

FANTASTIC FACTS

›› Old High Gallifreyan, the ancient language of the Time Lords, was first seen on screen in *The Deadly Assassin* (1976) but in fact hails from the groundbreaking 1972 book *The Making of Doctor Who*, where we first saw the Doctor's 'real name' written as a series of mysterious symbols. ›› No one ever said time travel was simple. The Doctor first met River Song in *Silence in the Library/Forest of the Dead* (2008). This was the first meeting for the Doctor, but the final one for River. In that story, River mentioned the crash of the Byzantium – the events we see unfold here. Now, we're far earlier in River's timestream, but later in the Doctor's. This is only his second meeting with River (that we know about, anyway...), but she still acts like she's already intimately familiar with him. As the Doctor says: 'We keep meeting in the wrong order.' ›› River knows how to pilot the TARDIS – even better than the Doctor does! She claims to have 'had lessons from the very best', but adds that it was a shame the Doctor was busy that day. However, in *The Pandorica Opens*, she reveals this may have just been a big tease, admitting it was the Doctor who taught her how to fly the ship. ›› So, just who is River? Amy thinks she knows: River is the Doctor's wife. But neither party is willing to either confirm or deny this suggestion. ›› The Weeping Angels were introduced in *Blink* (2007). The Doctor had one simple tip to protect yourself from their attack: don't blink! Here, though, we learn that it's not that straightforward, and not blinking could actually be the most dangerous tactic. Staring into the eyes of an Angel lets it into the watcher's mind, and the image of an Angel (a video clip, a photograph, even a drawing) can act just like the real thing.

"Even I don't know WHO RIVER REALLY IS!"

Alex Kingston, otherwise known as timey-wimey temptress River Song, exclusively reveals the contents of her little blue book...

HELLO sweetie! If we counted the ways we loved River Song we'd be counting for a very long time indeed. But we've only got four pages so we'd better get a grip.

You'll no doubt be pleased (but not in the least surprised) to hear that her Earthly alter ego, actress Alex Kingston, former star of the hit US hospital drama *ER*, is just as fabulous.

Basically, she's the sort of lady you want to take to lunch, to a cocktail bar, to see a show, to burgle a spaceship – it's no wonder the Doctor's so taken with her. Well, he will be. Eventually. Probably. And it might be the death of him. Possibly. Oh curse this wibbly-wobbly timey-wimey stuff!

But if we, the viewers, are being kept in the dark, what about Alex? Does she know all of River's secrets? And if so, will she be willing to spill them to *The Brilliant Book of Doctor Who*? Careful – there could be spoilers ahead. With any luck...

So, River Song – who's that girl?
Well, I'm glad you say girl and not old woman! She's an archaeologist, that's her profession. A time-travelling archaeologist because she's met the Doctor in the future, many futures, and has a very special relationship with that Doctor. She has her little blue book, which contains all her past adventures – which are the future adventures of our present Doctor. She's somebody who holds the Doctor very dear indeed. I can't say more than that!

Do you *know* who River is? Has Steven Moffat told you?
He's given me a fairly good idea. But, being Steven, he won't pin the character down completely. So I've got a fairly good sense of who she is, but then again I could be proven wrong. Steven always gives himself an open door to be able, potentially, to change tactics or ideas or stories.

FAQ

FULL NAME
Alexandra Elizabeth Kingston
DATE OF BIRTH
11 March 1963
HOME TOWN
Epsom, Surrey
FIRST WHO APPEARANCE
Silence in the Library, 2008
WHO FACT
Alex once revealed that she was turned down for a role on hit US show *Desperate Housewifes* for being 'too curvy'!

I don't think I've definitively been told by Steven who she is *exactly*.

Do you think she'll be back?
I *know* she'll be back. I mean, I've got many more journeys and adventures to go on with the Doctor, so River certainly will be back, yeah.

If you had a hallucinogenic lipstick, what would you use it for?
Oh, I think I'd use it for exactly the same thing that River uses it for – to get my own way! I mean, what else is it there for...?

When you're on set, what's *really* in that blue book?
Oh! Am I allowed to say this? Spoilers! Actually the blue book is incredible because it absolutely *is* what we say it is. It's full of River's scribblings about past adventures – there are pictures of the Doctors, there are extraordinary architectural drawings of buildings that she's seen on other planets. It's beautiful. The prop department spent a long time creating that book. »

We're asking the girls on the show to tell us a secret about the boys.
Oh my God. I don't think Matt *has* any secrets. You know that he's a brilliant footballer, don't you? And he has slightly bandy legs as a result. But that's not a secret, you can just look at them! Arthur Darvill and I have been out to see plays together in London. All I can tell you, and this isn't a secret but it's absolutely genuine, is that he's a really, really great guy. I thought he'd sort of think, 'Oh gosh, Alex, she's not my age or my generation, I don't want to hang with her,' but we had a fantastic night out in London. He's just a really nice person.

If you had a Pandorica, what would you keep in it?
Oooh... You ask such hard questions! I'd keep all of my life in it really, so that whenever I went into the Pandorica I could then travel back to certain times in my life that I wanted to revisit. I can't live for ever but at least then I could just keep going back in time and reliving my best moments. My greatest hits!

You've faced some of the biggest monsters in *Doctor Who* – which ones are your favourites?
Well the monsters that I used to find scariest as a child were the Cybermen. I don't know why but they *absolutely* terrified me. But I have to say that, since I've been doing *Doctor Who*, I find the Weeping Angels really terrifying. And particularly the last story we did with them, they were extraordinary. I think, as a child, if I was watching that episode I really would be terrified because it would make me constantly look at statues or gargoyles, constantly look and think, 'Are they really what I think they are? Or will they move when I don't look?' I think that's such a brilliant concept.

You took on a Dalek and made it beg you for mercy – that's pretty unique.
Haha! Well I'm not frightened of them! I mean I know how dangerous they are, but in this particular episode River also knows that that Dalek is still not quite fully functioning, so she does have a chance. The thing is, River Song is prepared to die for the Doctor. I mean, we know that because we've seen it. She's absolutely prepared to lay down her life for him. So she doesn't have that level of fear. I think it's as simple as that.

> "RIVER SONG IS PREPARED TO DIE FOR THE DOCTOR. WE KNOW THAT BECAUSE WE'VE SEEN IT"

We're determined to get some spoilers out of you – so try this one. Has Steven explained the 'taught by the best' to fly the TARDIS line? Or the identity of the 'best man' that River killed?
Well I certainly think when she says she's been taught by the best she's absolutely referring to the Doctor – but to *her* Doctor. In the past, in the episodes with David Tennant [*Silence in the Library/Forest of the Dead*, 2008] she talked about 'her Doctor' and that is, I guess, the Doctor that she has an amazing life with. And also, presumably, by the time she's found that Doctor, she's been through so many lifetimes, so many experiences, that I suppose, for her, Matt – and David of course – are still not quite fully formed Doctors. So I think she's absolutely referring to the Doctor when she says that. But when she's talking about having killed a man... I can't tell you any more about that because that would be giving stuff away. Spoilers, sweetie! Spoilers...
Foiled again! OK, what's on your MP3 player right now?
This is going to be really, really embarrassing but at the moment – and not necessarily because I want to but because it's what my daughter wants to listen to all the time – it's all the *Glee* soundtracks.
On that subject, River can be quite camp at times. Is that you or River?
Oh I think it's a bit of both. I mean, River *is* me. Actually, if I think about it, the first time you ever saw River she was quite camp then as well, and that's Steven's writing, I suppose. But I think Steven now has more of a sense of me, Alex, so I think it probably works both ways. He might write something that I'll interpret maybe in a slightly camp way. Haha!
Spoilers aside – we know when we're beaten! – when River comes back next year what would you most like to happen?
I would most like us to shoot in Morocco because I'm fed up of shooting night shoots in wet, muddy Wales! Or I'd settle for Barbados, the Caribbean, I don't care. But somewhere hot and exotic. Are you listening, Steven...?

River's cosmic closet

Alex shares the secrets of her arsenal of amazing outfits from Series Five...

Red shoes

Matt's got them. He kept them, not for himself personally but they're around because he wanted them to be on the set of the TARDIS for evermore. I think secretly he does want to try them on. They're a killer to walk in, is all I can say.

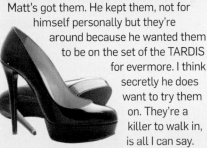

Byzantium

I think they got it from one of those vintage stores. I wasn't tempted to keep it, I wouldn't really have an opportunity to wear anything like that. I don't go to that many awards shows and if I do designers will usually say, 'Oh wear this for the night, will you?'

Combats

I definitely didn't want to keep the combats. Not after we finished with them. We got *so* muddy. You were walking sometimes with an extra 30 pounds of weight, squelching through clay, mud clinging to our boots. I was longing to get out of the combat gear by the end of filming that story, let's just put it that way.

Cat burglar

I actually wanted to have a pair of pussycat ears and a pussycat tail but they wouldn't let me have it. The producers were like, 'It's got to be serious'. I thought, 'Well, she *is* serious but she likes a bit of fun as well she's a cat burglar!' But they wouldn't let me. I could have had something sonic at the end of my tail!

Cleopatra

Oh lord, I look like Fenella Fielding! I just think I look like mutton dressed as lamb. It was fun to do and that's part of River's campery. It's like, 'What can we put her in next?' I'm longing to see what I'm going to be wearing in the next episode, that's for sure. I don't know where the costume came from – probably left over from *I, Claudius*.

Pandorica

With a sheep thrown over the top sometimes! Additional sheep! That was fabulous for being warm. The weather that particular night we were filming at Stonehenge was freezing cold. We had rain, we even had snow at some point in the early hours of the morning. So I was actually quite thrilled to have all those layers keeping me from icing up.

Legends of the Weeping Angels

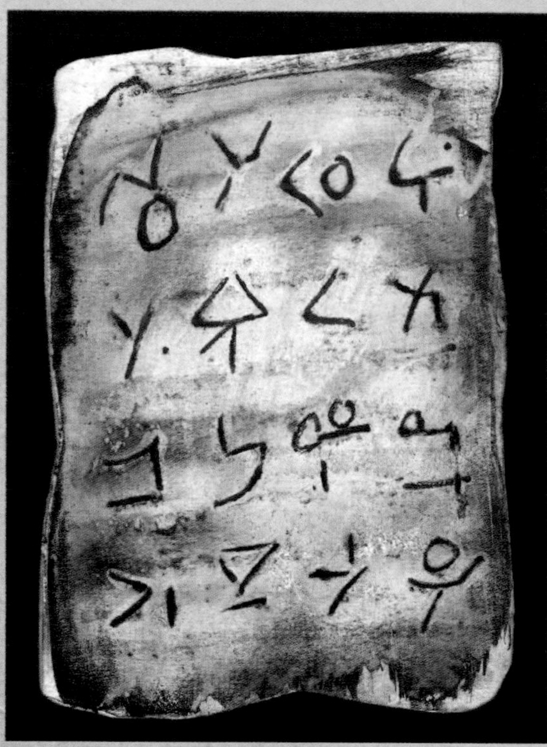

'It's behind you'

TRANSLATED FROM AN OLD HIGH GALLIFREYAN PROVERB

The Laugh of an Angel

A POEM BY ANON.

Whilst walking through an
Abney graveyard
In the dying days of September's summer
I heard an angel's laugh
But when I turned there was nothing there
And the graves were young and new.

'... And they ask us, what shall we do with the flock of angels that destroys our worlds and dims our suns? How shall we protect our colonies as they cower in the dark? How might we attempt to understand these creature's ancient minds, to prod and poke around in their thoughts, to learn how they think, how they live, what they do and why?

'And they ask us to take up arms against such creatures; creatures that cannot be harmed with sticks or stones, that cannot be swayed by our dulcet rhetoric, creatures that have lived longer than the very stars by whose warmth we build our matchstick empires, and will survive for ever after we have gone.

'And I reply; you fools. You seek to understand the angels? You dare to even name them? These are not the stuff of myths and legends. These are not the monsters beneath your bed or the fairy tales made flesh. Why, the very attempt to describe them in such a way is to underestimate them. These are not beings that the human mind can comprehend, what we see is merely an aspect of the very entropy of the universe itself! The angels are a force of nature, and to fight such a force would be as futile as to stand on the shore and demand that the ocean turn back its tide.

'Thank you, Mr Speaker.'

– Chancellor Hardy speaking at the New Moscow Rally, 14 November AD3215

The Mirrored Room

Discovered by the Hargreve expedition in a tomb beneath the Ioan burial mounds. The following images had been carved into the floor between two stone effigies of primitive religious iconography. Translated by Professor Josephine Thomas

In the morning we found a stone woman at the entrance to our village. We thought her to be dead and named her the Gorgon's victim.

But when we looked away, a sudden night fell across the world, and the sun flickered and faded in the sky as if it were a candle without air.

Only I survived to light my lantern, and by its light I saw the creature's true face. Overcome with fear, I fled to the mountains, the stone woman following.

I desecrated the tomb of our emperor. But his treasure was my only hope, and amongst his gold and jewels he had the finest collection of mirrors.

Creating a circle, I stood in the centre, praising our emperor for his vanity as I lured the stone woman towards me by shielding the lantern with my hand.

When I felt the woman's cold embrace I released the light, and the woman saw her image reflected a thousand times around her until she could move no more.

Then I looked into her mournful eyes and the sadness of her entrapment broke my heart.

So I decided to wait with her a while.

Whatever Happened to Charlie Cause?

Extracted from the ancient Earth social network, Blipper.

CClause- 15.27 12/06/09
Scouting out locations for film studies short. Zombie Vixens is officially go! Wooh! :D

CClause- 15.36 12/06/09
Spooky graveyard. I feel a night shoot coming on...

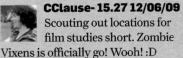

CClause- 15.36 12/06/09
Statues, awesome, always a good decoy for real monsters

CClause- 15.40 12/06/09
Who's fitter, me or the old bird? Blippervote!

CClause- 15.42 12/06/09
Wait, cancel that, my hair was RUBBISH. Try now...

No more search results.

EPISODE 5

Flesh and Stone

BY STEVEN MOFFAT

THE STORY

The Doctor, Amy, River and Octavian's men have escaped into the wreckage of the *Byzantium*. Under siege by the Angels, they embark upon a desperate escape – but not everyone's going to survive...

Something is growing in Amy's mind. The army of Angels is nearly at full strength. And there's a crack in the *Byzantium*'s wall. As the rupture in time and space tears open, people start to fall out of existence – and still the Angels are closing in.

Time is running out – for Amy, for the Doctor, for the universe itself...

FANTASTIC FACTS

» The title of this episode was dreamt up by Joshua Moffat, writer Steven Moffat's son. » River's story gets even more complicated: we learn here that she's been released from the Stormcage Containment Facility to aid Father Octavian in his mission to recover the Weeping Angel from the crashed *Byzantium*. At the end of this episode, she mentions that she'll see the Doctor again, 'when the Pandorica opens': indeed, we meet her next in *The Pandorica Opens*, where she's a prisoner in Stormcage. » But why was River locked up? Octavian reveals that she killed a great hero – someone whom River describes as the best man she's ever known. Could this be the Doctor? Surely not... » 'You, me, handcuffs – must it always end this way?' asks River. At the end of *Forest of the Dead* (2008), River handcuffed the Doctor so he couldn't stop her sacrificing her life to rescue the people 'saved' within the library's computer. Though she has no idea here, River's quip serves to remind us of her ultimate fate. » Having just left her in the forest, the Doctor returns to Amy – who has her eyes tight shut – to implore her to remember what he told her when she was 7 years old. Eagle-eyed viewers might be able to spot that the Doctor is suddenly wearing his jacket again, when we just saw him wander off into the forest without it. Now, of course, we know that the Doctor we see here is actually from the future, on a haphazard journey back through time to solve the problems created by the cracks in the universe. » When we met the Weeping Angels in *Blink* (2007), the Doctor called them 'the only psychopaths in the universe to kill you nicely': they transported their victims back in time and fed off the potential energy left by the displacement. But in this story, they use more brutal tactics. They snap the necks of their victims, tearing out their cerebral cortex to 'borrow' as a method of communication. Why the brutal tactics? Maybe Octavian and his friends are simply in their way. The Angels need to feed on energy to survive, and the cracks in time are a massive source of energy. Perhaps the Angels have sought one out to feed on it? Of course, not even they realise the true nature of the cracks, and how far out of their depth they are. » The Doctor starts to realise that something has shifted in the universe: time can be rewritten, even 'unwritten'. He mentions the gigantic CyberKing marching through the streets of Victorian London. This enormous machine – seen in *The Next Doctor* (2008) – was taller than anything in London. There's no way such a sight could have gone unrecorded by history – unless it never actually happened at all...

MAGIC MOMENT

THE DOCTOR: We've got comfy chairs, did I mention?
ANGEL BOB: We have no need of comfy chairs.
THE DOCTOR: I made him say comfy chairs.
AMY: (Laughing) Six.
THE DOCTOR: Okay, Bob, enough chat – here's what I want to know. What have you done to Amy?
ANGEL BOB: There is something in her eye.
THE DOCTOR: What's in her eye?
ANGEL BOB: We are.
AMY: What's he talking about? Doctor, I'm five. I mean – five. Fine. I'm fine.

BEHIND THE SCENES
STEVEN MOFFAT
Writer

The Weeping Angels are an undeniably creepy idea. Is it fun to write 'scary'? And how far can you take it in a family show?
Frights and scares are fine – we all laugh after we jump, we don't cry – but horrifying and traumatising is not. Scary like a rollercoaster or a ghost train is what *Doctor Who* does. Not scary like being followed on a dark night, or someone physically threatening you.

It's impossible to tell that these were the first episodes Matt Smith and Karen Gillan filmed for the series.
Well that's cos Matt and Karen are both so brilliant. I'm not being flippant – they are honestly incredible and we're lucky to have them. We really chucked them in at the deep end though. First day – rainy beach in Wales, press and paparrazi watching their every move, and they had to suddenly be the Doctor and Amy, standing on an alien planet, looking up at a crashed spaceship that wasn't there. And the pair of them just pulled it off like it was the easiest thing in the world. Did I mention how good they are...?

SPOT THE CRACK

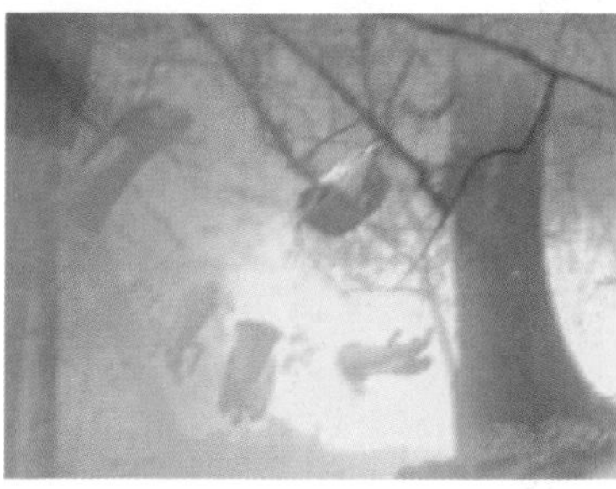

The crack – the biggest one yet seen – is on the wall inside the *Byzantium*'s secondary flight deck. It closes when the Angels fall into it.

CHANGE OF PLAN

In Steven Moffat's very first draft of Episode 5 – dated 12 March 2009 – there was no mention of the Pandorica opening. Instead, as she awaited transportation, River teased the Doctor with a very different taste of their future adventures...

RIVER: No sneak previews. Except this one. The next time you see me we'll be on the Bone Meadows of Antioch by Dyandra Falls. You'll step out the TARDIS and I'll slap you in the face for something you haven't done yet.
THE DOCTOR: I look forward to it.
RIVER: I remember it well.

FAMILIAR FACES

IAIN GLEN
Father Octavian

Iain starred in BBC One's 2009 dramatisation of *The Diary of Anne Frank*, playing Anne's father Otto.

MAKING DOCTOR WHO

AT THE centre of Upper Boat Studios sits the nattily named Blue Box Café. From the outside, it's a pretty innocent looking Portakabin. Inside, though, you'd swear it was bigger than it looked – plus, it serves good coffee. We're here to meet with *Doctor Who*'s executive producer, Beth Willis, to talk about how the series is made. What if, we ask, someone wanted to make their own vortex-hopping, action-adventure series for a Saturday night? What do they need to know? What goes into an episode of the show? Who's responsible for what? Stage by stage, minute by minute, exactly *how* do you make *Doctor Who*...?

Beth puffs out her cheeks. She's only got an hour, and it turns out there is a lot to get through. We've all seen editions of BBC Three's *Doctor Who Confidential*, which takes a weekly look at the making of the show, but there's even more to the story than even that highly detailed series can cover. *Doctor Who*'s production actually starts more than a year before it hits our TVs, and during the making of each 45-minute show, the episode is handed down through a dizzying array of departments. Each one adds its own invaluable contribution – and encounters its own problems to surmount. In fact, when you get to the end of this guide, you might wonder how any *Doctor Who* gets made at all.

Beth settles back onto the couch and clears her throat. She warns us from the off that she's going to have to zoom past the vital work of a number of people – the admin-wizards in the production office, the caterers, the drivers, the extras, the production coordinator, runners, camera department, sound recordists... She's keen not to miss anyone out, but to cover them all might 'take as long as it takes to actually make an episode!'

'OK,' she says, taking a deep breath, 'where do you want to begin?'

At the beginning...

1 STEVEN MOFFAT

Every episode of the series starts right at the top, with executive producer and lead writer Steven Moffat. He's the one who makes all the big decisions about the 'shape' of each season: what the running storyline of the season is, which old friends and foes might turn up, who stays, who goes. Once Steven has a plan in place for each episode, the work really begins...

2 CHOOSE WRITERS

Beth explains that the writers' availability can affect the arc of the series. 'It's a bit chicken-and-egg,' she says. 'There is a broad plan for each series; certain events have to happen at certain points.' Perhaps Steven wants a particular writer to tackle an episode featuring events which affect the main storyline of the series – a big twist, maybe, or a stunning revelation. Let's say that story is planned for the Episode 5 slot. But what if that writer isn't available to write it soon enough for that slot? Maybe he wants to, but because of his other commitments, it can't come any earlier than Episode 8. Steven has to go back to his plans and fiddle until the whole thing works again. Until another writer throws another spanner in the works, anyway!'

How far in advance are these kind of plans made? Beth explains: 'We discussed the storylines for our second series in April 2010.' So, about a year before the first episodes see the light of day, the writing work is already in motion.

3 WRITING

Each writer is commissioned and off they go to clatter at their keyboards to bring the stories to life. Throughout the process, Lindsey Alford and Caroline Henry, the script editors, remain in constant contact with the writers: it's their job to make sure everything is going smoothly, and to pass notes and comments back and forth between the writers and the producers. And then, even when the writers type 'THE END', it isn't really...

'We keep the writers contracted right up until the end of filming,' Beth says, 'just in case any last-minute changes need to be made.' The practicalities of filming frequently necessitate such changes. Maybe a vital location is suddenly unavailable, or an actor drops out, or a scene as written just won't work in the location chosen for filming. It's the writer's job to assess the problem and script a new scene to accommodate it.

For a perfect example of such a change, just look at *The Time of Angels*. Arriving on Alfava Metraxis, the Doctor sticks his head out of the TARDIS door and says that there's 'a slight chance of rain'. This little line was added to explain away the rather dreary filming conditions of the earlier location shoot, on a rainy beach in Wales.

Regardless of these last-minute modifications, there comes a point – still long before filming – where the script is considered 'finished enough' to pass on to other departments. This is where the pre-production process really begins...

4 THE PERFECT SCRIPT?

'You never get the perfect script before the other processes start,' says Beth. 'That's because the demands of pre-production always result in changes to the scripts.'

5.1 CASTING

Once they have a working version of the script, the casting director and the producers meet to discuss ideas for casting. Who should play the big villain? Who should populate the spaceship, alien world or sleepy village the Doctor finds himself in this week? Once some names are decided on, it's the casting director's job to contact actors' agents, to determine the availability and interest of possible stars, and to go about lining them up. It's also his job to set up any necessary auditions. Here's where an early possible problem can rear its head: what if the perfect actor isn't available on the planned filming dates? Usually, the dates will have to be changed to accommodate this – which is just the first of many production wrinkles that have to be ironed out...

5.2 DESIGN TEAM

The production designer and his team start making their own plans, based on the needs of the script. Meetings take place between the designer, director and locations manager, to see what work is involved in the episode. What sets need to be built in the studios? And what locations need to be altered and dressed to look the part? Sometimes, these two elements cross over: for example, a huge, abandoned warehouse might be the perfect place to house the cockpit and engine rooms of a broken-down spaceship. In this case, a set would have to be built at the location, blending the best aspects of the location itself with some sci-fi stylings.

5.3 LOCATION MANAGER

Doctor Who employs a full-time location manager, whose job it is to find, choose, negotiate and manage all the locations needed for filming. 'It's a huge, huge job,' says Beth. 'We can need anything from two to fifteen locations in a single episode.' The location manager needs to check all sorts of things: 'Is it all right to blow out the windows? Where do we park

the team's trucks and trailers? What are the practicalities of a team of 70 people working at that location?'

The production designer might want to make changes to a location, and the Location Manager has to handle that, seeking out the appropriate permissions and assuring the owners that no damage will be done. He also has to deal with the police, informing them of filming dates and locations, and sometimes asking them to stop traffic. If the filming involves a 'period' location – a street in Victorian London, for example – the Location Manager even has to ask local residents not to park their cars outside their homes!

As well as catering for the needs of the production team, the Location Manager has to keep the owners of any properties happy – and make sure the team clean up when filming has finished!

5.4 COSTUME AND MAKE-UP

'The other day,' Beth says, 'I walked into the toilets to find someone from costume washing a blonde wig for auditions for the Christmas special!' The work of the costume and make-up teams starts early, too. They take a look at the script and decide what clothes they need to buy or rent, and what costumes they might already have hanging in their extensive wardrobes. But, with *Doctor Who* adventures spanning everything from medieval times to the far future, their job often involves a great deal of stitching and sewing. 'They can't just go buy a load of clothes from Top Shop,' Beth adds. 'There are a lot of things that need to be made.'

5.5 THE MILL

You might think that the computer-generated effects are one of the last things to be added to a *Doctor Who* episode, but that's only partly true. The Mill, the effects house who carry out most of the series' dazzling CGI, get involved right at the start, having been sent another copy of that early working script. From that, The Mill makes a breakdown of what CGI is needed for that episode. Deciding what should be CGI and what should be physically achieved on set is 'a compromise that takes a long time to work out,' Beth explains. She cites Amy's battle with the disembodied head of a Cyberman in *The Pandorica Opens*: 'That was a mix of CGI and physical effects that ended up blending really well.'

5.6 MILLENNIUM FX

Speaking of physical effects, there's one final team who get a look at this early script: Millennium FX, the series' longstanding prosthetics team. If there are any monster masks or suits to be made (such as a Slitheen or a Cyberman), they need plenty of notice to get to work. 'It's a long process,' says Beth, 'and it can be reliant on casting, if it's a very detailed, close-fitting prosthetic like a Silurian mask.'

6 FIRST AD

Once the script is in something approaching its final state, and all the pre-production work is well under way, the episode is handed to the first assistant director. It's his responsibility to seek input from the other production departments and to take a long, hard look at the script, scene by scene, and turn all that information into a filming schedule. 'He needs to be realistic,' says Beth. 'He can't be optimistic, or conservative.' Too few days on the schedule and they could run out of time; too many, and they risk wasting money on days they don't need.

It's the first AD's job to ensure that everything – set design, casting, location filming, effects work, everything – fits together in a practical, workable schedule. Any number of problems can arise at this stage, requiring some nimble reactions from the other teams: there might be rewrites on the script, the casting director might announce that an actor can't work on certain dates, costumes could be still unmade, a location might only be available on the weekends... The first AD has to react to all these changes and keep his schedule watertight and bang up-to-date. Once the schedule is locked, it's also his job to communicate those dates to the whole production team – and to ensure they stick to them.

7 RECCE

'There are two days of recce,' Beth explains, 'and they're probably two of the most important days of the whole process!' On the recce, a small team (the location manager, producer and director among them) visits the planned filming locations and takes a look at them with a hyper-critical eye. Every practicality of filming there is examined, to make sure there are no nasty surprises when 'Action!' is called for the first time. A list of vital equipment is drawn up at this stage: maybe they'll need a crane to achieve some planned shots, for example, or something as simple as wooden boards might need to be laid over rough ground, so the Daleks can trundle smoothly into shot. The aim here is to make sure all teams get a chance to identify – and solve – potential problems before the cameras start rolling.

UPPER BOAT STUDIOS

Back in 2005, no one could have known how big a success the newly revived *Doctor Who* was going to be. But thanks to that first, smash-hit series – and because of the unique nature of the show's production – it soon became clear that it was going to need a home of its own, somewhere dedicated just to making *Doctor Who*. And so, from the ruins of an old car-parts factory, Upper Boat Studios was born.

The studios are an unassuming sight, looking like nothing more than a collection of warehouses. They are easy to miss even if you know what to look for. Just across the road sits a petrol station. Sometimes, lost supporting artists will call in, asking, 'Do you know where the *Doctor Who* studios are?' – and even the folk manning the pumps mere metres away have no idea what goes on in those anonymous-looking buildings.

All but one of the studios at Upper Boat are dedicated to *Doctor Who* and its spin-off *The Sarah Jane Adventures*. (*Torchwood* used to use these studios, too – in fact, the new TARDIS is built inside the shell of the old Hub.) The other studio is currently being used by outside productions, such as *Upstairs, Downstairs* and Steven Moffat's *Sherlock*.

The TARDIS itself sits in the largest of these studios. It's a big set and it needs all that room to breathe. Beth shows us around, and although she's worked in and around the set for months, it's clear she's in love with the TARDIS – and it's easy to see why. There are a myriad nooks and crannies to explore and even two whole staircases that we've never seen before on screen.

Next door to the TARDIS is the 'spare' studio used by other shows, and on the other side of that sits the studio housing the standing sets for *The Sarah Jane Adventures*: Sarah's attic, Rani's house, and Luke's bedroom. In fact, between them, the 'permanent' sets for both shows take up most of the space.

Across the way, you find another huge warehouse, this one housing an enormous prop store: shelf after shelf of weird odds and ends, all of it used to dress sets and locations during filming. The prop store also contains a number of locked rooms. First, there is a room of working firearms – it's pretty obvious why they're kept under lock and key. There's also a room to house all the 'functioning' props, things that have some sort of electronic or mechanical component such as the sonic screwdriver. Finally, there are two rooms which, between them, contain the masks and costumes for just about every monster the Doctor has ever faced. Dalek mutants, Slitheen, Silurians... the list goes on, but the scariest thing, without a doubt, is a fake David Tennant (used last in *The End of Time*). It's so lifelike, it's like he never left!

The final studio is empty when we see it. It's used for one-off sets, things that only need building to appear in one or two episodes. This studio also houses a floor-to-ceiling green screen, which is used for effects work.

Top it all off with the busy production offices, editing suites, green rooms, meeting rooms and, of course, the Blue Box Café, and that's Upper Boat. It's the biggest studio complex in Wales, and when you look at the size of the *Doctor Who* operation, it's easy to see why it needed such an extensive base for its production.

8.1 PRODUCTION MEETING

It's now just one week until filming starts. At a huge meeting of the whole production team, everyone is briefed on the final plans for the shoot, and any last-minute problems are ironed out. At this point, the wheels are really in motion...

8.2 SECOND AD

Meanwhile, the second AD is busy corralling the actors. It's his or her job to look after the stars, and to make sure everyone's in the right place at the right time. 'It has quite a creative component,' Beth adds. 'The second AD is responsible for finding and casting the supporting artists. If the script calls for fifty bald, five-foot men, he or she has to find them somewhere in Wales!'

8.2 READ-THROUGH

Also around this time, the whole cast for the episode, along with the writer and producers, gather around a huge table for a read-through. Everyone takes their part, acting out the whole episode in one long 'take', for the very first time. 'It's the only time the actors will read the script all the way through with all their fellow actors,' Beth says. Because the scenes for an episode are never filmed in order, and the Doctor may never actually run into Space Engineer No 2 on screen, it's really the only chance for these actors to meet. 'They can be sitting there with someone they'll never see again.'

The read-through offers a chance to get a proper idea of how the episode might turn out. A script is very good at telling you what people say, and what happens when, but until actors breathe life into those words, it's impossible to know how the episode feels. 'It's a good time to see what's feeling too fast, what's feeling funny, who has great chemistry,' Beth says –

and all these things, these emotional reactions to the performances, can result in further rewrites.

'It also gives Matt and Karen a chance to look forward,' Beth adds. The series' stars might actually be filming a different episode while the readthrough takes place – and even if they're not, the process of filming is so fragmented and confusing, it can be hard for them to see the wood for the trees when it comes to the stories they're creating. That's why a read-through can be invaluable: 'It helps them keep the shape of the whole series in their head.'

9 FILMING

The filming for an episode can take a couple of weeks, and is often carried out alongside one or two other episodes – a single director is usually assigned to one of these 'blocks' of stories. At this point, it's basically a case of following the first AD's schedule, pointing the camera at the actors, and shouting 'Action!'. The other teams have done their jobs, ensuring the actual filming goes as smoothly as possible.

'This is probably the most straightforward stage!' laughs Beth. 'But it's nerve-racking – everything is to play for. You have to get it done, and you're constantly reacting to changes in circumstances. Ideally, if everything goes smoothly, it should be a great time.'

And if everything doesn't go smoothly? 'The financial repercussions are huge...' she says. 'And once filming is over, that's it – you can't make any more changes.'

10 EDITING

Once shooting is complete, the editor and director take all the filmed material and sit in a darkened editing suite for a week, until a 'draft' edit is complete. They choose the best shots, and the best takes, and build them all together into a seamless telling of the story. Once this is complete, the episode is shown to the executive producers, who give their notes. The following day, these notes are incorporated in a new edit. The episode goes back and forth in this manner, until a final version emerges. But even now, with this 'locked' edit in hand, the work isn't nearly over...

11.1 INCIDENTAL MUSIC

The series' composer Murray Gold is handed this 'locked' version of the episode, from which he writes, arranges and records music for the episode (find out more on page 38).

11.2 SOUND DESIGN AND ADR

The sound design of an episode is a 'massive contribution', according to Beth. Not only does it add atmosphere and much-needed bleeps and bloops from the TARDIS console, it also enhances – and in some cases completes – the story.

ADR (Additional Dialogue Recording) is a big part of this: this is the process whereby the actors come into a recording studio to re-record lines, or record brand new ones to be added in the final edit. For example, an early two-minute scene might have to be cut from the episode for timing reasons, taking some necessary background information with it. In ADR, lines can be inserted into later scenes to fill in the blanks. Sometimes, too, the sound recording of a line may turn out to be slightly less than perfect – which is where ADR can come to the rescue. (ADR is most often – but not exclusively – used in shots where the actor's face is turned away from the camera, making it a little easier to fit in such lines, as the actor's lip movements can't easily be seen.)

A great deal of ADR material is recorded, but not all of it is used. 'The performance on the day is always the preferable take,' Beth says. 'You always get a better performance from the actor "live". And it's a real skill. Try to do it yourself! Particularly if the actor is not saying what they said at the time.' But even so, ADR is there for all those times when a line is ruined by a barking dog in the background, a jet passing overhead, or an ambulance siren blaring along a road in the distance.

11.3 COLOURING

Beth is the first to admit that the process of colouring an episode – sometimes called the grade – is 'like magic'. The colourist takes the final edit and goes through it frame by frame, over two days, digitally enhancing the picture. He matches the colour palette on different shots in the same scene, giving everything a consistent look. Perhaps one shot is darker than another, when they're both meant to take place in broad daylight. Or maybe this underground cavern just doesn't look gloomy enough. All these things can be fixed in the grade, as well as giving an episode a final polish, leaving it gleaming and perfect. Once the colourist has completed his first pass, the director joins him for day to give his or her input. This is then rounded out by further notes from the executive producers.

The capabilities of the technology used still amaze Beth. 'Can we have more colour in their faces? Make the sky bluer? Make the Silurian greener? It does seem that anything is possible. They can transform something, making it beautiful when it wasn't. It's exciting to see something so familiar change so much. It brings a new layer out of it, like restoring an old painting.'

11.4 CGI

Now they've got a copy of the final edit, The Mill can begin to marry their computer-generated effects with the picture on screen. 'The CGI can take weeks and weeks and weeks,' says Beth. And it's full of its own scheduling pitfalls...

'We shoot the Christmas special in July,' she explains. 'But that's still scarily tight for The Mill to achieve what they need to in time. They will receive the "locked" edit in August or September. Only two months for them to do their work is pretty frightening. If they fall behind, that could have a knock-on effect on the next series.'

The Mill's work is part of the final finessing of the episode, and Beth describes this whole process as a very exciting time, with everything coming together. 'It should all be downhill from the edit onwards. The music, sound, grade, CGI – they're all new elements that should make the episode better and better and better. It's all about enhancing it and creating the best possible show.'

12 AND FINALLY...

Add some credits and a 'Next Time' trailer – and you're done!

EPISODE 6

The Vampires of Venice

BY TOBY WHITHOUSE

THE STORY

The Doctor takes Amy and Rory on a romantic date to medieval Venice, to try to mend their relationship. But the lovers' tiff is soon forgotten when they discover a private school that seems to be turning girls into vampires.

Run by the sinister Rosanna Calvierri, the school's front as a vampire factory is a lie. Rosanna is a Sister of the Water, a refugee from a shattered world, and she's brought the last of her people with her. Using the girls from the school, she plans to repopulate the Earth with the Saturnyne race.

A storm is brewing. Venice will fall, and a new Saturnyne will rise from the ruins. Only the Doctor stands between the human race and a watery grave...

MAGIC MOMENT

ROSANNA: We can build a new society here, as others have. What do you say?.
THE DOCTOR: Where's Isabella?
ROSANNA: Isabella?
THE DOCTOR: The girl who saved my friend.
ROSANNA: Oh, deserters must be executed. Any general will tell you that. I need an answer, Doctor. A partnership. Any which way you choose.
THE DOCTOR: I don't think that's such a good idea, do you? I'm a Time Lord. You're a big fish. Think of the children.
ROSANNA: You were right. We're nothing alike. I shall bend the heavens to save my race, while you philosophise.
THE DOCTOR: This ends today. I will tear down the House of Calvierri, stone by stone... And you know why? You didn't know Isabella's name.

FAMILIAR FACES

HELEN McCRORY

Rosanna Calvierri

Helen stars as Narcissa Malfoy in the *Harry Potter* movies; she also played Cherie Blair in *The Queen*.

ALEX PRICE

Francesco Calvierri

Alex has been in *Merlin* and *Being Human*, and also narrated this year's editions of *Doctor Who Confidential*.

WHERE IN THE WORLD?

Medieval Venice was recreated in the tiny town of Trogir, Croatia. Trogir is classed as a World Heritage Site for its beautiful architecture, much of it built when the Venetian Empire ruled here.

SPOT THE CRACK

After the climactic storm, there's a suspiciously familiar shape in the clouds. Or are we just seeing things...?

NUMBER CRUNCHING

10,002 THE NUMBER OF SATURNYNE SURVIVORS LEFT IN THE UNIVERSE

1 ***The number of Time Lord survivors left in the universe***

BEHIND THE SCENES
TOBY WHITHOUSE

Writer

As we see when she confronts the Doctor about her plan, Rosanna has a very compelling motivation for a *Doctor Who* baddie...
I think every villain – even the Daleks, or the Weeping Angels – have what is to them a sound and legitimate motivation to do what they do. Rosanna's was possibly much nobler: there was no personal ambition in her plan, it wasn't a question of greed or even power. Ultimately, all she wanted to do was save her race. Her argument was that all she needed for that was one city, and one city would save an entire species. Whereas with most of the other villains you can say, 'Oh no, that's wrong', I think this is much more of a grey area – and I think that makes the character more interesting.

As well as battling alien fish-vampires, the Doctor also had to contend with the problems in Amy and Rory's relationship. How hard is it to deal with such 'mundane' topics in the world of *Doctor Who*?
The brief I was given was to write a big, romantic romp. They wanted it to be a romantic episode, hence the decision to set it in Venice – traditionally, a very romantic city. *Doctor Who* works at its best when very human and familiar, recognisable emotions and relationships are being played out against this huge background. It was great fun to set a domestic argument from 2010 in 1518 in Venice!

DELETED!

THE DOCTOR: Next stop Leadworth Register Office? Assuming that's how you get married in Leadworth. Maybe you just put a tourist in a Wicker Man.

FANTASTIC FACTS

❯❯ OK, so the vampires here aren't real vampires – but that doesn't mean the Doctor wouldn't know a real one if he saw it. The Great Vampire race were involved in a bloody war with the Time Lords in an ancient era known as the Dark Times. The Time Lords won, but – as we discovered in *State of Decay* (1981) – one of the creatures survived. Until the Doctor found it, defeated its servants, and staked it good and proper! ❯❯ Other vampire-like aliens met by the Doctor include the Haemovores (*The Curse of Fenric*, 1989) and the Plasmovores (*Smith and Jones*, 2007). You can find out a lot more about the Doctor's various vampiric encounters starting on page 64... ❯❯ This story features another perception filter – this one worn at the waist of Rosanna, and used to disguise her fish-like true appearance. (We can assume that Francesco is using one, too.) ❯❯ The Doctor carries an old library card, featuring a photograph of his first incarnation (played by William Hartnell). The name on the card is 'Dr J Smith', a reference to the Doctor's commonly used pseudonym John Smith (last used in *Human Nature* – we might assume it's now too painful a reminder of that period of his life). According to the card, Dr Smith lives at 76 Totter's Lane, which was the address of the junkyard where viewers first met the Doctor, back in the very first story *An Unearthly Child* (1963).

twitbook

Archive from 25th June 2010

Barry Whitaker uploaded photos to the album "Rory's Stag". *10 minutes ago.*

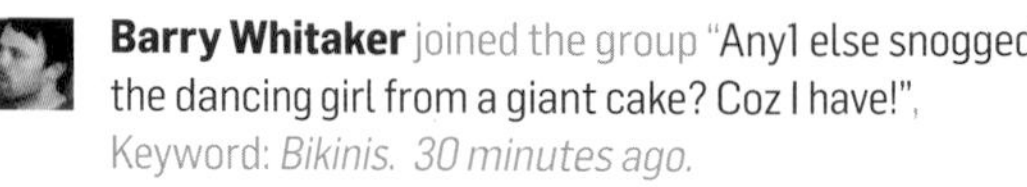

Barry Whitaker joined the group "Any1 else snogged the dancing girl from a giant cake? Coz I have!", Keyword: *Bikinis. 30 minutes ago.*

Jamie Thompson deleted his comment on Rory Williams' profile. *50 minutes ago.*

Jamie Thompson posted "To be fair, Amy is a great kisser! ;)" on Rory Williams' profile. *50 minutes ago.*

> **Barry Whitaker** commented "Dude, seriously?"

Rory Williams commented on the group "The 10 worst things that can happen at a stag do." *1 hour ago.*

Barry Whitaker updated his status "Just given my jumper to some random girl. It's well cold." *1 hour ago.*

Rory Williams joined the group "I hate surprises." *1 hour ago.*

Jake Johnson updated his status "learning to play darts at Rory's stag. The guy next to me is well hairy." *3 hours ago.*

> **Jamie Thompson** commented "Get off ur fone!"

> **Jake Johnson** commented "You too, lol! Anyway shh, the cake's here."

The Doctor answered "May be attending" on the event "THE Stag do". *Tomorrow*

Rory Williams joined the group "I love my fiancé so much I want to ask her to marry me all over again." *4 hours ago.*

Bradley Davis updated his status "Spent all day ironing transfers onto jumpers because the company mucked up the order. This is mental." *5 hours ago*

> **Rory Williams** commented "Hey, that's my catchphrase!"

Rory Williams updated his status. "Just finished reading a book on other dimensions. Mental!" *6 hours ago.*

> **Amy Pond** commented "Geek!"

Rory Williams posted "I love you. X" on Amy Pond's profile. *7 hours ago.*

> **Tim Salisbury** likes this.

Weird Nights Out – Rory's Stag

Uploaded by Barry Whitaker

Karen Jenkins "On the phone at your stag do Rory? Was it that bad?"

Jamie Thompson "Nah, he's calling a cab cos his party was TOO BANGING!"

Bradley Davis "Jamie, you were playing pool."

Barry Whitaker "What are the numbers on the back of the shirts supposed to mean Brad?"

Bradley Davis "In Jake's case it's how old he was when he first pulled."

Karen Jenkins "LOL, the guy next to you looks like Bill Bailey!"

Karen Jenkins "Awesome, wish I'd been there!"

Barry Whitaker "We can tell from the fact that you've commented on every. single. photo."

Karen Jenkins "Luv U 2 hun :p What pub were you in?"

Jamie Thompson "This is Leadworth, there's only one pub."

Karen Jenkins "Those t-shirts are cool, was it someone's idea or did you all decide to do the same thing by accident? Freaky!"

Barry Whitaker " *facepalm* "

Karen Jenkins "I want one!"

Karen Jenkins "Is that Rory's dad?"

Jamie Thompson "So who WAS that guy?"

Barry Whitaker "Some student mate of his from uni I reckon."

Jamie Thompson "Medics, they just dunno when to stop."

Barry Whitaker "I don't care, I hooked up with that girl from the cake cos of him ;) "

Bradley Davis "Really? You've not mentioned that, like, A MILLION TIMES."

Karen Jenkins "FIIIIIIIIIIIIIIITTTTTTTTT!"

SIGNORA CALVIERRI'S ACADEMY for YOUNG WOMEN

VENICE, CITY OF MYSTERY AND enchantment, fine art and festivities. What better place for young women to improve themselves in an atmosphere of tranquillity and refinement?

Signora Rosanna Calvierri has dedicated her life to the education and cultivation of maidens of humble origin, tutoring them personally in those attributes best befitting a lady of high standing.

Signora Calvierri considers her students to be her children, with Venice as their nursery. 'This city is so special to me,' she has often said, 'with its dark and narrow streets, and tranquil waters. No other city has been so welcoming to my family. No other city feels so much like our home.'

Here, at the Calvierri Academy, your daughter (legitimate or otherwise), niece, or ward shall enjoy an education in subjects most felicitous to a lady, including culinary skills, embroidery, poise, elocution, and fine dining.

Venice's most skilful seamstresses teach our pupils to craft all manner of garments, from gloves to cloaks, while Signor Francesco Calvierri, son to Signora Rosanna, takes a great personal interest in their well-being and their tuition in all subjects. Our pupils eat well, and they do not drink... wine.

Perhaps swimming lessons are all that we do not offer. After all, this is Venice. Everyone can swim!

Though the Academy is located in the heart of our great city, our students are protected from its more vulgar excesses and shielded from the baleful influence of street urchins and vagabonds. While the great cities of Europe and beyond are blighted by the terrible pestilence of the plague, here in the Academy our young women are of good health, not to mention a refined beauty which is the envy of all Venice!

Protected from vulgar excesses

After graduating from Signora Calvierri's Academy, our ladies are practically unrecognisable, even to their nearest and dearest! You may not believe the transformation that has occurred!

It matters not if a young lady is ill-educated, inexperienced, the proverbial 'fish out of water'. The House Of Calvierri accepts women of all circumstances and from all backgrounds, regardless of financial worth, providing they are youthful, in good health, and meet with the final approval of Signora Calvierri herself, and of course her beloved son, Signor Francesco.

Unbelievable transformation!

Former Students

'Before I attended Signora Calvierri's Academy, I was very poor and I ate very rarely. Now I feast regularly, and I enjoy it!'
SIGNORINA MARIA DA C___

'I was a shy and timid young thing, lacking in ambition, before attending Signora Calvierri's Academy, but now I know this world is for the taking!'
SIGNORINA SOFIA L__

'I was orphaned when just eight years old, and never knew there were so many opportunities in life, but now I have this unquenchable thirst... for knowledge.'
SIGNORINA CONSTANZA B____

The vampire chronicles

From every corner of time and space, our intrepid vampire hunter has unearthed documents which throw light on the many and varied bloodsucking monstrosities encountered by the Doctor on his travels...

THE RECORD OF RASSILON

The Vampire Army

In the First Days of Gallifrey, when Rassilon himself was young, the Lords of Time were threatened by a swarm of space Vampires: giant winged beasts whose fearsome hunger was such that a single Vampire could suck the life from an entire planet. And lo, Rassilon decreed that the Lords of Time should meet these Vampires in battle. Energy weapons were useless, because the monsters absorbed and transmuted the energy, using it to become stronger. Therefore Rassilon ordered the construction of bowships, swift vessels that fired a mighty bolt of steel that transfixed the monsters through the heart – for only if his heart be utterly destroyed will a Vampire die. So powerful were the bodies of these great creatures, and so fiercely did they cling to life, that they were impossible to kill, save by the use of bowships. Yet slain they all were and to the last one by the Lords of Time, the Lords of Time destroying them utterly. However, when the bodies were counted, the King Vampire, mightiest and most malevolent of all, had vanished even to his shadow, from time and space. Hence it is the directive of Rassilon that any Time Lord who comes upon this enemy of our people and of all living things shall use all his efforts to destroy him, even at the cost of his own life.

TARDIS Databank: Supplemental

Report uploaded by Time Lady historian Romanadvoratrelundar, Relative Dateline 13,121,980

There was of course a perfectly rational explanation behind all that superstitious nonsense about the King Vampire vanishing even to his shadow: the creature had simply escaped into a separate continuum known as E-Space, as the Doctor and I discovered when the TARDIS made planetfall on a sparsely populated world where the fugitive King Vampire had slept for millennia. The primitive human descendants of a long-lost colony ship had fallen under the Vampire's spell: the blood of murdered peasants sustained the creature in its sleep, while the ship's trio of flight officers were infected and became human vampires. Known as the Three Who Rule, Lord Zargo, Lady Camilla and Chancellor Aukon served their sleeping master for a thousand years until our arrival precipitated the Time of Arising. The Doctor ingeniously used one of the colony ship's scout vessels as a 'mighty bolt of steel', launching it on a trajectory which destroyed the Vampire's heart at the moment of its awakening. With the King Vampire dead at last, the Three Who Rule aged a thousand years in a matter of seconds and crumbled into dust.

JUDOON CASE FILE
NO. 31032007 / 179

EXPEDITION LEADERS: Judoon Officers Ka-Pa-Lu-Yes and Igg-Cha-Sbr-Sil-No.

OBJECTIVE: To capture and execute fugitive criminal of Plasmavore race.

INFORMATION ON PLASMAVORES: Shape-shifting race of bloodsuckers. Known to use Slab life forms for protection.

INFORMATION ON SUSPECT: Plasmavore criminal guilty of murder of Child Princess of Padrivole Regency 9.

OPERATIONAL REPORT: Suspect was tracked to planet Earth in population centre Lon-Don. Primitive human medical facility was isolated on nearby moon. Plasmavore suspect attempted to evade detection by ingesting human blood and absorbing genetic material, but was identified posing as elderly female human named Flo-Renz Fin-E-Gan. In apprehending suspect, Judoon Platoon received assistance of Time Lord Dok-Ta and human medic Ma-Tha-Jonz. Suspect attempted to destroy medical facility and planned to escape in Judoon ship, but was identified, apprehended and summarily disintegrated.

FILE STATUS:

CASE CLOSED

THE NINE TRAVELLERS

Notes for a Monograph by Professor Emilia Rumford

This magnificent Bronze Age stone circle in the ancient kingdom of Dumnonia has long been the subject of a dispute regarding the original number of stones: the survey of Dr Borlase in ~~1574~~ 1754 refers to the Nine Travellers, but earlier records allude instead to the Seven and the Six Travellers. The extraordinary truth about this discrepancy can now be revealed: from the very time of the circle's construction in around 2000 BC, three of the ancient standing stones were in fact alien monsters from outer space. Specifically they were Ogri, scions of a silicon-based life form hailing from the acid swamps of Ogros, a planet in Tau Ceti. Here on Earth the Ogri depended for their nourishment on globulin, a protein found in blood plasma, and they survived by draining the blood from human victims supplied by the followers of a pagan goddess called the Cailleach, who in reality was another alien, this time from the planet Diplos. Before her unmasking I knew her as my fellow archaeological colleague, Vivien Fay, but her true identity was Cessair of Diplos, a ruthless master criminal who had brought the Ogri to Earth four thousand years earlier when fleeing from galactic justice. When the alien law machines caught up with her, they carried out Cessair's sentence of perpetual imprisonment by transforming her into a new stone in the circle – and so, with the three Ogri now gone, we can settle once and for all on the Seven Travellers. Or can we?

This passage is NOT for publication. I do have my academic reputation to consider!

VISIT FRANKENSTEIN'S HOUSE OF HORRORS!

ROLL UP, ROLL UP! Here at the Festival of Ghana we've got spooks and ghouls and freaks and fools waiting to thrill you with the very latest in state-of-the-art automated entertainment. In Frankenstein's House of Horrors, our sinister cybernetic spectres will send a sizzle up your spine. Gaze aghast at the ghostly Grey Lady, the frightful Frankenstein's Monster and, deadliest of all, the demonically debonair Dracula! Yes, you'll come face to face with the Count himself, in the form of a robot so terrifying that he'll drain the blood from your veins, so chillingly realistic that he can fool anyone from rational schoolteachers to ruthless Daleks into believing that he's the real thing! But don't take our word for it – here's just some of the visitor feedback we've received since the Festival opened its doors back in 1996:

'More spooks to the square mile than the Tower of London!' – Ian Chesterton, London

'I feel as though my hair's turned white!' – Barbara Chesterton, London

'You won't believe what's in the secret tunnel!' – Vicki Troilus, Asia Minor

'Things that go bumpety-bumpety in the night, hmm? I am convinced that that house was neither tame, time, nor space. Nor Spain. And I'm not a mountain goat, and if you'd had your anti-radiation gloves, you could have lent her hers.'
– Dr John Smith, no fixed abode

The Ultima Project
27th May 1943

MOST SECRET

Following yesterday's dramatic events in Northumbria, the above project has been abandoned with immediate effect. Intelligence gathered from a classified source, codename 'The Doctor', suggests that Britain's secret plan to destabilise the Soviet government with a deadly chemical poison would have resulted in catastrophic long-term consequences for the entire planet: pollution of such a mysterious and unimaginable nature that it would ultimately result in the mutation of the human race into a species of blue-skinned, gill-breathing, bloodsucking humanoids known as Haemovores.

It is understood that a malevolent entity known as Fenric transported the last survivor of these Haemovores, known as the Ancient One, from Earth's distant future to its distant past, where it lurked for centuries beneath the waves of the North Sea, luring unwary mariners to their doom and converting them to its own kind. Yesterday Fenric released these creatures from their bonds and they rose from the sea at Maidens' Point, rampaging through the village and military base and claiming dozens of casualties. Fortunately for the future of humanity, the Ancient One took its revenge on Fenric by releasing the poison in a sealed chamber, destroying both itself and Fenric's human host. Thus was disaster averted and the future reshaped.

Yesterday's events are subject to a D-Notice, and a cover story is being prepared to explain that the Haemovore attack was merely a mass hallucination caused by a harmless leak of experimental gas into the local atmosphere. For reasons of national security, the true facts of the case are designated Top Secret in perpetuity. This file is to remain Classified indefinitely.

Today my old friend the Doctor called upon me and took a draught of Rhenish in my lodgings. He hath lately been in Venice, whereof he unfolded the most improbable fiction, and 'tis my sport thus to set it down.

A Sonnet, by Will Shakespeare

My mistress' girls cannot abide the sun,
Nor cast an image in Venetian glass.
Their shapely necks with crimson blood have run,
For monsters fang'd have taught Rosanna's class.
Shall I compare them to a Vampire? No!
Misleading is that term vernacular.
For Vampires are they not, though seeming so;
They share no common blood with Dracula.
Perceiving they were fish from Saturnyne,
The Doctor scaled a tall Venetian steeple
To disconnect an engine most malign
And overthrow these wretched Fishy People;
And thus reduced the Vampires plaguing Venice
To just another Underwater Menace.

DIRECTING DOCTOR WHO

WHAT do you think of when you think of a TV director? One of those fold-up fabric chairs? Megaphoned cries of 'Action!' and 'Cut!'? Peering through a frame of fingers as the perfect shot is set up? That stereotypical image, of the auteur marshalling actors and cameras for the perfect picture, isn't half the story – as you'll learn when **Ashley Way** takes us through the many responsibilities of a *Doctor Who* director.

'THE responsibility of a director is to take what's in black and white on the page and turn that into a visual and aural programme, to put it into pictures and into sound,' he says. 'That means that you're creatively responsible for everything you see and hear on screen.'

And that's what you might expect when you conjure up that image of a director on set. But, taking barely a breath, Ashley continues, describing the level of involvement his job actually entails.

'Therefore, I'll take a script, read it, work out what the locations need to be, what the props need to be, the costumes, who we cast – and then, on set, how you shoot that, where you put the camera, what the camera moves are, what the pace of the scene is, what the tone of the scene is...'

It's immediately clear that being a director is more than just 'taking a picture'. Their involvement is total, their input necessary at every stage of an episode's production – from long before the cameras start rolling.

'Initially, you get the script,' he says, 'and then your first involvement is when you meet the producers for your interview for the job. That's where you pitch your vision for the story, how you see the story unfolding visually and the tone of the story, and all the rest of it. That's where you agree with the producers on how things need to be – then you move on from there.'

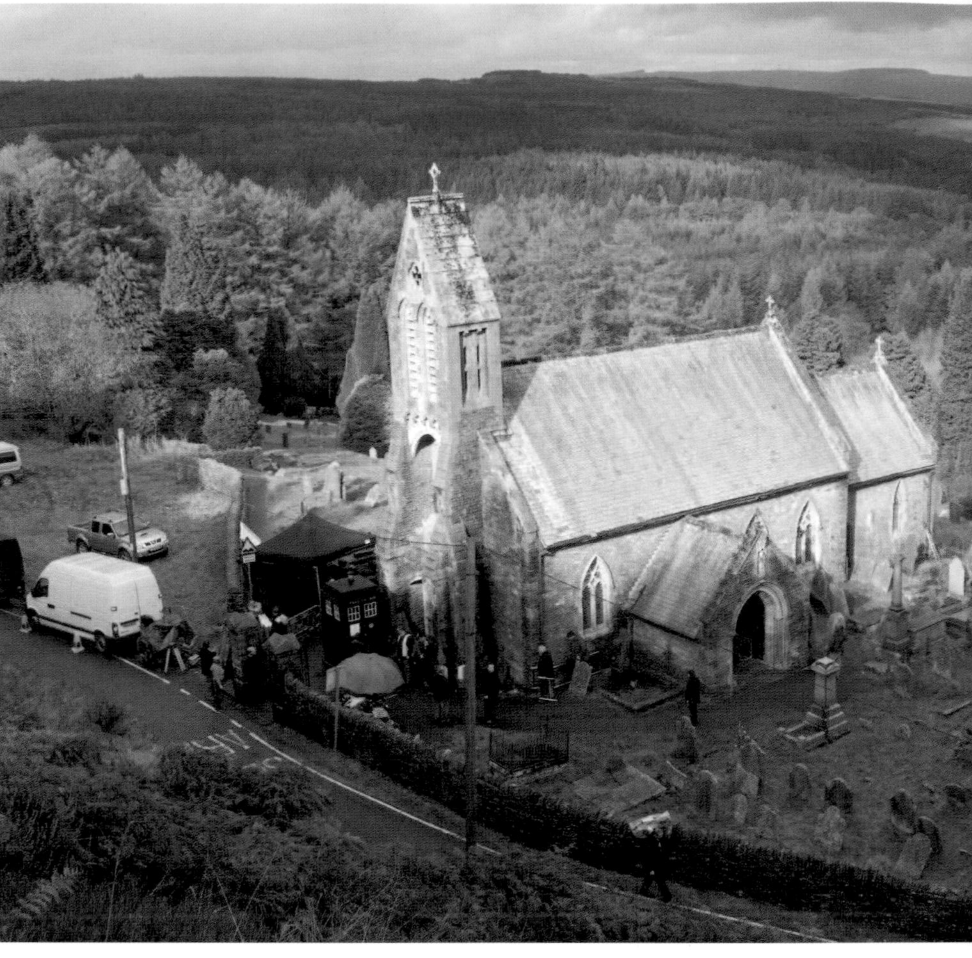

ASHLEY directed this year's two-part epic *The Hungry Earth/Cold Blood*, featuring a tiny Welsh mining village in crisis following the discovery of an ancient race of reptile people deep underground. He describes his pitch for the episodes as '*Signs* meets *Journey to the Centre of the Earth*. A fantasy adventure with a psychological edge. The script, as it read, was a real adventure romp, with these moments of strung-out tension.'

And a director's early involvement with the script often means more than just reading it...

'From a very early stage, as a director you're hopefully involved in the script, as well. You can give notes on how you think scenes might work better, or in a more visual way, or maybe sometimes where a story point is not clear. And the director comes into play with the pacing of the script, too.

'And of course, way before you have any kind of creative conversations with designers or the camera people involved, you're involved in casting as well. That's a huge part of the whole process – getting the right people for the roles. On something like *Doctor Who*, for instance, they always like to have "headline" talent, as it were. You get presented with a list of who's available and who'd be good for the role, and from that you discuss with the producers where you'd like to go with it, and you then make offers to the actors. Then you meet people for the other roles, the supporting roles if you like. Casting is an exhaustive process, but very rewarding when you get the right people. And getting the right people is key to getting the characters to come alive.'

Ashley was lucky on his episodes to have the 'headline' talent of Meera Syal as Dr Nasreen Chaudhry, along with a fine ensemble cast including Robert Pugh (Tony), Neve McIntosh (the Silurian warrior Alaya) and Stephen Moore (Silurian leader Eldane). With the script involving some high-stakes drama, as well as *Doctor Who*'s typical action and adventure, it was important to secure a group of such great actors for the episodes' varied roles. But who had the final say on casting them?

'It's kind of cheesy to say it, but it's very much a collaborative process,' Ashley says – explaining that this is true of just about every TV show. 'On *Doctor Who*, for instance, there's [executive producers] Steven Moffat, Beth Willis, and Piers Wenger, the producers, the casting director – and then the director! All of those people will have a say. And I'd say that eight times out of ten, everyone agrees on who's right for the role. If there's a very strong negative opinion to a piece of casting, then it needs working out further, but generally, like I say, it's a consensus of opinion. It's not as much of a bun fight as you might think!'

AS he talks, Ashley paints a picture of the director's deep involvement with many of the important decisions made in the production of an episode, and dealings with all sorts of teams and departments. In the making of *Doctor Who*, it seems, collaboration is king.

'Of course,' Ashley says. 'And collaboration is important because, although Steven has a very clear idea of where he wants the show to go and what he wants the show to do, everything needs to serve a common purpose. There needs to be a strong identity for something like *Doctor Who*, particularly because it is such a recognisable and successful programme. For that, everyone needs to pull in the right direction, everyone should be working together.'

Ashley picks out the editing process as a perfect example of this. With filming completed, the director and editor spend a few days building their final version of the episode – before revealing it to the executive producers for their input.

'It's definitely a collaborative process. You have lots of voices in there that need synchronising. It's kind of nerve-racking as well because, as a director, you've taken this story, you've shot it, and when you put it together in the edit and you show it to the execs for the first time, that's kind of like unveiling the painting. That's the time that someone sees what you've made – and then it's up for criticism and any changes they want to make.

'That's also when you see if the story's actually working, if the performances are working, if the tone and the pace are all right. So, that's the moment when you *rely* on an objective point of view from other people. It's different in film, but in television you can't be a 'maverick auteur', really, because there are a lot of other people involved in the decision-making process. You have to be a team player to make those things work, on a series especially. If you're doing a one-off drama then, of course, a strong, single voice for the director comes into play a lot more – but on a series, you need to address everyone else's concerns.'

So, in that regard, is *Doctor Who* pretty much like any other TV show?

'In that regard, yeah. But that said, on this latest series, particularly – from what I understand of other series and having worked on *Torchwood* and *The Sarah Jane Adventures* as well – they did encourage the director's own style a lot more. You were given free rein to run with your style and your interpretation, which was kind of refreshing – but also, like I say, nerve-racking when you show it to someone and it's up there for criticism. But there wasn't a generic style that we were forced into on *Doctor Who*, which was nice. You did get to interpret, which is unusual for a TV series.'

THIS wasn't the only big difference with the latest series of *Doctor Who*, though. There was also the small matter of the new leading man...

'As a director, when you go on to a series that's already up and running, you're encouraged to watch previous episodes,' Ashley says. 'But with Matt Smith being the new Doctor, all that was available of him onscreen were very rough cuts of other episodes. So, what I'd seen of Matt was reasonably disjointed, because no single episode had been completed by that point. I went in with my mind totally open, with no preconceived ideas or notions of how he was, of how he was playing the Doctor. And then it became clear, as soon as I'd met him and worked with him for a few days, that he's this incredibly devoted, very, very focused actor. He's got a very wide range, but also he was really keen to explore who the Doctor was, and all the very many different ways of playing the role.

'It was nice to work with someone who was so free and open to ideas,' he continues. 'I encouraged him to do that. A lot of the time, with TV production schedules, you have to nail things down and move on quickly. I just encouraged Matt to be a little freer, and maybe take a little more time to try different things. I think that was important, at that time, with him still kind of finding the role of the Doctor.

'Matt was incredibly charismatic – and what I love about him, and about his Doctor, is his look is sometimes very ambiguous. You watch him and you can see and read so many things in what he's doing – all of which are the right choices. Your eyes are glued to the screen. It's the same on set as it is as a viewer at home: I'm on set, watching him on the monitor screen, and it's mesmerising. You want to encourage him to play and find new things to do, which Matt is brilliant at doing.'

Here, Ashley raises one of the big dilemmas faced by all TV directors. How do you meet the demands of a busy filming schedule, while also allowing the actors the time and space to do their work to the best of their ability?

'It is a tight schedule,' Ashley says, 'but also you have a lot of big set-ups – not downtime exactly, but "in-between times", where they're setting up lighting or laying camera tracks. That gives you time to talk to the actors. It's you and the actors making that time, finding that time, when you can. Although, like I say, the schedule is hectic on *Doctor Who*, and you have to get through a lot in the day, there are moments in those days where you can work with the actors. The camera's not always turning.'

POLICE TELEPHONE
FREE
FOR USE OF
PUBLIC
ADVICE & ASSISTANCE
OBTAINABLE IMMEDIATELY
OFFICERS & CARS
RESPOND TO ALL CALLS
PULL TO OPEN

BUT even when the cameras are resting, there are still plenty of other things for a director to do. After all, the whole 'look' of an episode is the director's responsibility – and again, there's more than one person involved in those decisions.

Firstly, there's the production design, the sets that need building, the locations that need dressing...

'You have a very strong relationship with the production designer. My episodes were designed by Edward Thomas, who was the incumbent designer and who has been there for many years – and I've known Ed from years back anyway, so we knew how each other worked. I think the producer – my producer on those episodes was Peter Bennett – has lots of strong ideas as well. We worked together to decide how we saw the locations panning out, the look of the episodes, the colours we used.'

The colours? It may seem like something that wouldn't really need any thought – the TARDIS is blue, monsters are green, Amy's hair is red – but the colours seen throughout a single episode of *Doctor Who* are all carefully considered.

'Individual episodes have a colour palate,' Ashley explains. 'There might be an episode where you'd say, "Right, we won't use yellow in this episode"' – so, it doesn't look like colours are randomly spread across the screen. You restrict the colours. That gives you a really strong and definite look. On my episodes, we concentrated on the warmer colours – browns, oranges, reds – to give the episodes that warmed-up feel, the feeling of below ground – and also that life *above* ground was slightly warmer, being set ten years in the future.'

ONE of the key elements from Ashley's episodes were the 'monsters' themselves: Homo Reptilia, or Silurians, led by Eldane. Although the Silurians had been seen in the series before (they first appeared in 1970's *The Silurians*), this new tribe looked very different. Part of the reason behind this redesign was to let us see the actors' faces more clearly.

'Chris Chibnall had written these very emotional scripts, and there was a lot of dialogue, and a lot of different characters as well,' Ashley says. 'We really needed to sympathise with these characters, we really needed to love or hate them – which is difficult to do if they're all of the same generic design, or you can't see their eyes. We were very insistent in the design that you could see the real actor's eyes.

'But we did give them a mask, which wasn't in the original script. We knew these lizards had to be beautiful and sympathetic but also quite scary at times. The mask gave them that element of threat. And obviously, at a practical level, it allowed us to have lots of Silurians in the background that didn't need the expensive prosthetic make-up!'

WHEN you put it all together, directing *Doctor Who* looks like one heck of a challenge. Ashley reckons the hardest part of the job is 'realising the ambition of the show'. Taking a script, building a vision for it, and then making that vision work – there are a lot of things to juggle, a lot of things that can go wrong. But then, when it all goes right...

'It's hard work at the time,' Ashley admits, 'but when you see it in the edit or when the special effects go in, it's incredibly rewarding to see it *work*. And sometimes even when you're on set and you *know* a scene is a really good scene, it can be rewarding there and then – if you can see through the clouds of fatigue and frustration!

'But the director is the figurehead through which all the questions are put. That's not to say that the director is the ultimate voice in all those decisions, because obviously you to defer to Steven or the execs whenever necessary or whenever relevant, but the people on set need to know who to talk to when they've got questions. Therefore, you as a director have that responsibility to carry the show creatively.

'So, yes, it's a lot of responsibility and it's a big challenge – particularly on *Doctor Who*, where the design elements, the CG elements, the special effects, the performances are all very, very key. It's a lot of work – but it's great, really. And shows like this don't come along every day, so you've got to grab it when you can!'

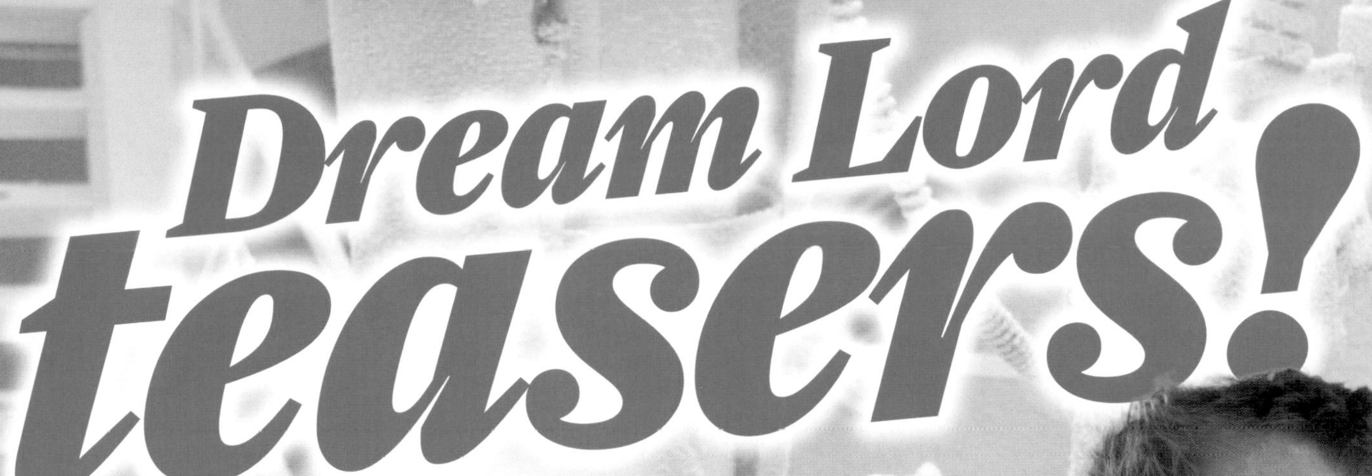

Dream Lord teasers!

Hello – it's the spooky old Dream Lord here, come to freak you out because that's just the sort of 'guy' I am. Being the hidden darker side of that lovable planet-saving scamp the Doctor, I have to amuse myself somehow when he's off somewhere being ever-so-cute. And, specially for all you Doctor-spotters out there, who love him and his ethically dubious crusade throughout all time and space, I've prepared – you might even say 'concocted' – a miscellany of misdirection. Concealed within the following statements are a smattering of truths about what's to come for our intrepid amigo on his Saturday night sorties on BBC One in 2011. (I'll be watching the darker side – ITV. At least I will when the transmissions reach my poor, stranded, pollinated form.) Everything else is a load of codswallop – fabrication – farrago – dream, geddit?! Try to keep up. And don't pretend you won't be poring over this page for the next few months pondering my fiendish fibs. Remember – once you read it, you can't un-read it. Ta-ta! (For now.)

» **THE DOCTOR WILL BE ON TRIAL – TWICE!** » WHO CONTROLS THE LIGHT SCULPTORS? » **YOU WON'T BELIEVE WHAT'S BURIED UNDER WEMBLEY STADIUM** » SCARED OF THE EYE IN SPACE? YOU SHOULD BE » **TAKE UP THY SINS AND WALK – SLOWLY** » 'THERE WON'T BE A PUB QUIZ ON TUESDAY BECAUSE THERE WON'T BE A PUB!' » **BEAU GESTE IS COOL** » BOW STREET RUNNERS ARE COOL » **BROMLEY-BY-BOW IS COOL** » 4 AUGUST 1982 – HAPPY BIRTHDAY, MA'AM » **SOME LIES ARE TOO MUCH FOR THE PSYCHIC PAPER** » 'I WON'T TAKE CALLS FROM *THAT* PRIME MINISTER' » **'MARC, WHERE ARE YOU?'** » **THE ONLY WATER IN THE FOREST IS THE RIVER** » WHAT AWAITS THE TARDIS AT THE ZERO POINT? » **'12 YEARS ON AND RORY'S STILL TERRIFIED OF GRANNY GRAINGER'** » 'I WAS LOST IN FRANCE' » **'HOW COULD A FELLOW GALLIFREYAN STOOP SO LOW?'** » HORROR OF BANGKOK » **'GIVE IT UP, SUEET KORN!'** » ARGONITE? HERE? » **AN ORDINARY BLOCK OF FLATS** » 'IF I SAW THEM WALKING DOWN THE HIGH STREET WHAT WOULD I THINK?' 'I DON'T THINK YOU'D THINK ANYTHING AT ALL, AMY.' » **FIND THE LADY – BEFORE SHE FINDS YOU!** » 'MARGARET! COME BACK!' » **THE DOCTOR DEFEATS THE SAHARA DESERT** » SUSANNAH'S STILL ALIVE » **MILL GREEN ON FIRE** » THE DOCTOR WILL GET MARRIED – TWICE! » **WHAT ARE THE DANGERS OF PORT OLVERON?** » 502, BUT NEVER 503 » **BEWARE OF THE KITES** » 'A PILLAR OF SALT, YES – BUT NOT BECAUSE SHE LOOKED BACK, LOOKING BACK IS GOOD!' » **THEY'LL HAVE TO GET A NEW NAME FOR THANKSGIVING** » PAY ATTENTION – IT'S NOT REALLY HER » **TREADING THROUGH THE SAND – ON THE ONE NIGHT THEY COME BACK** » THE SHUDDERING BRETHREN, THEY'LL STICK IN YOUR MIND » **'I'M MY OWN DOCTOR'** » OCTAVIAN WASN'T LYING » **MYSTERIOUS SEMBLANCE AT THE STRAND OF NIGHTMARES** » THE BONES OF THE TARDIS

EPISODE 7

Amy's Choice

BY SIMON NYE

THE STORY

It's five years in the future. Amy and Rory are married and have settled down in Leadworth, eagerly awaiting the arrival of their first child. And then the Doctor crashes back into their life. Rory discovers his patients at the old folk's home are actually venomous aliens, and they're out to kill...

Or –

It's the present day. The TARDIS has ground to a halt. Now, it's caught in the gravity of a cold star, falling towards its doom, freezing its occupants to death...

And in both worlds, the Dream Lord taunts and teases the Doctor and his friends. Only one of these realities is true. The other is just a dream. And if the Doctor, Amy and Rory die in the wrong one, they die for ever.

But is the answer that simple?

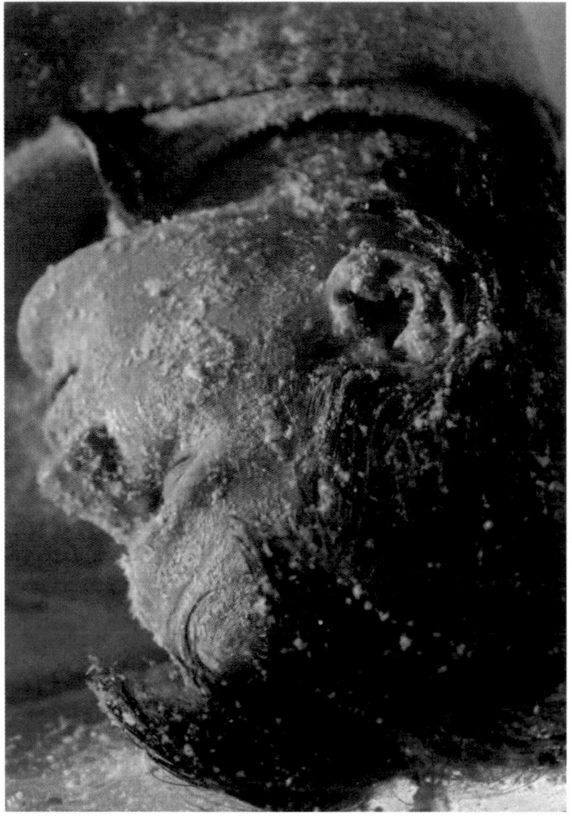

BEHIND THE SCENES

STEVEN MOFFAT

Executive Producer

An episode full of tricks, dreams, the real and the unreal... *Doctor Who* seems able to encompass so many formats.

It's what keeps it going, I think. A different show every week – even a different genre!

There's quite a disturbing undercurrent given the Dream Lord's real identity – do you think the Doctor *really* hates himself to the degree this episode implies?

We all hate ourselves sometimes, and we all have regrets. But the Doctor's nearly a thousand years old – that's an insane amount of regret. You have to remember that he's usually able to keep it all in check. That's a hell of a feat.

This episode forces Amy to look closely at her relationship with the Doctor. It feels quite different from those we've seen before. How would you describe it? Siblings, friends...?

Very good friends who fancy each other a bit. Hardly a brand new invention, it's out there everywhere. For the Doctor, though – and don't listen to fools, he's never been a man not to notice a pretty girl! – she'll always be 7-year-old Amelia. You'll notice he even calls her Amelia in moments of stress.

WHERE'S THE CRACK?

There's no crack to be seen in this episode – but then, so little of it takes place in the real world, maybe that's not so surprising.

DELETED!

The TARDIS is partially frosted. Amy is in a foetal position, rocking, hugging her knees.

THE DREAM LORD: You're supposed to be getting married tomorrow. What are you going to look like?

Amy's tears are turning to ice, sealing her eyelids.

AMY: Aghh.
THE DREAM LORD: The Doctor always leaves you on your own, doesn't he? Have you noticed? When you were small, and needed him. And since, whenever there's trouble. Is he trying to tell you something?

» The Doctor's first thought on being faced with the strange problem in this episode is that the TARDIS has 'jumped a time track'. This happened back in *The Space Museum* (1965), when the First Doctor and friends skip forward into a future where they've been preserved as exhibits in a museum. » The Dream Lord teases the Doctor over his mysterious relationship with Queen Elizabeth I. The Doctor hints at a... run-in with Elizabeth at the beginning of *The End of Time,* Part One (2009), and, towards the end of her reign, in *The Shakespeare Code* (2007), she seems to be out for the Doctor's blood. Further clues as to their relationship are given in *The Beast Below* (2010). » At one point, the Doctor goes hunting for tools beneath the TARDIS console. A little metal plaque there is inscribed with the words: 'TARDIS. Time And Relative Dimension In Space. Build Site: Gallifrey Blackhole Shipyard. Type 40. Build date: 1963. Authorised for use by qualified Time Lords only by the Shadow Proclamation. Misuse or theft of any TARDIS will result in extreme penalties and permanent exile.' The type number of the Doctor's TARDIS has been mentioned many times throughout the history of the show; its first mention was in *The Claws of Axos* (1971). The ship's build date – 1963 – was, of course, the year of the series' first broadcast. It's interesting that the Shadow Proclomation (seen in *The Stolen Earth/Journey's End* (2008)) are the ones who 'license' the Time Lords to travel in time. But then, they are intergalactic lawmakers, and the Time Lords aren't the only time-travelling race, so... Well, someone has to be the Space DVLA! » The reliability of the TARDIS Instruction Manual has always been a point of contention for the Doctor. Back in *The Pirate Planet* (1978), he tore out a page he didn't like – and here, he reveals that he threw the book into a supernova because he disagreed with it!

FANTASTIC FACTS

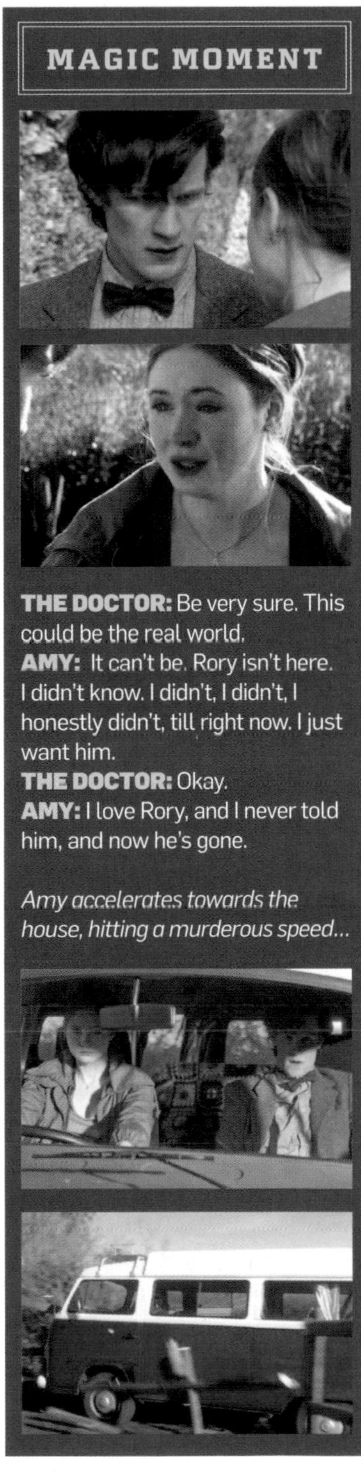

MAGIC MOMENT
THE DOCTOR: Be very sure. This could be the real world.
AMY: It can't be. Rory isn't here. I didn't know. I didn't, I didn't, I honestly didn't, till right now. I just want him.
THE DOCTOR: Okay.
AMY: I love Rory, and I never told him, and now he's gone.
Amy accelerates towards the house, hitting a murderous speed...

FAMILIAR FACES

TOBY JONES

The Dream Lord

Toby's film work includes roles in *Frost/Nixon* and the *Harry Potter* movies in which he provides the voice of Dobby.

"Matt Smith is a DANGER TO HIMSELF!"

Arthur Darvill looks back at Rory Williams's eventful first year aboard the TARDIS, and reveals a penchant for puns, posters and portliness...

The life of poor old Rory Williams has not been an easy one. As a child he was forced to dress up as an imaginary raggedy Doctor for his friend-who's-a girl Amy Pond. Years later, the hapless lad gets sort-of the night before his wedding to Amy, and then invited aboard a time machine by the not-after-all-imaginary Doctor. There, he finds that his wife-to-perhaps-be is willing to put off the morning's nuptuals indefinitely. That would floor most of us, but it was the easy bit for Rory. You probably get a new perspective on what trouble means when you then get killed twice, erased from history, resurrected as a plastic duplicate in an ancient Roman legion, forced to kill your girlfriend, left to guard her for 2,000 years and then thrown into an alternative timeline where none of that happened, except it did when your new bride remembers her Time Lord friend, and so do you. Phew!

When *The Brilliant Book of Doctor Who* first spoke to the (actually extremely cool) Arthur Darvill on the set of *The Big Bang*, he seemed blissfully unaware of the hype surrounding *Doctor Who*. Even months later, as we sat down for a catch-up just before a very special screening of Episode 12 in London, he was still pretty unaffected. Perhaps, as he turned the corner and a horde of well-informed fans descended upon him, outstretched arms packed with pictures and DVD sleeves to be signed, the impact of being a TARDIS traveller finally hit home! We'd have asked him, but frankly we legged it inside...

So, Arthur, you're now a fully fledged companion.

Well yeah, it looks like it.

And the first married couple in the TARDIS...

Yeah, how's that going to work? I think it's going to be a strange time. I mean, is it going to become really

domestic? Is Rory going to want to get a catflap in the TARDIS? See, I'm interested to know what Rory did for the 2,000 years he waited. I hope he's going to become really intelligent and has read loads of books. But whether that will change him or not... I think it's probably going to be a lot of Rory cleaning up after Amy. Trying to put a few posters up of his own and trying to make it his, but I don't think he'll ever really be allowed. I'm determined that Rory's not going to be pathetic, though. He's got to stand his ground at some point.

He's already more of a fighter by the end of the series.

Completely. There's been a *massive* change. Also you don't know what's gone on in the TARDIS, what they've talked about. At first, Rory's so in awe of the Doctor and scared of him, but actually he's got a lot of respect for him. He's shown him a life far more interesting than he had back home. I think Rory's so impressed that the Doctor's »

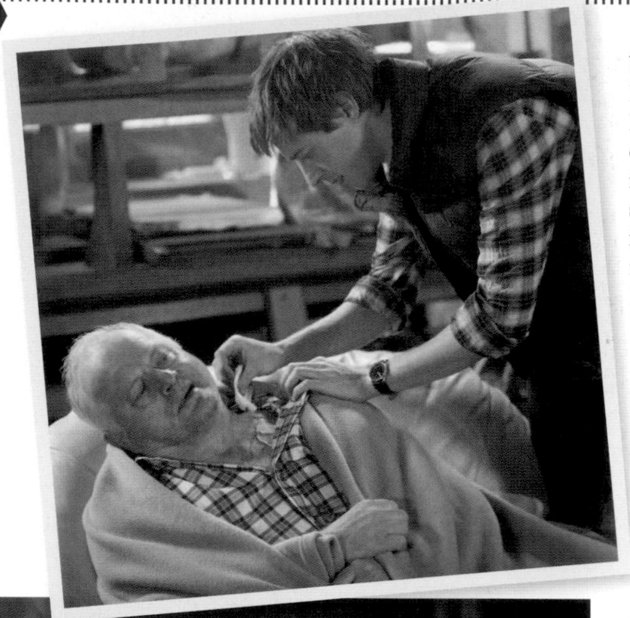

brought so much out of him, out of Rory, that he never knew existed. He could never have imagined dying and being sucked into a crack in time, coming back as a Roman soldier and waiting for 2,000 years for the woman he loves. That would never have happened without the Doctor, and in a way it's absolutely tragic that that happens, but also I don't know that Rory would go back and change anything.

So you think Rory remembers those 2,000 years?
Maybe he doesn't remember at the end of it all. Maybe it's better if he just forgets it all and carries on with his life. But imagine if he does – I think he'll have become a genius, read all the important books, been on the fringes of all the massive historical events. I mean, obviously he stayed very near the Pandorica, but he's been driving himself mad. He's read the paper ever day and done the crossword... He's used it to get more intelligent!

How has your first year of *Doctor Who* been?
It's amazing. It's only really just dawned on me how brilliant it's been. It's been weird having a few months away from it, where I've literally just gone off and forgotten about it. I think the scripts have been amazing and the people have been amazing. I don't think I've ever taken a step back and gone 'wow' up until now, really, I suppose with the prospect of doing it again coming up so soon. It's been great, not a bad thing to say about it.

If you had a Pandorica, what would you keep in it?
Haha! I don't know. Matt Smith?

Why would you put Matt in it?
He's a danger to himself and others! And the Pandorica's meant for the most feared thing in the universe. Matt's certainly the most feared thing in the props department.

Do you look at cracks differently now?
I suppose I do. It's so funny, just because I spent six months looking at that shape of crack, I suppose they catch my eye occasionally. I'm just glad that there aren't other worlds behind cracks in the road, so I can go, 'Yeah, that's a good crack, it's not going anywhere.'

Do you think Rory will be sticking with the bodywarmers next year?
Let's hope so. They're comfy things. I think that he's found something that he's comfortable in and he's really gone for it – there's no wavering for him now. I don't think Rory's suddenly going to become some kind of fashion icon.

Did you keep one of Rory's stag T-shirts?
No, I didn't keep anything. They don't let you keep a thing! I think it'd be a bit weird if I wore it out on a night out. It's like [*adopts nerdy voice*], 'Hey, look at me, I wore this in the show!'

What's been your favourite moment of the series?
Definitely coming back as a Roman solider. I thought it was going to be the swordfight in Episode 6 but no, just coming back and dressing up as a Roman soldier was so much fun.

When were you most impressed?
I think – because I drove myself – driving to Stonehenge. It was the middle of the night, we were on a night shoot and my satnav started going haywire and I didn't really know where I was going. Then, suddenly, because they'd lit it all up and it was quite misty, Stonehenge just appeared right ahead. It was like being in a film. I just drove

"EVERYONE'S TERRIBLE BEHAVIOUR IN CROATIA WAS HILARIOUS! IT WAS LIKE BEING ON A SCHOOL TRIP"

up and it was completely dark everywhere apart from these huge film lights pointing at Stonehenge, and all these people walking round as Roman soliders. I just drove up to it and thought, 'that is *brilliant*'. It was an amazing thing to do.

What's been your funniest moment?
The whole thing has been incredibly funny. Everyone's terrible behaviour in Croatia was hilarious! People behaved like they were on a school trip or something – the crew included. Everyone just had a brilliant laugh. Tony Curran, dressed as Van Gogh, floating around Croatia in his LA shades with his massive booming voice... Just amazing!

What would you most like to happen next season?
I think it'd be interesting to see what Rory could do now. I'm sure Steven Moffat's got far more clever ideas about it than any of us could possibly have, but I'd like to see Rory as a bit more of a hero. Maybe that's just my own ego talking, but I'd like to see Amy following Rory around for once.

FAQ

FULL NAME
Thomas Arthur Darvill
YEAR OF BIRTH
1982
HOME TOWN
Birmingham
FIRST WHO APPEARANCE
The Eleventh Hour, 2010
WHO FACT
Arthur is also a musician and composer, and has had his work performed at London's Globe Theatre – thankfully without any Carrionite visitations...

How do you amuse yourself on set between takes?
I drink a lot of coffee. Me, Matt and Karen get on really well, but it's got to the point where we're actually quite horrible to each other because we just don't think there's any point in being nice to each other all the time. So yeah, generally just being horrible to each other.

I hope you're just joking!
Yeah, it is all in jest. Or so I tell *them*. But I actually *do* hate both of them. But they think it's in jest, which is why I find it funny. Hahaha!

What's on your MP3 player?
Probably something from the latest Grizzly Bear. Karen's music taste is the most bizarre thing. One minute she's listening to Biffy Clyro and the next minute she's listening to the Spice Girls. I suppose that's because she's a girl.

Would you wear a bow tie?
I don't think you can now. Matt's made it cool but also no one can do it. It's like he's become the only person that can pull off a bow tie. Which is quite crafty. Unless you were in a dinner jacket, I suppose. Or you're kind of portly and you always wore a bow tie.

Do portly people have an immediate get-out clause on that?
Ha! I think so, yeah.

Portly people and Matt Smith. So he can get fat now if he likes?
Yeah, he can. If he can wear a bow tie and still be cool, he can do anything!

Does that mean you're the only person that can wear bodywarmers and still be cool?
Definitely. Well, me and Michael J Fox. I've got it written into my contract.

Finally, can you help us start a crazy *Doctor Who* rumour?
Let me think. What's not too dodgy...? It would be quite fun if Amy was actually the biggest baddie in the world and was actually a spy. Or maybe Amy and Rory could join together like a big Power Ranger! Maybe that. Or that... the Doctor's actually... um... a dog?

Dogtor Who?
Dogtor Who! Yes! He's actually a dog. If I was to come up with a convincing rumour it would definitely be accompanied by some sort of pun. So that's the one!

EPISODE 8

The Hungry Earth

BY CHRIS CHIBNALL

THE STORY

The Welsh valleys, 2020. Humanity's most advanced mining project has hit a snag. The earth itself seems to be fighting back, swallowing human victims and sending... *something* up to the surface.

So, it's a good job that the Doctor's arrived on the scene. While Rory investigates stories of corpses missing from their graves, the Doctor and Amy check out the drill – only for the ground to drag Amy down into its suffocating embrace.

But the earth is the least of their problems. As the Doctor gathers the terrified survivors together, they find themselves under siege from an ancient enemy of humankind. An ancient race the Doctor knows only too well...

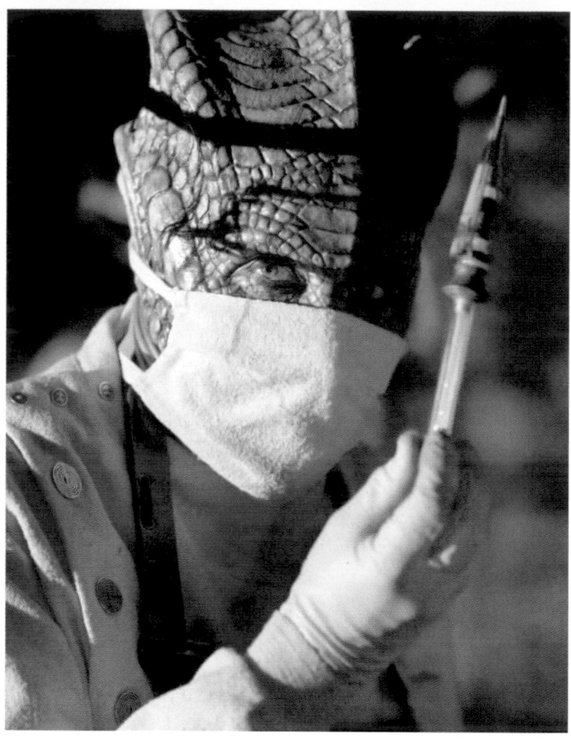

MAGIC MOMENT

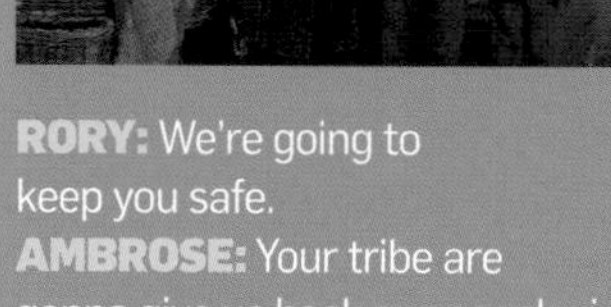

RORY: We're going to keep you safe.
AMBROSE: Your tribe are gonna give us back our people, in exchange for you.
ALAYA: Shall I tell you what's really going to happen, apes? One of you will kill me. My death shall ignite a war. And every stinking ape shall be wiped from the surface of my beloved planet.
TONY: We won't allow that to happen.
ALAYA: I know apes better than you know yourselves. I know which one of you will kill me. Do you?

FAMILIAR FACES

MEERA SYAL

Nasreen Chaudhry

An actress, comedian and writer, Meera's TV roles include *Goodness Gracious Me* and *The Kumars at No 42*.

ROBERT PUGH

Tony Mack

As well as a recurring part in *Prime Suspect*, Robert's also played the role of Jonah in the *Torchwood* episode *Adrift*.

UNSEEN ADVENTURES

It seems likely that the Doctor has met this branch of Homo Reptilia on at least one other occasion: he seems to know the limitations of their venom glands, suggesting he's experienced them before.

NUMBER CRUNCHING

300,000,000 *Years that have passed since the era of Homo Reptilia.*

2020 *HUMANITY WAKES HOMO REPTILIA.*

3020 An age of peaceful coexistence?

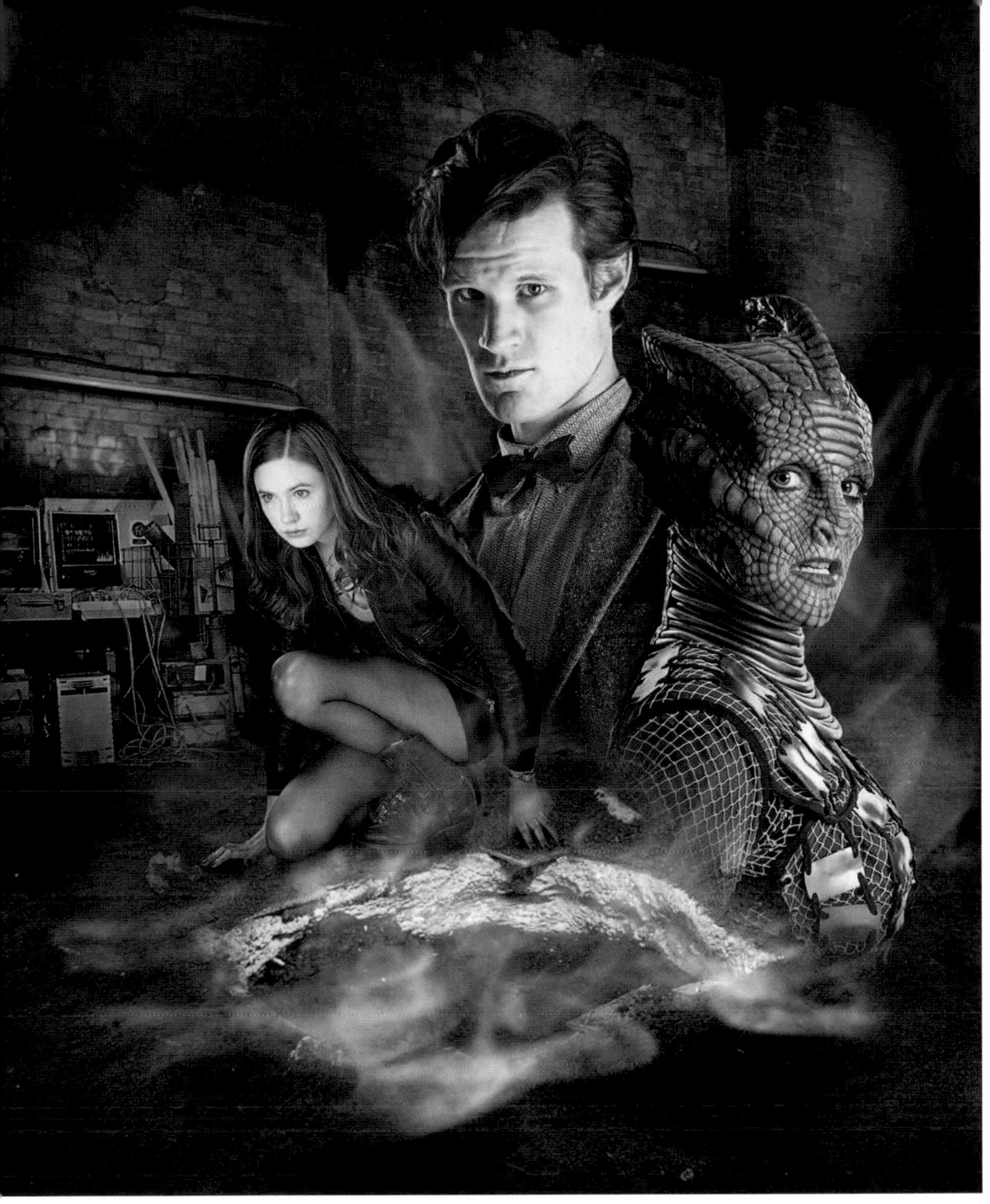

BEHIND THE SCENES

ASHLEY WAY

Director

As well as a whole new alien tribe, these episodes also required the creation of an undiscovered underground civilisation. That must have been tough...

Creating a city was, I suppose, the biggest challenge of these episodes. We didn't want to go down the route of being stuck in tunnels all the time, or building sets that we couldn't afford to build – so realising that city was a real challenge.

We had to find locations that couldn't be too Earthly – we had to find another world in Cardiff. And as wonderful and beautiful a city as Cardiff is – and I come from Cardiff, so hand on my heart I do mean that – the range of, for instance, big buildings that could be a Homo Reptilian Senate was very limited. We ended up using the Temple of Peace. Being five years into the series, if you're a big fan, you'll see that it's been used a few times before. So, the other challenge then – which was more for Production Designer Edward Thomas and myself – was to show that location in a new and fresh way.

FANTASTIC FACTS

» The working title for this episode was *The Ground Beneath Their Feet.* » The Doctor first met Homo Reptilia – then called Silurians – during his exile on Earth in his third incarnation, in the story *The Silurians* (1970). The tribe seen here know nothing of this earlier meeting, though the Doctor does reveal to them that the first human/Homo Reptilia contact ended in bloodshed. (The Brigadier, against the Doctor's wishes, bombed a Silurian settlement beneath Wenley Moor, killing many of the creatures and sealing it off from the surface world.) » In this episode, we see that Malokeh has been storing samples of surface life forms for study; he learns much about their biology, and is able to use his more advanced technology to manipulate the bacteria in human bodies without the use of drugs or surgery. In *The Silurians*, we learn that Homo Reptilia are skilled at genetic engineering, being able to 'create' dinosaurs, even though they had been extinct for millennia. » Homo Reptilia are only called 'Silurians' once in this episode. The Doctor says they were 'once known as the Silurian race – or, some would argue, Eocenes'. Strictly speaking, the term Silurian is inaccurate for Homo Reptilia, that period pre-dates reptiles by more than 200 million years. Eocenes isn't much better, though. The Eocene epoch started around ten million years after the Dinosaurs became extinct. Best just stick to Homo Reptilia. »

In the 1972 story *The Sea Devils*, the Third Doctor met the aquatic 'cousins' of the reptile men from *The Silurians*. They had allied themselves with the Master and were attacking shipping. These 'Sea Silurians' (as their debut adventure was almost called) returned, along with their land-lubber cousins, in *Warriors of the Deep* (1984).

DELETED!

AMY: I wanted to ask – me and Rory on the hillside. Future us. That's good, right? That happens. We get a happy ever after.
THE DOCTOR: As things stand, in this timestream. Time's not fixed, though, things might change...
AMY: What things?
THE DOCTOR: I don't know. Any things.
AMY: You like him, right? You think I'm doing the right thing? With the wedding.
THE DOCTOR: You're asking the oldest single man in the universe for marriage advice.
AMY: Yeah. See your point.

The Little Planet

Written by DAVID LLEWELLYN

Illustrations by ANTHONY DRY

ONCE upon a time, in the last days before we went into the Earth, there lived a young girl named Kaya. Kaya's father was a scientist, and her mother a soldier, and they lived in the northern territories.

This was the time when the Little Planet grew larger in our sky, and to Kaya and her friends it seemed the grown-ups spoke of little else. Each night it was there, the Little Planet, hovering in the star-speckled blackness like an unblinking white eye. And each night it drew closer to the Earth.

Sometimes the things the grown-ups said made no sense to Kaya. They spoke of 'gravity', and 'tidal waves', but she didn't really know what these words meant. All she knew was that when her parents spoke of them they looked very serious, and perhaps even afraid.

One night, Kaya's father sat her down and told her that they would have to leave their home, and soon.

'Leave?' Kaya asked. 'You mean to another house?'

Kaya's father shook his head. He looked sad. 'No, Kaya,' he replied. 'We're leaving the surface and going underground. Our engineers have built places deep below the earth where we can sleep until the world is safe again.'

'Safe?' asked Kaya. 'But why isn't it safe now?'

Her father closed his eyes and let out a sigh. 'The little white planet,' he explained. 'It's coming towards the Earth.'

'Will it hit us?'

'No, Kaya. But it will come very close, and when it does, the seas will rise and the air will grow thin. It won't be safe here for us. That's why we're going underground, so we can sleep there until it's safe again.'

Kaya nodded. She thought she understood him, but she was still afraid.

'And what about Leefa?' she said, looking up at her father with an expression of worry.

Her father shook his head. 'No,' he said. 'Leefa can't come with us. None of the mammals can.'

Kaya gasped. 'But why?' she cried. 'Why can't Leefa come?'

'Eldane has ordered it,' said her father. 'All pets are to remain on the surface.'

Kaya looked across the room to the cage in the far corner. There, nestled down and sleeping on a bed of straw, was her pet ape, Leefa.

'But he won't be safe on the surface,' she said. 'You said so yourself.'

'I know,' said her father. 'But these are the rules, Kaya. And you know yourself, you can't keep Leefa for ever. One day soon he would have grown to full size, and we would have to have let him go.'

Kaya nodded, but there were tears in her eyes.

WEEKS passed, and the Little Planet grew larger still. Kaya heard her parents talk of how the beaches in the south were being battered by the waves, how whole stretches of the coast, places they would sometimes visit in the hot seasons, were now underwater. Kaya's tribe lived high up in the mountains and far from the sea, and so she thought perhaps they would be safe from the tidal waves her father spoke about. Maybe they could stay above ground, and she could keep Leefa as her pet, and they wouldn't have to sleep below the surface.

When she told her father this, he shook his head. He told her that the Little Planet was like their own, that it had something called 'gravity'. On Earth it was gravity that made the rain fall, and stopped things from just floating off into the sky, but the Little Planet's gravity would pull at everything on Earth, all the water and the air, until the seas would rise up and the air would grow thin.

'So even if the sea didn't rise this far, the air would still be too thin for us to breathe, Kaya,' he said. 'We would suffocate.'

In the valley below their home, the engineers were still working on the shelters, and the work continued through the days and nights, the almost deafening noise of the machines echoing from the hillsides. It was so noisy, in fact, and the air so thick with smoke and dust, that Kaya hardly played outside with her friends any more. She preferred to spend her time inside with Leefa.

It was so sad she couldn't take him with her when they went into the shelter. Sometimes, when she looked at Leefa, and at the other apes, they reminded her of people. They had arms and legs like people, and faces like people. She could tell when Leefa was happy or sad, or when he was angry or upset. The noises he made could sometimes sound like words, though her father told her this was silly, because apes couldn't speak. Apes were animals, he said. When they were young they could be kept as pets, but when they grew older they belonged in zoos and laboratories. Some grown-ups even hunted apes for fun, but Kaya thought this was cruel, though she never said so out loud.

When her parents weren't in the same room as her, Kaya would sometimes try to teach Leefa words. She would crouch down beside his cage, and she would say the words over and over again, hoping he might say them back.

'Ka-ya...' she said, pointing at herself. 'My name is Kaya. Can you say Kaya?'

Leefa would just look at her and frown, and sometimes he would grunt, but he wouldn't say her name.

'Leefa,' said Kaya, pointing now at her pet through the bars of his cage. 'Your name is Leefa. Can you say Leefa?'

And still, Leefa would just frown at her and say nothing.

FINALLY, the day came when it was time for them to leave the surface. Kaya's home looked empty and bare. The only thing they were leaving behind was Leefa. Everything else they owned had already been taken down into the shelters.

'How long will we be asleep down there?' Kaya asked her father as he loaded the last of their crates onto a transporter.

'Not long,' her father replied. 'Just enough time for the air and the sea to settle back into place. A few weeks, perhaps. Then, when it's safe, the shelters will wake us up automatically.'

'But Leefa...' said Kaya.

Her father shook his head. 'Leefa won't be here when we come back,' he told her. 'You should say goodbye to him now, while you have the chance.'

Kaya nodded, and she crouched down besides Leefa's cage. Reaching in, she stroked the top of his head, and the little ape made a purring sound. When he looked at her, it was as if he knew they were leaving him. Kaya turned to her father.

'Can I let him out?' she asked. 'It's unfair, leaving him stuck in his cage.'

'Very well,' her father replied. 'Let him out.'

Kaya opened Leefa's cage, and in an instant, her pet jumped up, throwing his arms around her neck and holding her tightly. Kaya's father stepped forward, about to lift the animal off her, but Kaya shook her head.'

It's all right,' she said. 'He's just saying goodbye.'

Then she lifted Leefa away and placed him gently on the ground.

'Goodbye, Leefa,' she said. 'I'll miss you.'

Kaya's father placed one hand on her shoulder, and led her towards the door. Another transporter was waiting for them now, this one filled with other people of the tribe. They sat in rows, tightly packed together, some with their last belongings in their laps and at their feet.

Kaya and her parents left their home, looking back at it just once before they climbed on board, and then the transporter carried on its journey to the shelters.

Though she had watched the engineers working at the surface, and heard them work all day and night, nothing had prepared Kaya for what she saw there. They were taken down, deep below the surface, on floating discs, and finally they came to a dazzling underground city, more amazing than anything she had ever seen before. And she had never seen so many people. Climbing into their hibernation pods there were people from all across the northern territories, families like hers who must have travelled hundreds of miles, maybe more.

Because she was a soldier, Kaya's mother would be sleeping in a different part of the shelter, with the rest of the army, but she told Kaya they would see each other very soon. Then Kaya's father took her through to their hibernation pods. Her father's friend, Malohkeh, was already there, waiting for them, and he told her how to climb inside and make herself comfortable.

'Nothing to be afraid of,' he said, with a warm smile. 'I'm sure you'll have sweet dreams!'

As the glass door closed around her, Kaya saw her father waving at her and smiling, and he stayed there, still waving, until she was fast asleep.

•••••••

High above the entrance to the shelters, on the mountainside where Kaya and her family had lived, the little ape reached a rocky ledge and sat down. It frowned as the last of the transporters disappeared into the shadows of the cave, and the valley became silent.

Leefa grunted twice, and with his arm outstretched he pointed towards the cave. Then he made a sound like no other he had made before.

'Ka-ya,' he said, and then, louder than before, '*Kaya!*'

•••••••

The next day the Little Planet came close to the Earth, just as our scientists had predicted, but the seas did not rise and the air did not grow thin. Instead, the Little Planet settled into Earth's orbit, becoming its moon.

With no disaster, the systems that should have woken us when all was safe did not work, and so we slept. And while we slept, the animals on the surface, the warm-bloods, the mammals and the birds, survived and flourished, and greatest and most powerful of all these were the apes. In time one of their species, the ones we call humans, would conquer the world and claim it as their own. They would build cities and explore the deepest parts of the sea and the dark void of space, even setting foot upon the Little Planet itself.

Little would they know that we were far beneath them, still sleeping, and waiting. 

EPISODE 9

Cold Blood

BY CHRIS CHIBNALL

THE STORY

Humans and Homo Reptila creep closer towards war, with the future ownership of planet Earth at stake. The Doctor is stuck in the middle, desperately helping both sides to see reason. Who will make the first move towards peace? Who can be trusted? And who will betray their race?

The Doctor sees a glimmer of hope as level heads start to prevail – but the tense stand-off quickly descends into violence. Homo Reptilia turn on each other as the humans frantically try to return to the surface.

But the threat of war isn't the Doctor's only problem. There's a crack in the rock of the subterranean city – the same crack from Amy's bedroom wall, from Churchill's bunker, from the *Byzantium*. It's still following Amy, and this time it will take something she loves...

MAGIC MOMENT

ELDANE Toxic fumigation. An emergency failsafe meant to protect my species from infection. A warning signal to occupy cryochambers. After that, citywide fumigation, by toxic gas. Then the city chuts down.
THE DOCTOR Eldane, are you sure about this, ?
ELDANE: My priority is my race's survival. The Earth isn't ready for us to return yet.
THE DOCTOR: No. But maybe it should be. So, here's a deal. Everybody listening. Eldane, you activate shutdown. I'll amend the system, set your alarm for a thousand years' time. A thousand years to sort the planet out. To be ready. Pass it on. As legend, or prophesy, or religion, but somehow make it known. This planet is to be shared.

DELETED!

RORY: I never used to believe in anything. Except for the healing power of strong, sweet tea. But being with the Doctor, the wonders he's shown us – it's given me... faith. I see why Amy kept waiting for him. Cos now I believe there are far greater things waiting in the universe than we can ever imagine.
ALAYA: No. All that awaits you is death.
RORY: Then maybe I'll find wonders beyond that, too.

SPOT THE CRACK

The crack appears in the rocky walls of the underground city as the Doctor and his friends are escaping – and promptly devours the dying Rory.

WHERE IN THE WORLD?

The imposing conference hall where Eldane, Amy and Nasreen discuss the future of the Earth is inside the Welsh National Temple of Peace and Health in Cardiff. This same location was also seen in *The End of the World* (2005), *Gridlock* (2007) and *The Fires of Pompeii* (2008).

BEHIND THE SCENES
ASHLEY WAY

Director

The Homo Reptilia in these episodes look significantly different to the Silurians the Doctor has met before. What was the thinking behind the new design?

We were very aware at the time that they weren't particularly faithful to the old Silurians from the 1970s, but the viewers really needed to sympathise with the characters. We needed to see the actors' faces. The original Silurians looked much more reptilian – and reptile's eyes are towards the sides of their heads. You had to immediately move away from that classic Silurian look, where the eyes were pushed out to the sides of the face. It would have been impossible, of course, to physically move an actor's eyes, so we had to go with a basically human face – and everything else came from that.

We discussed whether to have a human mouth or not, and then decided we really should – there's so much dialogue. We could have gone with that elongated, almost fish-like mouth of the previous Silurians, but again we thought it was important to understand this race and feel for this race, so we went with a different look. It's contentious, I guess, to fans, but it really had to work for this story. We wanted them to be beautiful as well as dangerous.

FAMILIAR FACES
STEPHEN MOORE

Eldane

Stephen's role as the Homo Reptilia leader isn't his first brush with BBC sci-fi. Back in 1981, he starred as the voice of Marvin the Paranoid Android in both the radio and TV versions of Douglas Adams's *The Hitchhiker's Guide to the Galaxy.*

FANTASTIC FACTS

» The last time the Doctor met Homo Reptilia – in *Warriors of the Deep* (1984) – their small invasion force was defeated by the use of a poisonous gas (hexachromite). Here, it is Eldane who uses a similar tactic to force his warrior caste to abandon their fight with the Doctor. » So, did humanity and Homo Reptilia ever manage to coexist peacefully? Here, the Doctor gives the humans a deadline of 1,000 years to share the planet with its ancient inhabitants. The events of *Warriors of the Deep* (which – we can assume – involved another solitary, dislocated tribe of Silurians) happened in 2084, well before the 3020 alarm call, so we must keep our fingers crossed. » Rory's death is only the sixth time we have seen one of the Doctor's companions killed on screen (and the fourth to later be revealed as only temporary!). The 1965–1966 story *The Daleks' Master Plan* saw Trojan handmaiden Katarina killed during an epic battle to prevent the use of a deadly Time Destructor. The 1982 Cybermen story *Earthshock* saw the death of mathematical genius Adric in a crashing space freighter. We also saw Peri Brown killed in *Mindwarp* (1986), but it was later revealed to be a trick. Grace Holloway and Chang-Lee died in the TV Movie (1996) but were swiftly resurrected when the TARDIS attained a temporal orbit. Finally, *Titanic* waitress Astrid Peth sacrificed herself for the Doctor in *Voyage of the Damned* (2007).

DOCTOR WHO | ART DEPARTMENT

THE SILURIANS

EPIC *Doctor Who* two-parter *The Hungry Earth/Cold Blood* featured creatures which first appeared in the show an astonishing 40 years ago. 1970's *The Silurians* first pitted the subterranean, humanoid reptiles against Jon Pertwee as the Doctor. The creatures then returned for a rematch in 1984's *Warriors of the Deep*, which saw Peter Davison in the show's lead role. While the Silurians looked subtly different in each of those TV appearances, they would change more dramatically for *Doctor Who* in 2010.

Neill Gorton runs Millennium FX, the company which has handled *Doctor Who*'s weird and wonderful prosthetic creations since the show returned to BBC One in 2005. Since then, Millennium have reinvented various classic monsters, including Davros, the Cybermen and the Sontarans. The Silurians represented a new challenge, especially as Gorton and co's initial design tactic was soon forced to make a sudden left-turn...

'We started off down the route of taking a look at the old version of the Silurians and then updating them,' says Neill. 'I figured out how we could make them work better. You're looking at something from the 1970s and 1980s, where there were a lot of limitations, in terms of technology, materials and techniques. For instance, the old Silurians ended up having a flashing light on their head as a third eye, because otherwise how would you know which one of them was speaking? They became Daleks, in that sense. They didn't move: they were just rubber heads without character or emotion. I wanted to do them as a mixed effect, with prosthetics around the performer's mouth, but with animatronic eyes.'

'It was still a Silurian, but sleeker and much more up-to-date, with a better design. We just made them look cooler and more for this generation than the last.'

Neill created a concept sculpture of a Silurian head, known as a maquette. 'We often do these,' he explains, 'because we can photograph them from different angles and then paint it on a computer screen, rather than painting the actual maquette.'

While Neill sculpted away, however, writer Chris Chibnall's scripts were nearing completion. It soon became clear that, while Neill's design was top-notch, it might not necessarily be the right look for these particular stories.

'Chris and Steven Moffat came back to us,' recalls Neill, 'saying they wanted a total overhaul. So we had to ditch the old design! Obviously, the fanboy and monster-maker side of me goes, 'Ohhh, I'd love to do those other ones'. But our job isn't to please ourselves – it's to service the script! And once I *read* the script, I could totally understood why. I totally saw their reasoning: they wanted a much more human element. When the Doctor's talking to the captured Silurian, Alaya, it's a much more performance-driven thing, partly because they can have proper eye contact. And when the humans and Silurians are sitting there, talking about the future of the Earth,

HEAT RAYS

The Silurians' weapons in *The Hungry Earth/Cold Blood* were designed by *Doctor Who*'s art department. At writer Chris Chibnall's request, they were loosely modelled on devices sported by the Silurians' aquatic cousins the Sea Devils, who appeared both in 1972's *The Sea Devils* and 1984's *Warriors of the Deep*.

"The brief was to keep the weapon design similar," says Who production designer Edward Thomas, "so that the 'flat face' remained the same. We textured the body of the gun in the same vein as much of the set: a volcanic rock with molten light sources within. The gun felt like an organic force rather than a killing machine, although in the right hands that's exactly what it was!"

there's got to be common ground between them. It's important for the Silurians to look like people – but reptiles as opposed to monsters.'

'So we took all the conceptual work we'd done previously,' he says with a laugh, 'and filed it in the bin! Then we started again and looked at what we could do with keeping as human a face as possible, but making it as interesting as possible. Lizard people have been done to death, so you just need to find something interesting. We ended up with a different head-shape, while keeping the human-like face. We also had characters, like Eldane, who were older – so we had to show age in a reptile face! That's harder to do with monsters. So we leant more towards giving them more of a dinosaur feel, basically giving the Silurians a human face with scales on. The script also handily specified that this was another branch of the same race, which explained why they looked different.'

IN order to get more Silurians on screen, Neill and co employed a technique they'd previously used with the Sontarans and the Sycorax.

Continued on page 87

MADE-UP MONSTER

Emmy Award-winning make-up artist **Davy Jones** tells us, step-by-step, how he transformed actress Neve McIntosh into not one but two Silurians for *The Hungry Earth* and *Cold Blood*...

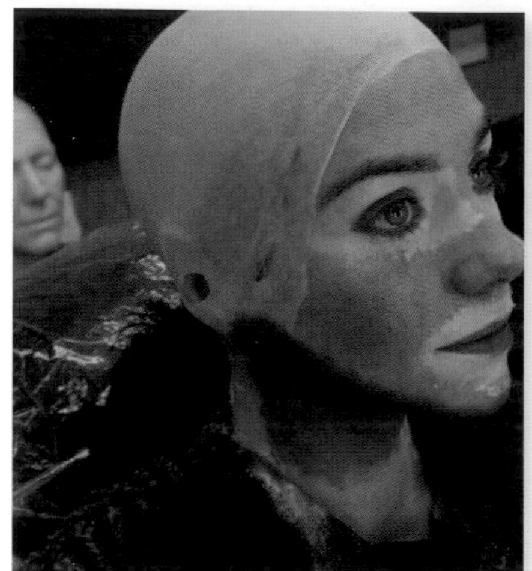

1 'I worked on the first series of *Doctor Who* with my wife Lin, so it's nice to come back and do the odd job for Millennium FX, the company who handle the show's prosthetics. In this picture, you can see the bald cap I used to protect Neve's hair. Around her eyes and mouth is what we call Pax paint, which is like a glue emulsion and acrylic paint mixed together. This stuff ensures that, when the prosthetics are put on later, there's no chance of seeing any human flesh tones. Dick Smith invented Pax paint – the guy who worked on *The Exorcist*.'

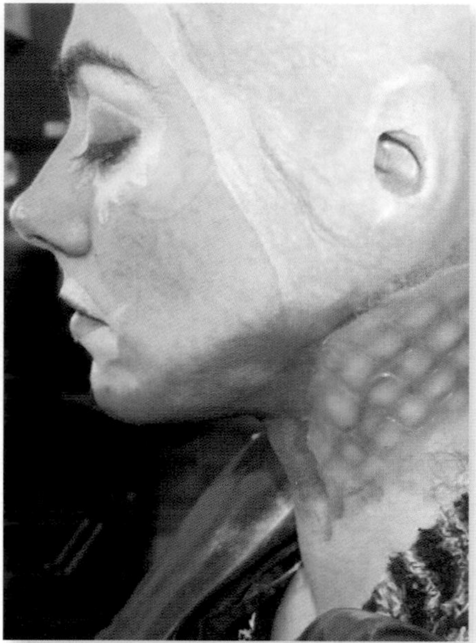

2 'In this picture, you can see the first prosthetic appliance, on Neve's neck. It's all done in stages and everything overlaps, so you very much need a system. I'd worked with Neve before on a BBC series called *Bodies*, so that helped our working relationship. She was great. It's always a bonus if an actor loves their make-up and really gets something out of it.'

3 'Here, I've applied the back head-piece, which overlaps the neck-piece. It's designed so that you can only see scales, even if Neve were to tilt her head forward. You'll notice I've slightly changed the colour of the eyes and mouth paint here, in order to match the pieces. Also, I didn't want it too dark around the eyes because Neve has so much expression there. Neve couldn't stop looking in the mirror, because she couldn't believe it was really her. When she was out of make-up on set, people assumed she was an extra, because they didn't recognise her!'

4 'What I'm doing here, is turning the Alaya head into Restac's, with a red airbrush. I'm also making sure that there's no distinction between the front and back pieces! The back-piece is reusable because it's quite tough, but we needed new front and neck-pieces each day. This whole process initially took about three hours, but we managed to make it faster. Restac generally took a little longer to do than Alaya, because I had to airbrush red on top of green... and I'm quite pedantic!'

5 'Here's Restac, fully coloured. We put a scar over her eye, to further differentiate between her and her sister Alaya. The front and back-pieces of her head prosthetics have been matched up and there's not a bit of human flesh to be seen. If you look at her eyes in this picture and see the pink bits... before each shot on-set I'd apply a green kohl pencil, to fill that in. So many things could potentially give us away, and I wasn't about to take that chance.'

'The Silurians needed to have moulds made of their faces, to fit them perfectly,' he says, 'and when those pieces have to be replaced for each new day of shooting, that becomes very expensive. We had our four lead Silurian characters – including one actress, Neve McIntosh, playing both Alaya and her sister Restac. But when it comes to producing a small army of Silurians, you can't afford to put everybody in prosthetic make-ups. The budget would be crazy! So that's where we came up with the metal face-mask, which could hide the face and make it simpler. We could have a crowd of them, but not have to apply custom make-up every day. Neve playing two parts also helped, because we could use the same mould, rather than make two custom-made moulds for two actresses. Her two characters being related serves the story too, because one of the reasons for the peace talks' failure is Restac's anger at the death of her sister.'

The creation of Silurian head-moulds was a complex procedure which Neill neatly sums up as 'a real faff! I was going cross-eyed, sculpting scales! Every one of them's got to be done by hand. You'll be pleased with work you've done on one side of the head, then remember that the other side has to be a mirror image. Sculpting scales is a real, absolute headache because of all that tiny, tiny detail. It drives you mad, and the only way to do it is by hand.'

Neill's understandably proud of the results. 'Every time you do a redesign, you get comment from fans, positive or otherwise! I've seen people saying, 'Oh, the Silurians don't look like the old ones', but most people seem to like them. There are always a few people who want them to look exactly like the old ones. That even happened with the Sontarans, which looked almost identical to the old ones! There are always a few people who don't like change: that's par for the course.'

'The only time we didn't have a single negative comment was Davros! That's the only time I never heard anyone say they preferred the older version. I think Julian Bleach's performance was so on the money that no one was even thinking about it!'

EPISODE 10

Vincent and the Doctor

BY RICHARD CURTIS

THE STORY

When the Doctor and Amy see a creepy face in a painting hanging in the Musée d'Orsay gallery, he takes them on a trip back in time to meet one of the greatest artists ever – Vincent van Gogh.

But, as Amy finds out when she meets Vincent, the phrase 'tortured artist' was never more appropriate. Struggling with his depression and loneliness, Vincent is a hated outcast. And when a string of brutal killings shakes the Provencal town in which he lives, the painter finds himself at the heart of a horrifying mystery.

The real killer is, in fact, the alien creature hidden in the painting – a Krafayis, an invisible monster which only Vincent can see.

Can the Doctor fight off the Krafayis and save the town? And, even if he succeeds, what hope is there for a broken man like Vincent?

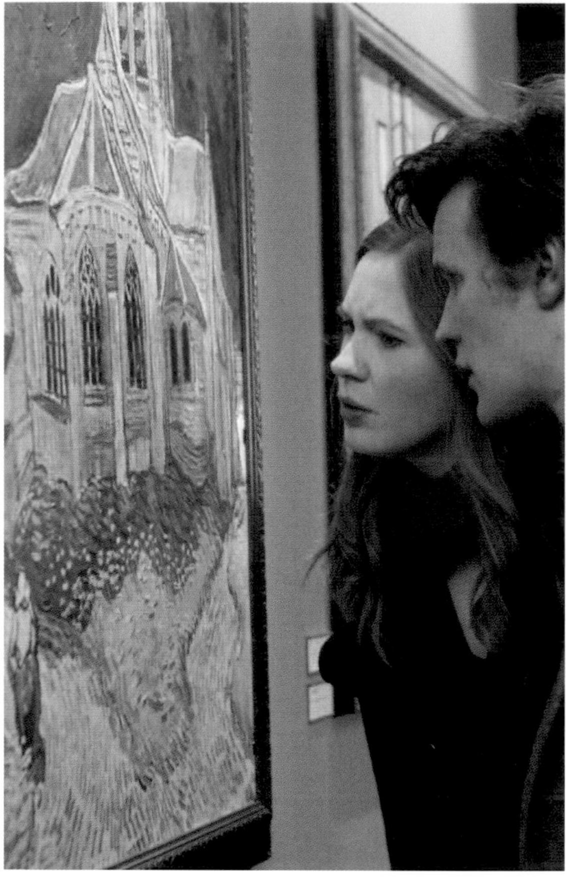

MAGIC MOMENT

It's night. Vincent lies with the Doctor and Amy, beneath the tangled branches of the olive trees...

VINCENT: Look at the sky – it's not dark, and black, and without character. The black is in fact deep blue. And over there, lighter blue. And blowing through the blueness and the blackness, the wind swirling through the air – and then, shining, burning, bursting through, the stars! Can't you see how they roar their light? Everywhere we look, the complex magic of nature blazes before our eyes.
THE DOCTOR: I've seen many things, my friend – but you're right, nothing quite as wonderful as the things you see.

DELETED!

THE DOCTOR: One of the great mistakes people make is to think that artists are, on the whole, making stuff up. We all know that painters notice things in life that most people don't notice. But they also see really weird stuff that's actually there. Most people think they're figments of the artist's imagination – but they're not...

WHERE IN THE WORLD?

This episode shared a filming block in Croatia with *The Vampires of Venice*, and many of the scenes set in Provence were filmed in and around the town of Trogir.

NUMBER CRUNCHING

1853 VINCENT IS BORN

1890 VINCENT DIES

1 THE NUMBER OF PAINTINGS HE SOLD IN THAT TIME

BEHIND THE SCENES

STEVEN MOFFAT

Executive Producer

The Doctor's made quite a regular thing of meeting historical 'celebrities' since his return in 2005...
Be honest, if you had a time machine, it's what you'd do – you'd go and meet famous people. If we never did it, people would ask why.

Generally, *Doctor Who* has 'happy endings' – does breaking this mould make for more powerful TV?
Oh, there are enough sad endings in *Doctor Who*, I think. Someone just pointed out to me that *The Big Bang* is the first genuinely happy ending to a season finale since the show came back. But emotional punch is one of the things we do – and when we do, we go big on it.

RICHARD CURTIS

Writer

What tempted you into writing for *Doctor Who*?
I've done a lot of what you might call 'high profile' things over the years, but it's such a pleasure to work on something that my kids love! Plus I'm very interested in Van Gogh as a person, and *Doctor Who* doesn't shy away from the difficult aspects of his life. We see the Doctor meet a man in crisis, and Tony Curran gives a truly great performance as Vincent. The whole thing has been a real delight.

FAMILIAR FACES

TONY CURRAN

Vincent Van Gogh

Tony won critical acclaim – and a couple of awards – for his role in the 2006 movie *Red Road*.

FANTASTIC FACTS

» In early versions of the script, the Krafayis was actually a monster from a Time Lord fairy tale. The Doctor recognised it from Vincent's painting, having seen it long ago as a picture in a storybook. » In the café, when they meet for the first time, Vincent – who sounds Scottish – asks Amy if she's Dutch, too. This is despite the fact that we can assume everyone here is talking French! The clever psychic translation carried out by the TARDIS must colour people's voices with accents which they find recognisable – and this feature works both ways, which is why Vincent, when he hears Amy's Scottish accent, assumes she is from the same country as him. A similar thing happened to Donna in *The Fires of Pompeii* (2008) when a stallholder in ancient Pompeii assumed her greeting of 'Veni, vidi, vici' meant she must be Welsh...

Vincent Van Gogh

1853-1890

VINCENT VAN GOGH was born in Groot-Zundert, the Netherlands, in 1853. His father, Theodorus van Gogh, was a church minister, and Vincent was named after his grandfather. Until 1864, Vincent was taught at home by the family governess, but at the age of 11 he was sent to a boarding school in Zevenbergen, 20 miles away from his hometown.

After studying art in Tilburg, Vincent found employment with Goupil & Cie, art dealers, who sent him to work in London and Paris. Though he was successful in this career he did not enjoy it, and by the age of 23 he was a supply teacher in rural England.

Vincent was a restless character, and after less than a year of teaching he had decided to become a pastor, like his father. His family sent him to Amsterdam to study theology, but he failed the entrance exams, and went instead to work as a missionary in the Belgian town of Petit Wasmes. It was there that he began sketching the farmers and coal miners that he saw every day.

WHILE LIVING IN Belgium, Vincent lived in virtual squalor and was troubled by a depression that would plague him for the rest of his short life. At one point his father, Theodorus, considered having him committed to a lunatic asylum.

Eventually, supported by his brother Theo, Vincent went to study under the Dutch artist Willem Roelofs, who encouraged him to attend the Royal Academy of Art. It was there that he began to perfect his style but, though his painting was improving, his personal life was often turbulent. A series of disastrous love affairs, along with the death of his father in 1885, drove him deeper into despair. That spring, Vincent completed his painting *The Potato Eaters*, now considered his first major work, and, helped by his art dealer brother Theo, he was beginning to get attention on the bustling Paris art scene. Later that year he moved to Antwerp, where he studied colour theory, taking inspiration from the paintings of Paul Rubens and classical Japanese woodcuts.

FROM ANTWERP, HE travelled to Paris where he socialised with the up-and-coming artists of the day, including Henri Toulouse-Lautrec, and there he was exposed to the works of the Impressionists (Pierre-August Renoir, Claude Monet) and Neo-Impressionists (George Seurat), artistic styles which would be a major influence on his work. In Paris, Vincent lived with his brother Theo, but their relationship became strained by Vincent's heavy drinking and partying with his new-found artist friends.

In 1887 the brothers were introduced to the artist Paul Gauguin, and Vincent and Gauguin became good friends, exchanging paintings and ideas, often painting the same subjects and scenes in friendly competition with one another. By February 1888, however, Vincent was exhausted. Hard work (he had completed over 200 paintings in Paris) and alcoholism had taken their toll. He travelled south to Arles, in the hope that a warmer climate might improve his health.

After the grey cityscapes of Paris, the bright and colourful countryside of Arles proved an inspiration for Vincent. His paintings became more vibrant and his use of colour in them more daring. It was while staying there that he painted some of his most famous works, including *The Night Café*, *The Café Terrace*, and the many still life paintings of sunflowers.

Eventually, in October 1888, Gauguin joined him in Arles, but their relationship deteriorated over arguments about art, and Vincent's increasingly erratic behaviour. After just two months their friendship came to an end, when Vincent threatened his friend with a razor blade. Gauguin left Arles for good, never to see Vincent again, while Vincent, in a drunken and delirious rage, mutilated one of his own ears.

He was hospitalised for a while, and only returned to his home in Arles for a brief spell, before his neighbours in the town (who called him 'fou roux' – the redheaded madman) signed a petition to have him evicted. Still suffering terribly with depression, Vincent left Arles and was admitted to an asylum twenty miles away, in Saint-Rémy-de-Provence. While at the asylum Vincent was often allowed out on walks, and he continued painting. Despite ill-health, his reputation was growing, though he had yet to enjoy any real success.

VINCENT LEFT ARLES to live in Auvers-sur-Oise, near Paris, to be nearer both his brother and a doctor who had been recommended to him, but despite this his depression worsened. On 27 July 1890, aged just 37, Vincent van Gogh shot himself, and died of his injuries two days later.

Though, during his lifetime, Vincent sold only one or two of his paintings, after his death his reputation grew. His work would inspire many artists in the twentieth century, and in 1987, less than a century after his death, his painting *Still Life: Vase With Fifteen Sunflowers* sold at auction for almost $40,000,000.

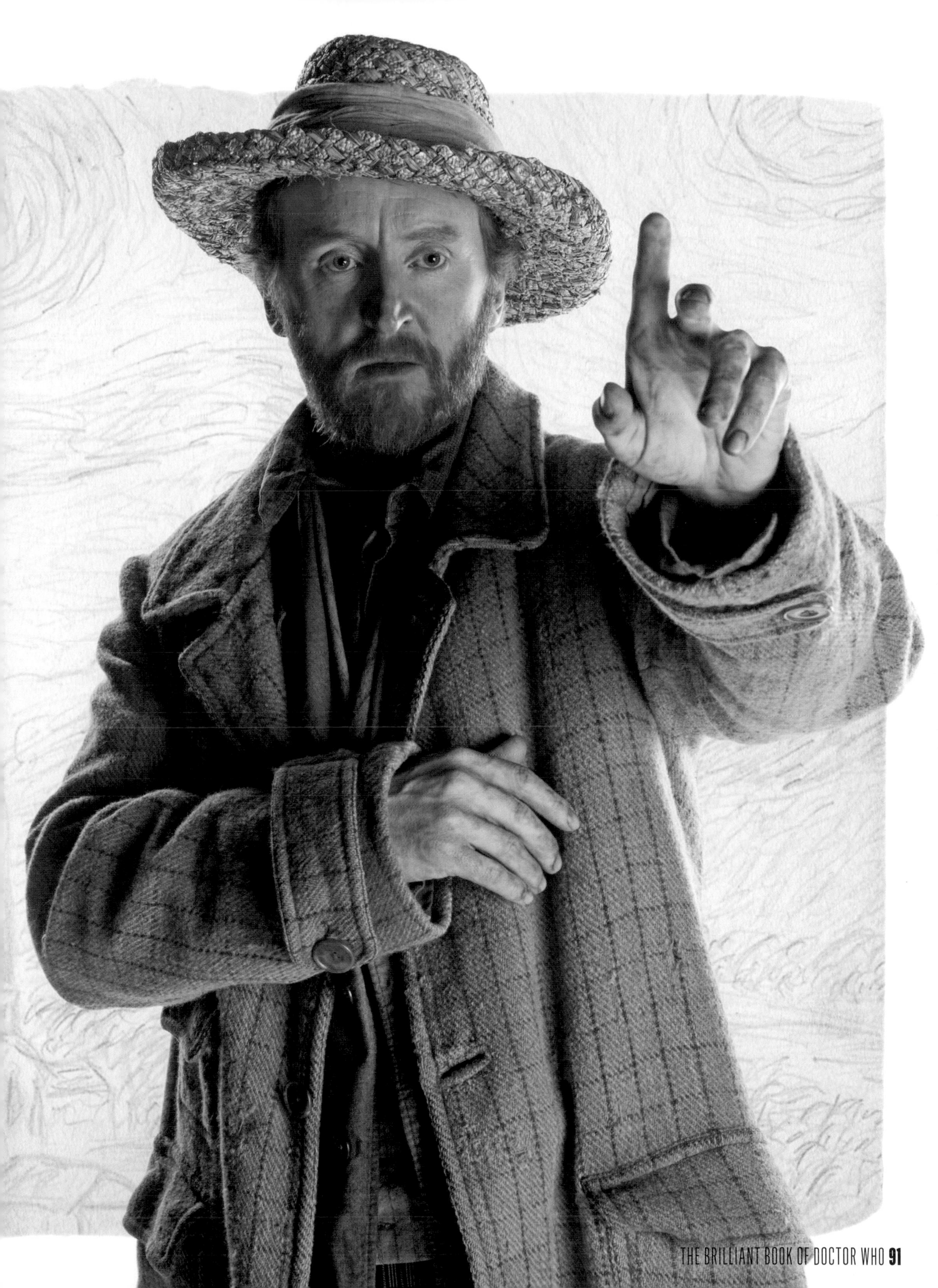

HOW TO WRITE *FOR* DOCTOR WHO

By GARETH ROBERTS , writer of *The Lodger*

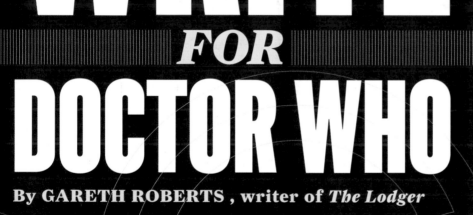

WRITING for *Doctor Who* is a tougher job than you'd think, and writing about writing for *Doctor Who* is only slightly less tough. There is no other programme on television like *Doctor Who*, and its requirements are strange, hard to define, and often contradictory. It must be intelligent and complex, but easy to understand and with jokes that 6-year-olds can get. It must have an emotional depth and some intellectual substance, but it must also have all the lurid thrill of the tackiest 1950s B-movie exploitation creature-feature that you ever did see. The hero is a 900-year-old Time Lord who is the cleverest and most knowledgeable man in the universe, but who is also innocent, curious, naughty and always being surprised. It must move between being cute, shocking, heartbreaking and cheeky in the space of a quarter-page of script. Still want to have a go? Then read and write on!

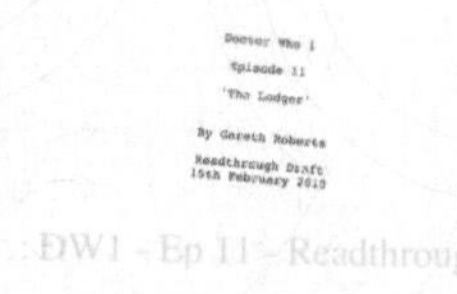
Doctor Who 1
Episode 11
'The Lodger'
By Gareth Roberts
Readthrough Draft
15th February 2010

DW1 - Ep 11 - Readthrough

THE GENERAL STUFF

TIP 1

DON'T JUST WANT TO WRITE *DOCTOR WHO*

There's a world out there. *Your* world. You see the world a little (or possibly a lot) differently from anyone else. Don't worry, you're not unique, everybody does. Which *does* actually make you unique, if you see what I mean.

And the more you write, about whatever gets you going – whether it's cats, wine, the funny thing you saw in the street that set your imagination off – the better you'll get at telling the world the unique way you see it (and the better you'll be able to write *Doctor Who* when the call from Steven Moffat inevitably comes).

TIP 2

WATCH AND READ

This is a fun tip. Watch as much TV and read as many books as you can. Think about how the story works (or doesn't) and how effective the dialogue is (or isn't). You'll be making enough mistakes of your own, but this is a nice way to try and avoid repeating anybody else's.

Now having completed steps one and two, which will probably take you at least ten years (sorry, but they'll be good ones, if poor ones, and much later you'll want them back because everything seemed so simple then), you can go on to write for *Doctor Who*.

THE SPECIFIC *DOCTOR WHO* STUFF

TIP 3

KEEP IT SIMPLE

You need to have just enough story for 42 minutes of screen time. Not too much and not too little. (Unless you're doing a two-part story, then you need enough for about 80 minutes. And if you're doing a two-parter, you should be giving me tips, so stop reading this immediately.) A modern TV audience can process a lot of information very quickly. Very, *very* quickly. Think about how much action and depth there is in an episode like *The Vampires of Venice* – every scene contains a narrative point to propel that story along. Toby Whithouse's script covers a big range of ideas and emotions; Rory and Amy's relationship and how it relates to the Doctor, the ethics of Rosanna's plan, the Doctor's position as the last of his own race, the loss of Guido's daughter and his revenge. And it's packed full of action and big moments; the girl Vampires chasing the Doctor, Amy's decision to go into the Academy single-handed, the final struggle to thwart the Saturnynes' plan. Those are just three of about fifty-seven. But the basic plot from which all that invention springs is very, very simple and easy to understand. For *Doctor Who*, it's always better to have a simple central idea that you can riff on. Even Steven Moffat's two-part finalé, which is packed full of incident and apparent complication, comes from the very simple, graspable idea of the Pandorica. So basically – have one really great central idea and then do everything you possibly can do with it. Don't have two or more.

TIP 4

USE YOUR OWN CHARACTERS

(and don't reveal the Doctor's actually called Roy Robins or anything)

It's always better to dream up something of your own – new characters and monsters. The universe is a big place, and the Doctor always needs new foes and friends. Also, the series is about the situations the Doctor comes into. It's rarely about the Doctor himself, who is best kept at a certain mysterious distance. We don't know exactly who he is for the very good reason that it keeps us interested in him. So if you've got theories about the Time War, his family, or why he left Gallifrey in the first place, etc (and we all have – mine are laughable) keep them to yourself. A mysterious hint is worth one million revelations.

TIP 5

TELL US WHAT'S GOING ON

In any other form of writing, even in other science-fiction or fantasty TV shows, it's a golden rule that you can let the audience work out what's going on for themselves. For some reason nobody quite understands, that doesn't work in *Doctor Who*. Perhaps it's because the action moves so fast that the audience has to be kept up to speed? Characters in the series genuinely need to react to significant events with very clear lines of dialogue such as 'It's overloading!' or 'The Daleks have teleported back to their ship!' or 'The TARDIS is out of control!' Nobody knows why this is essential in *Doctor Who*, and the last thing you should do in any other TV show. It just is.

TIP 6

KEEP THE DOCTOR AND AMY CENTRAL

Even if your episode is nominally all about one other character (Shakespeare or Van Gogh, for example), we need to relate to them through the characters we already know – the Doctor, Amy and Rory. Think of how much Richard Curtis uses Amy's reactions to the story of Van Gogh, or how central the Doctor is to Mark Gatiss's characterisation of Churchill. In any story, scenes without any of the regular characters must be very few and far between. Usually they will involve villains looking at our characters on a screen and plotting a terrible fate for them. We in the business call these the '*Who is this one they call Doc-tor?*' scenes. That may have sounded a bit flippant, but it's actually *vital*.

TIP 7

KEEP IT MOVING! ACTION! PERIL!

There is never any hanging around in *Doctor Who*. Nobody is *ever* bored or sleepy (except when it's the work of the evil Dream Lord). And things happen – lots of things, one after the other, faster than anything else on the telly.

TIP 8

GIVE IT SOME HEART

The story must have high emotional stakes. *Doctor Who* was always like this, like any other drama, but different emotions become fashionable over time. In the post-war generation, when *Doctor Who* first began, people were just glad to be alive. (We think we're a lot more modern and sophisticated now, of course, but in fact there are areas *Doctor Who* used to go into – violence, horror and regular criticism of religion – which we can't get away with today. It's all fashion!) When *Doctor Who* returned in 2005, it was Russell T Davies's biggest job to prove that it had a place in modern television. He succeeded so well that other shows now aspire to be *Doctor Who*, and Steven Moffat can push it even further. There must be serious consequences and high stakes for the characters, regular and non-regular.

TIP 9

PUT YOURSELF INTO IT

Although you're writing for a series, don't feel the need to slavishly follow the rules or copy other writers' work. You can make your individual voice as a writer heard in *Doctor Who* – you should hopefully be able to get yourself across while keeping to the limits of the series. You can feel the difference in scripts by different writers, and yours should be no different.

Congratulations! You now know how to write *Doctor Who*. Turn over to find out what happens next

THE PROCESS

HERE'S how a script makes it to the screen on *Doctor Who*. There are different challenges every time but this is what always happens...

1 You meet up with Steven Moffat, the executive producers Beth and Piers, and the script editor. Steven will have worked out a fairly secure outline for that particular series as a whole, with notes on the entire run of thirteen episodes. He'll know the mix and flow of each episode; what kind of story that will be told that week. And he'll be writing the key, cornerstone episodes himself – certainly the opener and the big finale, the 'event' episodes. (But he keeps all the big things secret.)

2 The stories in *Doctor Who* tend to divide roughly into four categories – Contemporary (*The Eleventh Hour, The Lodger*), Historical (*The Vampires of Venice, Victory of the Daleks*), Futuristic (*The Beast Below, The Time of Angels*) and, occasionally, Sideways (*Amy's Choice*). A writer sometimes brings their own idea to the mix (as I did with *The Lodger*), but more usually Steven will have a starting-point to begin from.

3 This is only the beginning of the meetings. You start to bandy ideas around, and then go off to write a storyline – a fairly brief sketch of the plot of your episode. This goes back to Steven and co, who will have notes that could range from 'Great, go ahead!' to 'Oh dear, let's start again!' Once everyone is happy with the storyline, the writer sets to work on the first draft.

4 You usually get about a month to write a first draft. A totally blank page can be the most daunting moment of the entire process. Different writers have different ways of working – both Steven and Russell T Davies work painstakingly, writing every scene from scratch in order. I like to write a 'skeleton' version of the entire script's structure, then go back to the start and fill in all the gaps. But when the month is up, you'll tap the fatal, final 'Send' button on your email, and off the first draft goes to Cardiff. You will immediately realise what could have been better, now that it's too late.

5 Then everybody will tell you what you've got wrong, and hopefully what you've got right. Now begins the heart of the process – rewrites. You'll get notes from the script editor, and at this early stage probably another meeting to discuss what to aim for in the next draft. Don't be disheartened about rewriting – it's all about making what is hopefully already a good script even better, bringing out every last ounce of potential drama, humour and emotion and getting it up on screen. Television is a very technical business, and *Doctor Who* obviously more so than any other drama, so notes can also relate to what can be achieved and what can't. (I once put a flying car in a first draft script and got a note from Steven – 'We're making twelve other episodes this year, did I not mention?') Every script is different – in my time on *Doctor Who*, I've had to start virtually from the beginning again after a first draft (*The Unicorn and the Wasp*), and on another occasion (*The Lodger*) started with a structure that never changed although a lot of the emphases and details shifted.

6 And the rewriting begins! There'll be at least another eight drafts, with notes batting back and forth after each one. At this point, it's time for me to big up the script editors – some people think that nowadays they are note-takers or glorified secretaries. Piffle! I've worked with script editor Lindsey Alford on three *Who* scripts, and she's always coming up with great ideas and solutions to seemingly insurmountable problems. A script editor is invaluable, your first point of contact with the production, always there at the end of the phone.

7 But there'll be ideas from Steven too! He has an amazing ability to think up answers to script problems. He once texted me when I was in Sainsbury's with an incredibly elegant solution to a plot dilemma. It was doubly impressive because, as we all know, there is never a mobile signal in Sainsbury's.

In *The Lodger*, Steven came up with the answer to the mystery of what was upstairs – my original solution featured an elderly person possessed by an alien who was building a faulty time engine. When *Amy's Choice* was confirmed as Episode 7 in the line-up of the series the 'villain' had to change, as Simon Nye's earlier script featured a very similar enemy. Steven seemingly effortlessly thought up the idea of the automatic crash system of the 'bad TARDIS' to fulfil the same function, and he also came up with the idea that there never was an 'upstairs' to Craig's flat to give the episode an added lift as it neared the end. He's very clever. Doesn't it make you sick?

8 As production gets closer, there'll be what we call a Tone Meeting. This is a day when Steven leads the heads of all the different departments that make *Doctor Who* – costume, special effects, art, design, production managers – through the script, page by page, looking mostly at the technical aspects. This is fun for the writer because it means you get out of the house and into a sweaty room with no air-conditioning. By this stage filming locations are being decided upon, designs for monsters and sets have been created, and numerous decisions must be taken as to how the demands of the script can be achieved. Most importantly it's when the writer meets the director of the episode. It's your opportunity to communicate exactly what you want to the director, who will have ideas to communicate back to you. The whole thing starts to feel more real – what's been living in your head and in your computer is starting to take shape.

9 But the rewrites haven't stopped, oh no. There may be a whole raft of practical considerations to be factored in – perhaps you have to lose a location (as happened in *The Lodger* – the 'can explosion' time loop originally happened in a pub). Or perhaps effects you thought could only be achieved with CGI can be done practically on set, or vice versa. Back to the script!

10 And then, about a month later – and after more rewrites probably – it's almost time to start shooting, and the cast gathers for a read-through. This can be a nerve-wracking experience for a writer, as you sit in anticipation wondering what everyone thinks of your work. When people laugh at your jokes, or get gripped by a dramatic scene, it's such a relief. This is your opportunity to have one last good look at the script – what jokes don't work? Is an actor hitting a particular line in the right way? If an actor's having trouble getting a line of dialogue out, is it your fault and do you need to make it simpler, more sayable? There's another meeting afterwards to iron all those points down – and another meeting means more notes and more rewrites.

11 Then, at last, production begins. Your script starts shooting, and at the end of every day you can pick up rushes of the filming from the internet. This is your chance to keep an eye on the production and see how everything's going, and feed back if a performance is wrongly pitched or a scene doesn't meet your expectations. Luckily this has never happened to me on *Doctor Who*, honest!

12 When the shoot is over, the director and editor disappear into a darkened room at BBC Wales and produce a first rough cut of the episode. It's your turn to give notes, alongside Steven and company. Here is where you see entire scenes cut for reasons of time – or, rarely, you need to go away and write some more scenes to be filmed later to fill up the timeslot.

13 When the episode is edited to everybody's satisfaction, it's 'locked' – with every scene and shot finalized. Now post-production can begin, with special effects being added and Murray Gold coming up with another amazing score. For the writer this stage means working on the ADR (Additional Dialogue Recording). There may be moments when people should be heard talking in the background, or when a particular plot point isn't clear, so the writer has to step in and fill the gaps. For example, for *The Lodger* I had to provide additional dialogue for the Doctor on the phone in Craig's call centre, and for Amy in the opening TARDIS scene, which Matt and Karen recorded weeks after the initial filming.

14 And that's it! The episode is finished and ready to go out on BBC One. Invite all your friends round when it's on and hover anxiously about, waiting to see if they will react in the right way.

15 So there you go – you're armed with the inside information on writing for *Doctor Who*. Good luck! It really is the best job in the world.

EPISODE 11

The Lodger

BY GARETH ROBERTS

THE STORY

A temperamental TARDIS kicks the Doctor out, then goes flying off into the Vortex with Amy trapped on board. The ship can't materialise properly – something is stopping it. And if the Doctor wants to save Amy, he's going to have to find out what's causing the problem.

Stuck in present-day Essex, the Doctor does what any self-respecting, 907-year-old, alien kookball would do. He blends in. Badly. He becomes the flatmate of Craig, a sofa-loving nobody who can't quite tell his friend Sophie how much he loves her. Sophie, meanwhile, feels her Colchester life is going nowhere, so she dreams of an exciting new life saving monkeys in the rainforest. The Doctor can see that they belong together – but can they?

What's worse, unless the Doctor can get the two of them to come to their senses, an alien intelligence in the non-existent flat upstairs is going to cause the destruction of the entire solar system...

So. Who's for a kickabout?

DELETED!

SOPHIE: Well done saving the company.
CRAIG: Sorry. I've done what?
SOPHIE: The Doctor used your notes at the meeting. Didn't he tell you? He found that stuff in your desk, your mad plan. You'll get all the credit, a promotion.

WHERE'S THE CRACK?

The crack in time tears through the wall of Craig's flat, just behind the fridge. Does this mean that poor Craig and Sophie got sucked through and deleted from history...?

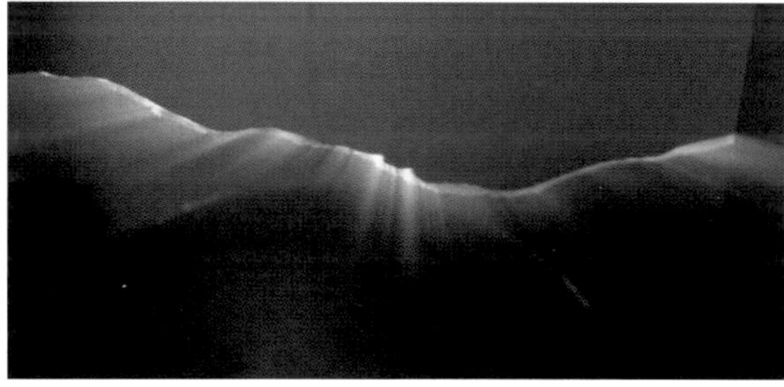

MAGIC MOMENT

The Doctor, Sophie and Craig share a bottle of wine while they discuss Sophie's dream career...

THE DOCTOR: Well, perhaps that's you, then. Perhaps you'll just have to stay here, secure and a little bit miserable till the day you drop. Better than trying and failing, eh?
SOPHIE: You think I'd fail?
THE DOCTOR: Oh, everybody's got dreams, Sophie, very few are going to achieve them. So why pretend? Perhaps, in the whole wide universe, a call centre is about where you should be.
SOPHIE: Why are you saying that? That's horrible!
THE DOCTOR: Is it true?
SOPHIE: Of course it's not true. I am not staying in a call centre all my life – I can do anything I want!

Sophie realises.

SOPHIE: Oh! Yeah! Right! Oh my God, did you see what he just did?
CRAIG: No, sorry, what's happening? Are you going to live with monkeys now?
THE DOCTOR: It's a big old world, Sophie. Work out what's really keeping you here, eh?

NUMBER CRUNCHING

6,000,400,036 THE NUMBER TO BEAT

BEHIND THE SCENES

GARETH ROBERTS

Writer

Could you live with Craig as a flatmate?

Oh yes. I think Craig is the epitome of 'decent bloke' and 'good friend'. I can picture me snuggling up on his sofa to watch *Carry On Abroad* or something, with pizza and booze naturally factored in too. If he fell in love with me, though, I would want to know. And I'd get rid of that strange spooky picture in his hallway. Who the heck is that?

Could you live with the Doctor as a flatmate?

I can't see that working. I think I'd lose patience a lot sooner than Craig did, and the Doctor gets embroiled in deadly danger far too often for my liking. I like my routines, and sharing with the Doctor would inevitably lead to disruption, interruption, alien attack and my gory death.

FANTASTIC FACTS

» The Doctor gives the current population of the Earth as 6,000,400,026. The most recent estimate from the United Nations puts it at 6,800,000,000. Maybe the Doctor has subtracted a few to account for all the people who've fallen through the cracks in time? » We see another perception filter in operation, this time giving Craig's house the appearance of having a second storey that doesn't actually exist. This is the first time we've seen a perception filter used to make something visible: in *The Sound of Drums*/*The Last of the Time Lords* (2007), for example, the filters were used to make the Doctor and his friends disappear, just like the filter around the door of Prisoner Zero's room in *The Eleventh Hour*. » The Doctor turns out to be pretty good at football – which is not all that surprising, given Matt Smith's original career plan. As a youngster, he wanted to be a professional footballer, going on to play for the youth teams of Nottingham Forest, Leicester City and Northampton Town. When a back injury prevented him from following this dream, one of his teachers snapped him up to appear in a stage adaptation of *Twelve Angry Men* – and Matt never looked back! » This story was based loosely on a comic strip, also called *The Lodger*, by Gareth Roberts, which was published in *Doctor Who Magazine* in 2007. » The working titles for this episode were *Something at the Top of the Stairs* and *Don't Go Up the Stairs*. » The original villain in early drafts of this story was Meglos, a shape-changing, cactus-like Zolpha-Thuran whom the Fourth Doctor battled in *Meglos* (1980). He was to have taken over the body of the elderly lady who lived in the upstairs flat, so Steven Moffat cheekily suggested the episode should be titled *Mrs Meglos*. He soon changed his mind...

UNSEEN ADVENTURES

» The Doctor spent some time in Paris in the 18th century, learning to cook. He later used his culinary skills to impress Craig.

FAMILIAR FACES

JAMES CORDEN

Craig Owens

James is best known as the co-creator and star of comedies *Gavin & Stacey* and *Horne and Corden*.

The fabulous, fantastic gallery of CHARACTERS THAT *NEARLY* MADE IT INTO *THE LODGER* *but didn't for some reason*

PRESENTED BY THE WRITER, MR GARETH ROBERTS

THE DOCTOR SAYS: Nothing is as simple as it seems. All events are connected to all other events in a mysterious pattern. Here are the people and things behind the people and things I met when I stayed with Craig. (Not literally behind, you know what I mean.) See if you can spot the spooky old hand of Destiny weaving through and linking these people and events ... PS Don't worry if you can't, I can't, it's just for fun. PPS: But if you do, write in, it might be important. PPPS: I don't know where you should write in to.

CRAIG'S MUM

Craig's mum lives in Southend. When her son complained to her during his twice-weekly phone calls about 'noise coming from the upstairs flat' she thought it was very odd. 'How very odd,' she thought.

CAPTAIN OF CROWN & ANCHOR

A very happy man. The following Saturday, Sean, captain of the King's Arms pub league football team, gave the following pep-talk to his players – 'We did well last week but, even though the Doctor's gone, we can still do good – he made us better players, better people. Let's get out there and annihilate the Crown & Anchor!'
The final score: Crown & Anchor 7, King's Arms 0.

MELINA

Sophie's fourth best friend, who thinks she is Sophie's best friend. Always having a 'crisis'. Her most recent crises include 1. Tearing her new skirt on a railing 2. Splitting up with her boyfriend Dylan (see below) after lots of tears 3. Getting back with her boyfriend after lots of tears 4. Thinking she was about to get sacked 5. Thinking she was going to be promoted 6. Realising she was going to be neither sacked nor promoted.

THE DOCTOR SAYS: You call any of those a crisis? She should try saving the entire universe from falling Silence after her TARDIS explodes. All right, perhaps number 3 counts as a crisis, yes, fair dos, admittedly we've all been there.

DYLAN

Boyfriend of Melina (see left). Hobbies include splitting up with Melina, getting back with Melina, arguing with Melina, hiding from Melina, lying to Melina, telling the truth to Melina, apologising to Melina for telling the truth to Melina, sewing.

THE OLIGARCH OF LAMMASTEEN

The natives of Lammasteen have a technology unique in the universe – they can create apparently 'technological' devices by balancing the resonances of shapes exactly, an arcane science using the mystical power of bits and bobs. After he saved Lammasteen from a terrible plague, the Oligarch presented the Doctor with a toaster, which he mistook for a shower.

THE DOCTOR SAYS: I was lightly browned before I realised.

ELLEN de SMITH

Fearless conceptual artist, dedicated to breaking down barriers in art. In a freakish coincidence, her latest work (pictured) was actually entitled *Ooh, Ain't Modern Society Awful*.

CLARE

Sophie's third best friend, who thinks she is Sophie's second best friend. Knows Dylan (left) well, and shares his hobby of lying to Melina.

THE DOCTOR SAYS: What a tangled web these humans can weave. My life is so much more straightforward, as I was telling Amy and Rory only the other day after reverse–transitioning the flux neutrinos of a sentient crystal quasar that was threatening to engulf an entire galaxy by repolarising its light spectra.)

MARK

Craig's former flatmate, who received £2 million in a legacy on the death of his uncle, Doctor Pond. He had never heard of this uncle before, and neither had anyone in his family, and neither had any government agency, but the Archbishop of Canterbury was prepared to vouch for his existence. There is a dent in the wall of Mark's room where he banged his head after one too many nights of pizza-booze-telly spent watching Craig and Sophie not getting off with each other.

MONSIEUR LE CHEF

Taught the Doctor to cook shortly after the French Revolution. His repertoire consists of omelettes *fines herbes* and several other things that he would have taught the Doctor to cook if he had not been cyluvionised by the Cyluvions shortly afterwards. Luckily he was de-cyluvionised later, by which time the Doctor had already gone.

THE CAT'S OWNER

Mrs Joan Morgan, who lives at 43 Aickman Road and owns the cat. Ever since the Doctor's stay she has noticed a slight change in her pet's behaviour. Whenever she strokes the cat's head she gets a vague, confused, dreamy image consisting of police boxes, Time Wars and beautiful young women. She has now started wearing a bow tie and carrying an electric toothbrush in her pocket wherever she goes. 'Still don't know why!' she jokes to her supportive friends.

CAPTAIN TROY HANDSOME

In a freakish coincidence, there is actually a 'Captain Troy Handsome', who pilots two flights a week on the Mars-Venus rocket run in the 26th century. Tragically the Handsome family are all really ugly. But amusingly, Troy's co-pilot on the rocket run, Lieuetenant Virgil Ugly, is really ugly too.

DOM IN MALTA

Member of the King's Arms pub league team, and Craig's best friend who is a boy, Dom went on holiday to Malta during the events of *The Lodger* and missed everything. Secretly in love with Craig, which saved him from the attentions of the Man Upstairs whenever he came round to talk about football and look dreamily into Craig's oblivious eyes. Returned from Malta to find Craig and Sophie together to his double horror, because he also secretly loves Sophie. Gave up in despair and went to save monkeys (see below).

THE DOCTOR SAYS: I'm glad I didn't have to sort that out.

SAD MONKEYS

The monkey sanctuary never heard back from Sophie, who preferred to stay working with Craig at Brandon's Information Solutions. But Dom (see above) arrived to work with bewildered orang-utans, and luckily fell in love with a woman called Jackie and a man called Bill, both of whom loved him back. The monkeys loved him too, but not in the same way.

SINDA CALLISTA

The Doctor planned to take Amy to the fifth moon of Sinda Callista, one of the universe's holiday hotspots. The Doctor's attempts to take a holiday always end in disaster, but strangely the period in which their stay would have taken place were it not for the diversion from the faulty time engine in Aickman Road was blissfully happy, sunny and totally uneventful.

THE DOCTOR SAYS: Knew it!

PART TWO

Archibald Sneop was the prosecutor. He went into a long speech, explaining how the use of synthetic genomes had been expressly forbidden. Most of what he had to say was drearily familiar. He spoke as though it was drearily familiar.

From their narrow structures, members of the judiciary emerged, a grim and grimy-looking lot, to be shown in to their places by androids. Shokerandit was unceremoniously ushered out of the room.

Once they were all settled, the relevant Laws were read out.

A brief extract from the record of Dino Scanlon's adventure in the parched land was shown.

The Doctor was then called as principal witness for the defence. He came forward briskly and without hesitation began speaking. 'I speak for the Yumwelt, who find themselves threatened by your newly proposed edict. The Yumwelt was established in Germany as a charitable organisation and now flourishes here along the WestCoast, for everyone's benefit.'

A voice from the audience called scornfully, 'They're peddling dreams, that's all!'

'Oh, much more than that,' said the Doctor. 'Their work's of huge importance. 'Popular psychology', you might call it. But their objectives are to cure the sicknesses brought on by the cramps and pressures of your overcrowded societies without use of medication of any kind that might have side effects; and without an often prolonged involvement with psychotherapy or psychoanalysis. You mustn't let their work be destroyed by a financial penalty created by people who have no understanding of that.'

'They use a regenerative machine called a Separator. It lets a sleeping patient experience the non-cognitive freedoms of

inner-space. It lets them dream. 'Umwelt' is simply a German word for 'environment'. But you knew that, right?'

A member of the judiciary said, 'This sleeping patient. What is the point? How can it help in the way you describe?'

'Ah – good question.' The Doctor raised his finger skywards. 'How does sleep help any of us banish the cares and humdrums of everyday life? In this case, the patients can chose their method of unawakeness. Don't you all owe yourselves some relief from your cramped and crowded lives? Your individual umwelts, your own personal worlds, are enclosed within generation-wide umwelts. This present-day umwelt would have seemed unbearable to people only thirty years ago, just as the life-style of your great grandfathers' time would prove unbearable to your present-day selves. This is – if I can borrow another useful German word...' He paused, as if considering, then decided: 'And I think I can – this is the Zeitgeist at work, ever-shifting. Think of your strikes, your riots, your record unemployment figures... You take them for granted, though they warp and distort your lives.'

The jurists frowned and muttered, but the Doctor continued:

'You're just like dogs on leads. The dog pads through the streets, but it's entirely without liberty. It stops when its master stops. It goes on when he goes on. It follows the route he chooses. Don't you think that dog, from frustration, would sometimes love to take a bite out of a passing leg? So why doesn't it? Out of good nature, or because it fears reprisals?'

The muttering increased, and the Doctor went on:

'So you're all dragged along by the Zeitgeist. The Separator, the Yumwelt machine, frees you. It allows you to escape, to whatever imaginary world, happy or wretched, which best expresses your inner universe – often a universe concealed even from your conscious selves. Yes, it lets you dream. Do none of you have dreams? Do none of you want to find yourself free in a non-world? Just for a while? This dreaming, this liberty, this freedom harms no one. It brings you greater freedom than a holiday in Southern Spain. It lets you enact your ambitions, see beyond the horizon, imagine the possible.'

The leader of the Judicial body rose to his feet.

'This vulgar likening of us humans to dogs on a lead provides an insight into the harm this Yumwelt machine can do. Moral harm. Safe from scrutiny, the perpetrator can indulge whatever sin he likes, and cannot be checked for it.'

The Doctor did not bother to conceal his anger. 'No, no, no. That's how your mind works, is it? Always thinking about crime and selfishness. Well, let's take another look, shall we? Let's all have a gander at this great sin. Like a CCTV, the Separator records every imaginary experience, as you've seen. Well, look again. And this time, actually pay attention to what you see.'

The Doctor busied himself at a screen at the front of the courtroom.

'Have you heard of the nations of Satorn and Napplekar?' he demanded. 'No? You're too busy tightening the Zeitgeist round your own throats. All right, then see how sorrow of this present umwelt exorcises the sorrowing of our latest customer...'

The Doctor switched on.

•••••

There lay the barren waste, stretching into a distance blurred by heat. No living soul, no habitation. And there came that stub of train, rolling along its track. The poor, the homeless, clung prostrate to its roof, faces down. The clip lasted for less than a minute.

•••••

The Doctor switched off...

An uneasy silence filled the court. 'The Separator isn't some gimmick you can just outlaw. It translates. It reveals. Self-knowledge comes as a shock. A smidgeon of harmless polysynthia on recovery is a small price to pay for better understanding of how your psyches work.'

The Doctor seemed to grow taller as he spoke: 'You cannot, in the name of humanity, ban the use of the Separator, using this ounce of polysynthia as a pretext. We all know that isn't what you're really afraid of, what you are trying to outlaw.'

Ignoring what the Doctor was saying, the judges were holding a whispered conversation. Then the leader spoke out.

'Laws exist to be obeyed. The witness has admitted to the distribution and use of polysynthia. Doctor, you are arrested as a criminal!'

•••••

He didn't fight or struggle. But four men came to overpower him. One man, gasping from the exertion, breathed foul breath into the Doctor's face. The court rose as he was marched from the chamber. He caught sight of Amy, frightened and alone, as the lackeys dragged him into an elevator. The elevator began to sink, then stopped again abruptly. The doors opened. Six men entered, grim in uniform, full of determination.

'Out you go, chums,' one of them ordered, throwing up his arm. 'Police here now.'

The four holding the Doctor hesitated. Whereupon the newly entered leader roared with anger and assisted them out with his boot. The doors clanged shut and again the elevator began to descend.

'So, what happens now?' the Doctor demanded. 'Who are you lot, anyway?'

'Don't worry,' the other replied. 'You're going to be OK. There's more than one law around here.'

'I'm always OK,' the Doctor told him.

The cage was falling. It stopped with a jolt. The doors creaked open.

A man stood there, aiming a rifle, braced to kill. A shot echoed through the cellar. The man fell on his face, kicked with one leg and was still.

Shokerandit emerged from the shadows. 'Is no more badness from that man.'

The Doctor was aghast. He made a dash for it but was immediately seized, as the three men in the elevator recovered from the shock of the killing.

'Take it easy,' came the order. Two of the men grasped his arms as they went forward. Their footsteps echoed on stone. Shokerandit had re-slung his rifle. He bowed to the men as they passed.

'Not too much violent, I hope,' he said as they went by, tremulous looks on their faces. 'Now you be good,' he told them.

•••••

The place was dark and enclosed, low of ceiling, with a single bar of light burning overhead. Several lorries, some of them fitted with weapons, were parked here, their bulks reflected on the gleaming stone floor. A man in overalls, propped with an elbow against one of the vehicles, beckoned the Doctor and his escort over.

'Here we go,' said the leader, cheerfully. 'You're not going to get shot, after all, Doctor, you may be glad to hear.'

The vehicle was compartmented. The man in the overalls was evidently the driver. He motioned the Doctor to climb in beside him. The others climbed in the back.

The lorry started up immediately. 'Hey, what about my friends?' the Doctor exclaimed. 'Amy and the lawyer, where are they? I can't leave here without them.'

'They'll be OK,' said the driver, staring ahead.

'Have you got Shokerandit on board?'

'He'll be OK too. Says he was born in Kairo. Where's Kairo?'

'They are all being properly looked after,' said a female voice from behind where the Doctor was sitting. He recognised it. He said nothing. The voice belonged unmistakably to Mayor Billiant. He waited. The truck had already gained a side road. It was moving too fast to invite a jump.

'I am speaking to you from a small reinforced cabinet just behind your head,' said the Mayor. 'This is not a transmission. I am here in person and we are taking you back to the Yumwelt workshops. You understand?'

He felt only hostility towards her. 'I assume you're doing this in your own interest, not mine.'

An answer came after a moment's silence. 'Doctor, I must apologise. I keep bad company. Those judges who condemned you for the polysynthia are themselves in the pay of the criminal gangs. They do not favour competition of any kind.'

'And they act as your financiers, and keep you in power,' the Doctor realised. 'If what you say is true.'

'I do not always lie.' She was silent. Then she said, 'You speak of me as being in power. Not at all. Perhaps that was the case in my first term in office. Now I have no power. I am a prisoner... a prisoner of such men as you had to deal with.'

He said nothing.

'Speak, will you, man? It's true – as you've seen – there are some few men who are on my side, who stand for law and order.'

Again, he did not speak.

It was almost daylight. He recognised the shabby environs through which they were passing. Soon they would, so it seemed, be back at the Yumwelt workshops.

Her voice came again, sounding almost tearful. 'I was happy. I loved a good man. But had some little ambition. Ambition but no sense... Doctor, I know you are a righteous man, a defender of what is good. You've got to help me.'

But he resisted her appeal. 'Got? Got to help you? What makes you think that?'

'Oh, oh, please forgive me – I'm too used to giving orders. I beg you to help me.'

Then she added, 'What is this ambition I had? It acts like a leech. You can't be happy. You get something, then you desire more of it.'

In a tone of agreement, he said, 'Mmm, a familiar cliché.'

Gravel crunched under their wheels and the vehicle came to a halt.

The Doctor climbed down. Shokerandit emerged from the rear.

He said, shaking his head in grief, 'Men is bad company in there. Too much of swearing, to anger Great God!'

Carmody Jacobs came hurrying out of the workshop, giving a cheer of welcome. He embraced the Doctor.

And in that second, the Doctor came to a decision; that however much Billiant lied, however much he personally disliked her, he would help her if he could. This woman was in trouble. She probably lied because she was afraid. Besides, she had got him out of that fearful legal establishment. Yes, he would willingly give her assistance.

His hearts were made glad by this fresh determination. He helped her out of the side of the vehicle. They stood looking at each other, weighing each other up. Suddenly she smiled at him. Something in her stiff posture faded away. A communication without words took place.

Billiant's men came jumping from the back of the lorry.

'Maybe you could guard this place for us,' Billiant suggested to the head man.

'I'll have some coffee coming up for you in a minute or two,' said Carmody. 'And my thanks for all your help.'

Taking the mayor's arm, the Doctor led her into the Yumwelt building. The hallway was reasonably smart, with two leather sofas facing each other from either wall. Carmody called to the servant to produce coffee for the men and for the Doctor and Mayor Billiant. Sensing the Doctor's change of mood towards her, Billiant asked that the Doctor would call her Fay.

'Well, Fay, what can we do to help you?' He spoke seriously, leaning towards her with a forearm on his knee. 'I assume you don't plan to return to that fortress of yours? But whatever else happens, I want Amy back safe and sound.'

'When was this umwelt made with the rail track running across the desert?' She gave him a piercing look as she asked the question.

'Couple of days ago.'

His answer evidently pleased her. 'Maybe you can help me – if I confess to my stupidity.'

A tray full of cartons of coffee was presented to her. She accepted a carton, smiling gratefully at the servant. She sipped the liquid. It seemed she was trying to think what she should say next. The Doctor waited, saying nothing.

'I've been foolish. Very foolish... A criminally foolish woman.'

He pointed out that she probably did not believe what she was saying. It was a form of pretence. 'Pretence or protection, warding off the fear that others might call you foolish. You get it in first to disarm them. It's an old trick.'

'Forget it!' She dismissed the charge. 'It was just by accident that you brought that particular umwelt with you, was it?'

He agreed it was, watching her intently. 'It happened to be their most recent product. He paid for it to be made.'

'An umwelt contains the essence of a person. Is that the case?'

'Yes. Well, sort of. But the mind-body situation can shift overnight and give a different picture. Or a different detail, or a different colouration. The next day might be very different. You never know – you might wake up tomorrow and believe that you really are foolish.' The Doctor said this with a laugh.

She considered the matter before saying that now he would think she was being silly, but she recognised the person – the personality – who had projected that astonishing umwelt with the rail running across the desert. Recognised it beyond doubt, she asserted.

He told her he thought that unlikely.

'What do I care what you think? I simply know!' This was said with something of her old passion.

The Doctor was curious about her obsession with the train-wilderness umwelt. Suddenly a light shone. 'It's the man you were looking for. Your soul-mate. That's what you believe, isn't it?!'

Fay Billiant seized both of the Doctor's hands with both of her own hands. She flung back her head. 'Yes, yes, of course. Who else could it be? We quarrelled and like a fool I kicked him out. My Dino! He's been in a spiritual wilderness ever since. It's clear in this umwelt.'

The Doctor frowned. 'What in particular is clear?'

'Oh, don't you see? A man travelling through endless desolation. Surely that must mean he is still missing me?'

She plunged into confessional mode. Yes, she told him, it was years ago. She met Dino. He was building a summer house for her parents in their garden. They fell in love. They were youngsters then, when love fills all of life, when you are blind to the future.

They went to live by the ocean. Dino

fished. She collected shells. They set up a little shack on the shore, sold snacks and fizzy drinks to holiday-makers. They swam when the sun was setting, although the water was always cold. They loved each other and slept on a gaudy Indian blanket spread on the boards of an old boat house. It was an idyllic life. They really had nothing and wanted nothing. No ambition but to be with one another.

Then along came Rugaby. Wasted but good-looking, thin as a well-scrubbed plank.

Rugaby was steeped in politics. He assured them their way of life was part of a great world protest movement. He sang protest songs to the seaside crowd, accompanying himself with a tambourine.

'*Let me tell you truly I'm the rule of the unruly.*
Freedom's more than anything.
Life don't bother me unduly -
Long as I can sing
I'm Big President, Big King...'

Rugaby could sing. Rugaby could dance. Rugaby could sleep curled up like a cat.

'It's an old story,' Fay Billiant told the Doctor. 'We had it too good. No thought for the morrow. The boys fought over me. I was kind of thrilled at that, idiot that I was. Rugaby beat up Dino with a length of wood. I went off with him. That was when I discovered what he was really like... He needed money. He'd do anything to get it.'

The Doctor listened patiently. It was all familiar enough. Too late, she had realised what a good man Dino was. But there was no going back. She shed Rugaby and clawed her way into the grimy politics of Arpeggio City.

She did once get a chauffeur to drive her back to their old haunts by the ocean. They were still there, and the waves and sand and the shells, as white as ever, were still there. Dino of course was long gone. The boat house still stood, empty. Empty, that is, but for their old Indian blanket, hanging on a nail. She had cried then. Years ago. Tears came to her eyes as she spoke of crying now.

At last the Doctor told Fay she had to pull herself together. Then she could go in search of Dino. She should get it clear in her head that if she found him he would be much changed. Yumwelt held his address on his receipt.

'You're going to get rid of me,' Fay sneered. 'You got something else to do.'

'Of course.'

'You think I'm trash.'

'It doesn't matter what I think. I'll get Carmody to give you a free whirl on the Separator and you can see yourself as you really are.'

The railway ran straight as if for ever. Two people, a man and a woman, were travelling in the leading carriage. On either side of the train they saw when they looked out small rugged hills, some with dangerous cliff sides.

The woman was young, with dyed blonde hair. Next to her sat a man entirely covered by a woven Indian rug, so that his features could not be seen.

When the engine whistle sounded, the woman peered out ahead. They were about to enter a green and leafy wood, where lofty trees grew like arches over the track. The sun had broken out from behind cloud, setting young birds to flight. A sense of glory and achievement filled her as they plunged among the foliage.

The Doctor's buggy was taking him with Amy back to Arpeggio City. They had said goodbye to Carmody Jacobs and received a final blessing from Shokerandit. There remained more skulduggery to be tackled in the city. And in all other cities on the map.

"I'm in a constant STATE OF PANIC!"

Steven Moffat is the big boss of *Doctor Who* – executive producer, head writer and de facto showrunner. And we want answers from him!

Setting up an interview with Steven Moffat isn't easy. For the last few weeks (actually, it must be months by now), he's been locked away, writing the 2010 Christmas Special, the opening episodes of Series six, and the overall plan for the season as a whole. Even *The Brilliant Book of Doctor Who* has to take second place to all that!

But we can nag with the best of them. And eventually our perseverence is rewarded with an hour in the great man's company. There's so much to ask, and so little time. So let's get on with it...

Hi Steven. Now it's all over, how do you feel the 2010 series of *Doctor Who* went?

In production terms? It was just what I thought it would be – but what I thought it would be was murderous. It's absolutely non-stop, no days off at all – which is tricky when you've got kids. In terms of the show going out? The great joy and the hugest surprise was how quickly Matt was accepted as the Doctor. I thought we'd have about six weeks of proper resistance, given the popularity of David [Tennant], but Matt just seemed to walk it. There were two reviews on the first day saying, 'Best Doctor ever'.

When did it hit home? At what point did you sit back and say to yourself, 'I think we might have nailed it.'

There were a number of moments where I thought, god, this is pretty good. Which, incidentally, is not the same as thinking it's going to be a success. I remember watching a rough assembly of the 'fish custard' scene from *The Eleventh Hour*, with Matt and little Caitlin *[Blackwood, playing the 7-year-old Amy]*, and just thinking, this is absolutely brilliant! That's such an important scene. It's the scene that nails Matt as the Doctor. You can't not love him after that.

As head writer, did you ever find that something was beyond you? Anything that you thought, 'I don't know how to write my way out of this'?

Oh, just about all the time. That's the condition of writing. I'm in a constant state of panic. Really, genuinely, on every script, I'm saying to myself, 'How can I fix it? How can I fit all the things that are meant to happen into the space I've got left? They're all just standing around talking. This is boring! This is rubbish! And yet they've got to stand around talking, because we've got no money left. Help!' It's a constant struggle, really and truly, on every script, whether I'm writing one of my own or fiddling around with somebody else's. I never believe I'm going to be able to finish it until I actually do.

But you're not exactly new to this writing lark. You must have known that, ultimately, you wouldn't mess it up?

I knew that I could do it, yes. I knew that it'd be disgustingly hard, but also that I had form – if that doesn't sound appallingly arrogant – so I didn't spend a lot of time worrying about it. In the week before Episode 1 went out, I suppose it sort of hit home a bit. 'If I mess this up, that's it for television and me.' I had everyone round to the house on the Saturday, all sitting there on the floor and the sofas, watching it and loving it – except Matt and me, who

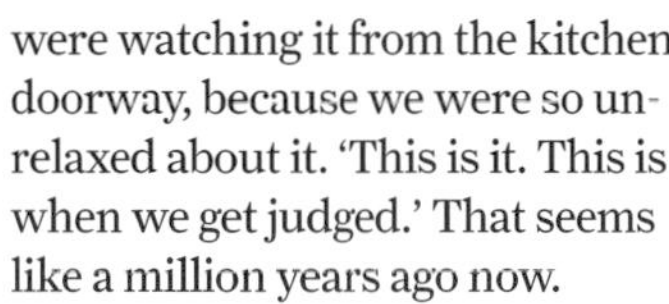

were watching it from the kitchen doorway, because we were so un-relaxed about it. 'This is it. This is when we get judged.' That seems like a million years ago now.

You sat and watched most of the series with your kids. Did that give you a fresh perspective on any episodes?

Hmm, yeah. They were much more interested in the Dream Lord *[in Amy's Choice]* than I thought they might be. I thought that might be pushing it for them.

In what sense?

Well, 'is it a dream or not' is a hoary old cliché. But it was a brand new story to them. I sort of thought, a fairly obviously cheapo episode without a proper monster – we might be in trouble here. But they were properly intrigued by it.

When making 'cheapo' episodes like *Amy's Choice* or *The Lodger*, don't you worry that the BBC might turn around and go, 'If you can make *Doctor Who* on this money, we'll have more of that, please,' and cut your budget?

No, we've been very clear about the cost of episodes like that – they're a huge risk... This is a flagship show. It's an expensive show to make. It gets money more easily than some other shows do, but it's still nowhere near what you really need to make a show like this. There's no such thing as a cheap episode of *Doctor Who*. It's not possible. *The Lodger* wasn't cheap, just cheaper. We built Craig's flat. That's a big set. By the standards of most TV drama, it was actually quite expensive. And it's *Doctor Who* with no monsters, and *Doctor Who* with no monsters is *Doctor Who* with no toys. To make a cheap episode of *Doctor Who* is the least effective economy in the world.

What prompted the Dalek redesign?

That was prompted by me walking into the prop room, and realising that we only had three Daleks.

They're our Big Bad, and we had three of 'em! We need loads and loads of Daleks. How could I justify asking for half a dozen more? I thought, I'll claim it's a new race of Daleks! The fact is, we're not going to lose the old Daleks. We're keeping them. They're coming back. We'll just use them all at once, and have different ranks. All I've done is give the Daleks an officer class.

It was still a pretty brave decision. You can't have been surprised that it split opinion.

It didn't really bother me. I kind of figured that if we got away with an entirely new cast and production team, and some people were complaining about a lick of paint, then that'd be a massive relief. The fans did very well being rushed through a series of huge changes; something was bound to stick in their throats. Was it brave? Was it dangerous? No. Rock-climbing is dangerous. Skydiving is dangerous. Painting a Dalek yellow is not dangerous. It's just a prop.

Let's talk about Matt and Karen. Did how you wrote for the Doctor and Amy change as the series progressed, once you'd seen how Matt and Karen were making the parts their own?

It was quite sudden with Karen, because she's Scottish, and tall, and beautiful, and we knew that's what Amy Pond was like, and yet there's a nuttiness to her that played against Amy's slight grumpiness quite nicely. But with Matt? As I said to him at the beginning, if he's a little bit David-y to start with, then that makes sense, because he used to be David. Any moments of David that shone through in the writing or in Matt's performance are absolutely legitimate and proper. As time's gone on, and Matt has grown more confident, I've realised what a funny Doctor he is. He's completely, barking mad. I'm writing Matt's second series now, and I'm putting more 'daft Doctor' jokes in there, and doing hilarious things that I sort of associate with Patrick Troughton and Tom Baker's Doctors. Matt is a young, funky new Doctor, but also a throwback to the idea of the Doctor as an eccentric professor and mad boffin. He seems chaotic. He doesn't seem to be in charge at all, and makes huge, bumbling errors, but that stimulates him to do something even cleverer, because he's such a genius. He would drive Christopher Eccleston and David Tennant's Doctors insane, if he was in the TARDIS with them. He would break everything, trip over everything, his plans would be stupid, and he'd forget what he was doing halfway through. I'm loving all that.

FAQ

FULL NAME
Steven Moffat
DATE OF BIRTH
18 November 1961
HOME TOWN
Paisley, Scotland
FIRST WHO CREDIT
The Empty Child, 2005
WHO FACT
Before writing for *Doctor Who* proper, Steven penned a star-studded spoof of the show for Comic Relief in 1999, which saw the Doctor played by (among others) Rowan Atkinson, Joanna Lumley and Hugh Grant!

In the months following the announcement of Matt's casting, there was plenty of speculation about how he would play the part, some people doubting whether he was even up to it. You must have been thinking, oh, shut up!

Well, it's good to be on a show that's talked about. I've worked on plenty of shows where no one really gives a damn. I think it's quite nice when we get followed by tabloids, or when newspapers lie about our ratings for the hell of it. Of course, everyone had a view on the new Doctor. In a way, the fact that he was controversial was good. Look at Daniel Craig, when he was cast as James Bond. He went through the same process of being absolutely vilified, until people actually saw him, and then everybody loved him. It makes it more exciting. Had we cast somebody where people would have immediately gone, 'What a good choice! Yes, he'll be splendid,' and they'd have been right, there would have been no showbiz moment. There's a moment of genuine showbiz when people realise that this young fella we've cast can absolutely do it. I do think, having seen his audition, that Matt was a safe choice, but he didn't feel like it because he was so young, and such an odd-looking fella.

Does he mind you calling him odd-looking?

Haha! I'd like to look odd in the way Matt looks odd! It seems to work for him.

He's probably crying on the inside.

Nah, he enjoys it. That's what we do, and he's very secure in what he is. He knows that he's certainly not going to be cast as James Bond. He's handsome in a sort of weird, exaggerated way. He knows that he's appropriate casting for Doctor Who. He's in no doubt about how he comes over. He revels in it. Matt and I just adore each other.

It's unusual, in television, for a scriptwriter to be in the spotlight almost as much as the lead actors. Is that something you're comfortable with?

By writers' standards, you get a quite phenomenal amount of attention, don't you? Normally, it's only the pretty people who get the attention, but here the ugly one gets it too! But I'm kind of relieved when I don't. You don't want to be photographed next to Matt and Karen. Have you seen them? It's like the two most beautiful people in the world, and a genetic experiment. I hate it. I can't wait for them to say, 'Could you move aside now, Mr Moffat?' I just think, oh please, no, don't let anyone see this.

It's interesting how, a couple of years ago, we were starting to get used to the idea that Doctor Who companions didn't have to be young, gorgeous, and scantily-clad – but now that Karen is in the show, that traditional notion of the Who girl, complete with mini-skirt and impractical footwear, seems as crucial a component as the TARDIS, the monsters, or the sonic screwdriver.

Well... no, it's not against the rules for a companion to be great-looking. The show has a long history of sexy girls. The most hilarious stupidity ever from the *Daily Mail* is when they ran a piece, earlier this year, asking, 'Since when were Doctor Who companions sexy?' From the very beginning! Idiots.

If the absolute best person to play Amy hadn't been as glamorous as Karen, and probably the next contender wasn't, would you have cast Karen anyway?

No. But Karen had to get the part, because she blew us away. If anything, we did think, are girls going to like her? Her model looks were not in her favour, put it that way. What you really want is someone extraordinarily beautiful, but who does an impersonation of the girl next door. The moment you've got this flame-haired, 5' 11" Amy Pond, that goes out the window. But it still works, because there's something slightly uncoordinated about Karen, something utterly charming, despite her looks, and of course she's an amazingly good actress.

Amy is a bit of a handful, though. She tried to snog the Doctor on her wedding day. Twice! Does that make her harder to like?

Well, clearly it doesn't, because she's so popular – but I think it's important to distinguish between approving of somebody and liking them. Are your favourite friends the ones you approve of the most? Is the person in the world you love the most also the most impeccably behaved?

Ha ha, well, um –

You see? You laughed when I said it. You don't like people because you think they're decently behaved, upstanding citizens, and a fine example to the young. That's not how you choose your friends. So Amy's very naughty.

The crooked-smile crack that the Doctor first encountered in Amy's bedroom wall – that must have involved a phenomenal amount of forward-planning.

Yes, and panic. The tricky thing was where I had to write bits of Episode 13 before I'd written Episode 12. But it seems more complicated than it actually is, like all good tricks. Of course you have to pay attention, but why the hell not? Why shouldn't telly be like that? I haven't actually encountered anyone who didn't get it, only people who explain to me that other people won't have got it. 'A lot of people won't have understood that,' they say, then always add, 'But I got it, of course.'

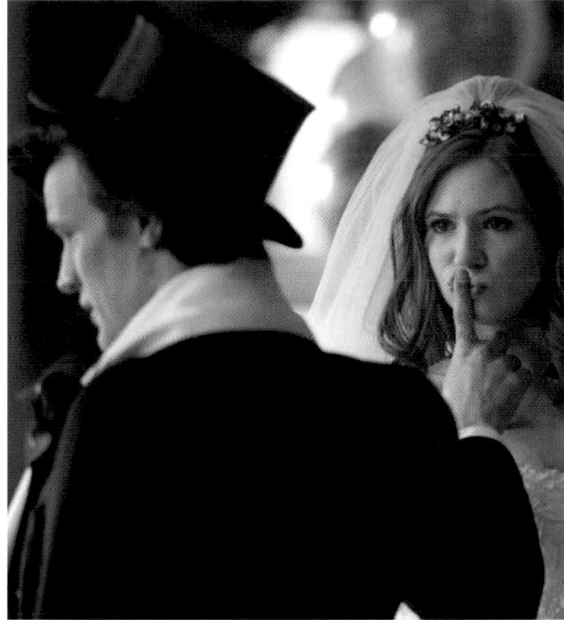

What can you tell us about the 2010 Christmas Special?

This one's incredibly Christmassy. That's true of the previous ones, but I wanted to go for broke – it's absolutely the most Christmassy thing you'll ever see. It's a huge, sentimental, lovely, jeopardy-driven story. It's the Christmas Special I'd like to see. It's like a compilation of every Christmas movie. A big Christmas treat. But that doesn't mean it's without scares, and that doesn't mean it's without heartbreak. It has genuine tragedy in it.

Can next series top the 2010 one? That's the challenge, isn't it?

It is, yes, and you always think that, otherwise you wouldn't bother continuing. There are always enough things that you got wrong... no, let me rephrase that. There are always enough things that you got right that you think you should have got right more often. We fell through the doors as complete neophytes, with the Weeping Angels episodes, which were the first to be shot – not that it particularly shows, but we really didn't know what we were doing. And now we do.

Will the story threads left hanging last series – 'the silence will fall', the alliance of monsters, why the TARDIS exploded – be resolved in 2011?

Yes. Absolutely. Nothing will be left hanging for ever. Some things will be addressed relatively quickly. We're going straight into the Silence, and what they are. There's been a sort of tradition, which I semi-followed with the crack, of there just being a sort of meme through the series, and I think, actually, a bigger mystery, and a bigger story, is possible now. I'm going to handle it slightly differently next year.

And will we find out who River Song is?

Yes. Yes, you will. That's absolutely coming. You're going to find out very soon, and that means we have to do it next series, really.

Have you always known who she is?

I've known for a very, very long time.

I'd always presumed that you had a good idea of who she was – maybe the Doctor's wife, maybe not – when you introduced her in *Silence in the Library* [2008], but then changed your mind when you decided to bring her back. Am I right?

Well... the critical thing here is, I want to explain who she is, not explain away who she is. If you don't deliver on most people's expectations, and you just say, 'Ooh, she's a specially programmed android who believes she's the Doctor's wife,' people will go, 'Well, that's a cheat.' You can't do that.

Hang on – so she *is* the Doctor's wife...?

Haha! I'm not saying that. I just mean you've got to explain it, and make a real story of it. Before I'd finished the Library two-parter, River Song's story came to me. I started at the beginning, the notion of how these circumstances could come about, how it could possibly be the case that any of what I had in mind is true... and I think it's a good story. It's a really good story. And it's sort of the story of next year...

"RIVER'S STORY IS A REALLY GOOD STORY. AND IT'S SORT OF THE STORY OF NEXT YEAR..."

EPISODE 12

The Pandorica Opens

BY STEVEN MOFFAT

THE STORY

There's a message being broadcast all through time and space and, with the aid of his friends, the message finally gets to the Doctor. The Pandorica is opening. The TARDIS is in grave danger.

The Pandorica is a prison for the most feared being in all creation. But it's a myth, a fairy tale – so why is it sitting under Stonehenge? Worse still, all of the Doctor's greatest adversaries are converging on the stone circle. He can't let the Pandorica, and whatever it contains, fall into their hands...

But the Doctor has fallen into a trap. His enemies have built the Pandorica as a prison, to lock away their Time Lord foe for all eternity. But they soon learn to be careful what you wish for...

Even that's only part of the problem: the cracks in time now threaten the end of all reality, and it's the TARDIS that causes it all. How can the Doctor stop the destruction of all time and space when he's trapped within a fairy tale?

WHERE'S THE CRACK?

The crack shatters a screen on the TARDIS console, while River is trying to pilot the ship to safety.

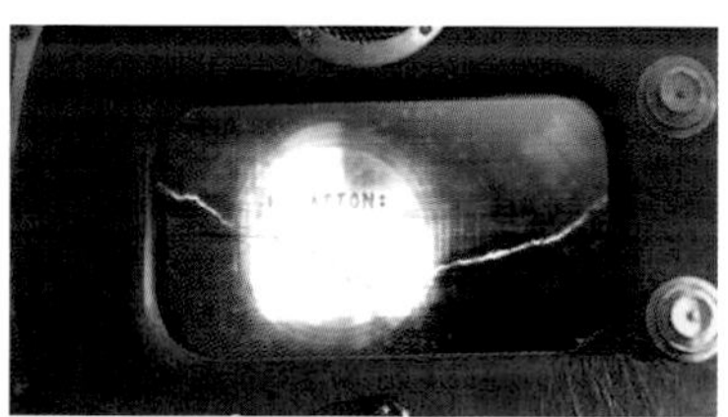

WHERE IN THE WORLD?

Doctor Who is one of very few TV programmes lucky enough to have been allowed to film at Stonehenge itself. (Stonehenge also appeared – but just as stock footage, and only briefly – in the 1996 *Doctor Who* TV movie.)

MAGIC MOMENT

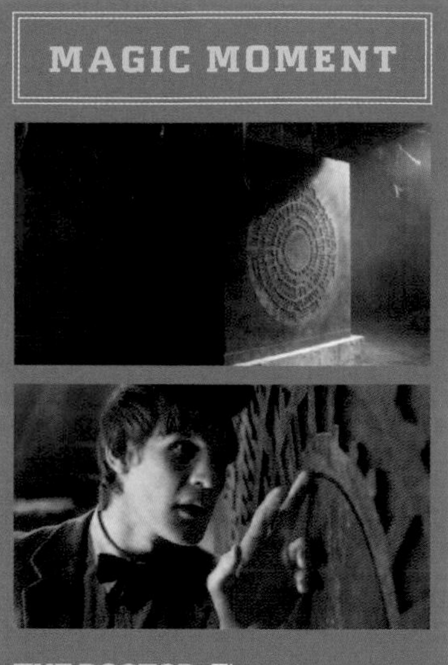

THE DOCTOR: There was a goblin, or a trickster, or a warrior. A nameless, terrible thing, soaked in the blood of a billion galaxies. The most feared being in all the cosmos. And nothing could stop it, or hold it, or reason with it. One day, it would just drop out of the sky and tear down your world.
AMY: How did it end up in there?
THE DOCTOR: You know fairy tales. A good wizard tricked it.
RIVER: I hate good wizards in fairy tales. They always turn out to be him.

NUMBER CRUNCHING

12,000 The number of ships in a typical Dalek battlefleet

3 The element of surprise

BEHIND THE SCENES

STEVEN MOFFAT

Writer

Was it hard to arrange the filming at Stonehenge?
It's surprising how many doors *Doctor Who* can open – there are fans everywhere!

How hard did you, the production team and the publicists have to work to keep Rory's return a secret?
Pretty hard – *Doctor Who* is one of the favourite subjects for newspapers and online gossip, in case you hadn't noticed. But it's more just reminding people who work on the show not to be careless. In the end there was a BAFTA screening of Episode 12, and I just asked the people who attended not to give it away – and they didn't.

Was it fun coming up with probably the biggest *Doctor Who* cliffhanger ever?
Well it was pretty much the cliffhanger for the whole season up to that point. Every episode had been building up to that moment, so I had to make sure I didn't blow it. I don't think anyone could have worked out exactly what happened next. It took me a while...

FANTASTIC FACTS

» In this episode we get a whistle-stop tour of the universe, meeting some of the Doctor friends from earlier episodes in this series: there's Vincent van Gogh (from *Vincent and the Doctor*), Bracewell and Churchill (from *Victory of the Daleks*), Liz 10 (from *The Beast Below*) and River Song. » River says that Stonehenge has 'been here thousands of years, no one knows exactly how long'. Archaeologists can't agree on a precise date for the stone circle's construction: estimates vary from 3000 BC to 2200 BC. » The River that the Doctor meets here is from earlier still in her time line. Remember that, in *Flesh and Stone*, River already had knowledge of the events of this episode? So, we continue our own backward trajectory along River's history. When we first see her in this episode, she's locked in the Stormcage Containment Facility, from which she was released earlier this series. » To help her hop around through time, River manages to get hold of a Vortex Manipulator, which once belonged to 'a handsome Time Agent'. Captain Jack Harkness, prior to meeting the Doctor back in *The Empty Child/The Doctor Dances* (2005), worked as a Time Agent, and he too owns a wrist-mounted Vortex Manipulator. Since *The Parting of the Ways* (2005), Jack has been indestructible and, when we last saw him in *The End of Time*, Part 2 (2010), he was bar-crawling his way across the galaxy. Coincidence...? » The alliance of races that have gathered to defeat the Doctor include (deep breath): Daleks (from many stories), Cybermen (similarly ubiquitous), Sontarans (last seen in *The Sontaran Stratagem/The Poison Sky*, 2008), Terileptils (reptiles from *The Visitation*, 1982), Slitheen (first met in *Aliens of London/World War Three*, 2005), Chelonians (from Gareth Roberts' 1993 *Doctor Who* novel, *The Highest Science*), Nestenes (last encountered in *Rose*, 2005), Drahvins (a race of warrior women, from *Galaxy 4*, 1965), Sycorax (from *The Christmas Invasion*, 2005), Haemo-Goths (never seen before!), Zygons (from *Terror of the Zygons*, 1975), Atraxi (from *The Eleventh Hour*), and Draconians (from *Frontier in Space*, 1973). Though not mentioned, there are blink-and-you'll-miss-'em cameos including Roboforms (*The Runaway Bride*, 2006), a Hoix (*Love & Monsters*, 2006), an Uvodni (from *The Sarah Jane Adventures*), Weevils and a Blowfish from *Torchwood*, the Silurians (from *The Hungry Earth/Cold Blood*) and the Judoon (last seen in *The Stolen Earth/Journey's End*, 2008).

DELETED!

THE DOCTOR: Hello, Stonehenge! Who takes the Pandorica, takes the universe – but bad news everyone, cos guess who!? Blue box? Check. Comedy hair? Check. Oncoming Storm? Check, check, check! Yes, girls, it's the Doctor! And who all needs a comfort break? So let's see, who have we got here tonight. Oh, it's the Daleks! And the Cybermen! Hello, handle-heads! And the Sontarans. Sontar-ha! Sontar-hoo! They're bald and they're butch and there's never any girls. Listen, fellas, your mother and I know, it's fine. Sontar-whee!

The Brilliant Book braves the *Doctor Who* studio floor for an exclusive look at the filming of TV's most challenging show...

MEETING MONSTERS

I'M underneath Stonehenge. In my hurry to get out of a monster's way, I've stumbled back and there's a loud cracking noise. Oops. I look up at my companion, who gives me a stern look.

'You broke the Pandorica,' he sighs.

I look down – not at the absolutely giant (and somewhat intimidating) box/trap but at a rock beside it which, in my defence, looks so authentic that I thought it would be OK to stand on. Fortunately it's still just about in one piece, but then it's hardly surprising that I thought it was real given that the entire Underhenge – for that is what this particular set is called – is so incredibly detailed that you can't help but think it's actually made of ancient stone.

It's so convincing that, even though I know we've walked into a large studio in Cardiff's Upper Boat, where *Doctor Who* is filmed, when I see the light at the top of the steps leading up from the Underhenge I walk towards it, expecting to pop out into the Welsh daylight!

This might actually be the coolest 'not real' place ever. It's dusty and creepy – the dust actually catches in your throat. In a small chamber off to the side there are guns. Lots and lots of big guns, all covered in cobwebs, that I know I shouldn't touch but touch anyway. You'd do the same.

The set is so authentic that it even has that 'old' smell about it. I'll be honest with you, I'm trying to keep my cool but really I'm spellbound, wondering what it would be like if I really travelled in the TARDIS.

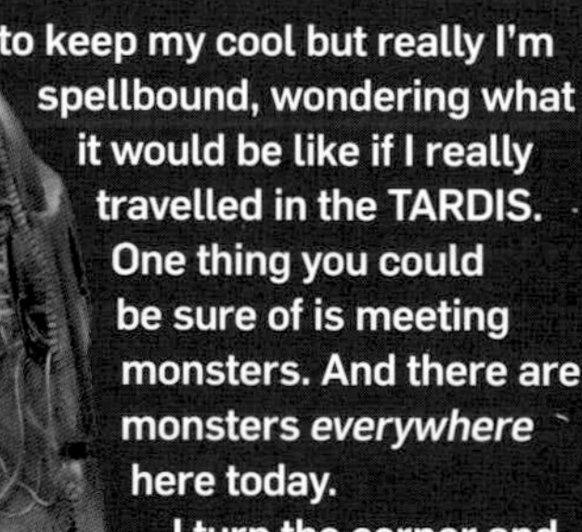

One thing you could be sure of is meeting monsters. And there are monsters *everywhere* here today.

I turn the corner and I'm face to face with a Dalek. It's huge and scary despite being the most colourful thing in this dark chamber. There are the remains of a Cyberman impaled on a huge wooden door. 'As you do,' a special effects person notes as he walks past. 'Just another day in the office...'

BUT where there are monsters there's usually the Doctor. And, in the form of actor Matt Smith, he's currently checking out the Pandorica, filming the scenes where he, Amy and River Song are trying to figure out what's inside.

'Have I got my sonic out?' Matt asks someone nearby. 'Probably,' he's told. Matt flips the sonic screwdriver up in the air and catches it repeatedly. The sonic lights up green and Matt grins. Sonics are cool. Karen Gillan looks on, smiling indulgently.

Another scene is just about to begin filming. The cast are chatting about the film *Dr Strangelove* and Matt talks about a spaceship instead of a plane. Being a time traveller is clearly getting to him.

The chatting soon stops as Karen gets attacked by a Cyberman. She films close-ups, banging the Cyber-head off the sturdy walls of the set, and then a stunt double dressed in a copy of Karen's costume steps in for the more dangerous shots as Amy is pulled to the floor by writhing Cyber-tentacles.

As one Amy watches another Amy tumble to the floor, Rory arrives – Arthur Darvill dispelling some of the spooky atmosphere as his fetching Roman armour is clattering particularly loudly.

JUST outside of this fantastical chamber there are many more adventures to be had. Around the corner are the remains of the exploded TARDIS console room from *The Eleventh Hour* (it still smells a bit singed), Amelia Pond's bedroom, and more monsters – Roman Nestene Duplicates to be accurate.

But there's something even nastier nearby. Hidden away down the winding corridors is a room so terrifying that even Steven Moffat's children won't go in without Matt Smith beside them. This is The Cupboard of Doom. The big boss's kids have been pestering him during filming to sneak a look, so I tag along as well. But I walk a few paces behind them – just to be on the safe side.

To get there we have to walk through huge storage bays. Imagine a giant warehouse that has everything from *Doctor Who ever* in it, sitting on row upon row of shelves. You could literally spend all week in here and not get even close to being bored.

But the Cupboard of Doom beckons. It's actually a largish room with brown paper taped over all the windows. And it's locked. Steven's kids look noticeably peeved. Steven tells them the paper is on the windows so the Weeping Angels can move around inside without people seeing them. They look noticeably less peeved and just a smidge scared...

I DECIDE to head over to another studio – the Underhenge is filling up with monsters, so finding somewhere quieter (where I'm not in the way or breaking vital props) means I can investigate more thoroughly.

Various shots are being filmed on small sets erected around the old TARDIS. Closed down and in the dark, with rubble strewn everywhere, the control room seems sad. I give the darkened console a reassuring pat. My fingers come back black. It really *is* singed. I knew I wasn't imagining that burnt smell...

I look up and my mouth drops open. There's a stone Dalek bearing down on me. It's being filmed against a green backdrop so that the special effects wizards can make it fly outside the National

Museum in the final episode. It casts a giant shadow as it rises up.

I scurry over to Amelia's bedroom, where Karen's cousin, Caitlin Blackwood, is tucked up under the covers preparing to film her last scenes for this series. There are children's drawings, signed 'Amelia', of a burning house with lots of ladybirds – might this be a clue to future adventures?

With her scenes complete, Caitlin jumps out of bed as Karen comes to make her an offer that no one would refuse. 'Do you want to go for an adventure in the TARDIS?' she asks. 'How exciting!'

And it *is* exciting, whether you're 10 like Caitlin or, er, slightly older like me. We both run around pressing buttons and pulling levers. There's a plaque on the console telling you what type of TARDIS it is, and warning that anyone who steals the time capsule could be expelled! There are little references to time everywhere. There's also a Bunsen burner and machinery from Magpie Electricals... All the timey-wimey things twirl around and lights flash. It's brilliant fun and all thoughts of monsters are temporarily banished. The Doctor's mallet is there, attached by a rope.

Karen rings a bell and tries to explain to Caitlin what various parts of the TARDIS are. 'This is a mad professor's thing,' she says, 'and this lever is for pulling, and that switch does something major to the flying process.'

Caitlin's having none of it, and asks where K-9 is. Karen looks slightly confused for a second. 'K-9? What, the dog thing?' she says, looking around as though half expecting to find the Doctor's old robot companion secreted somewhere on the huge set.

Karen's called for filming and we head back towards the neighbouring studio to take in Matt's last scene filmed for these episodes – the opening moments where the Doctor and Amy step out of the TARDIS and see River's message on the cliff. Except this time it's just a big green studio – the alien jungle will be added later.

Steven Moffat watches them do take after take, each time with a variation on delivery of the lines. 'Karen thinks she does a better "va-voom" than me!' Matt shouts at his boss. Steven grins.

They continue with their green screen acting, looking up at what will eventually be a cliff. At the moment it's a stick with white tape on it. That's the magic of television.

IT'S almost time for me to go, but I want to take one last look at the brilliant Pandorica chamber which is, sadly, due to be taken apart in a few days to make way for yet another a new set. It's non-stop here at Upper Boat – and although filming is coming to an end on Episode 13, there's still episodes 7 and 11 to do. Even behind the scenes, time doesn't behave itself on *Doctor Who*.

I pass yet more monsters on the way out – there are extras everywhere, not to mention doubles of all the regular cast, which gets very confusing. The director, who is insisting that he has to get inside a Dalek just to ensure that the shot is correct (yeah, yeah, we've all heard that excuse!) comes bounding over to say hello. It's his first time working on *Doctor Who* and, in addition to getting to work with nearly every *Doctor Who* baddie ever, he's also one of the nicest people you could hope to meet. 'Fun, isn't it?' he says with a massive smile on his face. 'And it's my job!'

Taking one last look around, I can't help but envy him. It looks like the best job *ever*.

EPISODE 13

The Big Bang

BY STEVEN MOFFAT

THE STORY

Little Amelia Pond is a troubled child. There's a crack in her bedroom wall, and no stars in the sky. But her life's going to get weirder when she gets a note telling her to check out the Pandorica at the National Museum...

Sneaking around the museum in the dead of night, she opens the huge, black box – out of which tumbles the grown-up Amy Pond, along with a whole heap of complications.

The universe is ending. Time is running out. And the TARDIS is trapped in a time loop, its explosion shattering the skin of creation. But it's OK – the Doctor has a plan. Just kick start a new Big Bang to recreate the universe! The cracks will close and everything will go back to normal.

There's just one problem. He'll be wiped out of existence for ever. All that will be left is a fairy tale in a little girl's memory...

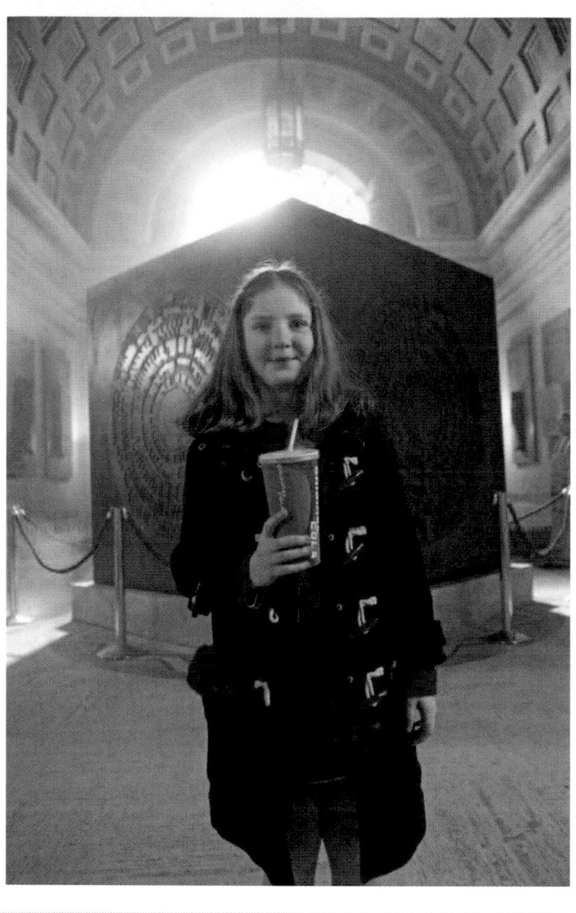

MAGIC MOMENT

The Doctor sits at little Amelia's bedside, like he's reading her a bedtime story...

THE DOCTOR: When you wake up, you'll have a mum and dad, and you won't even remember me. Well. You'll remember me a little. I'll be a story in your head, but that's okay. We're all stories in the end. Just make it a good one, eh? Cos it was, you know, it was the best. A daft old man who stole a magic box and ran away. Did I ever tell you that I stole it? Well, I borrowed it – I was always gonna take it back. Oh that box, Amy. You'll dream about that box, it'll never leave you. Big and little at the same time. Brand new and ancient. And the bluest blue ever. And the times we had, eh...? Would've had... Never had. In your dreams, they'll still be there. The Doctor. And Amy Pond. And the days that never came...

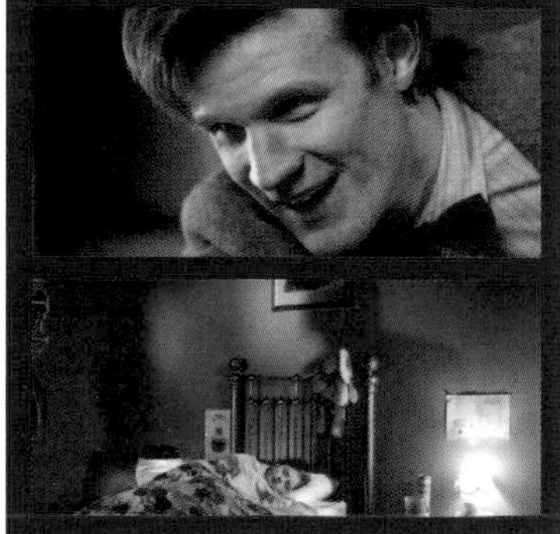

DELETED!

AMY: I love you.
RORY: I love you too, but this isn't me – I'm a plastic thing, I'm a copy of me...
AMY: Who doesn't age, and can keep going for two thousand years?
RORY: Yeah.
AMY: Result!
RORY: You'll age and I won't.
AMY: I'm back in your life, babes. You'll age!

WHERE'S THE CRACK?

It's hard to miss! Not only has it caused the Total Event Collapse, but the crack follows the Doctor back through time as he fades into non-existence...

NUMBER CRUNCHING

0 *The number of stars in the sky*

2 **The number of times the universe has been created**

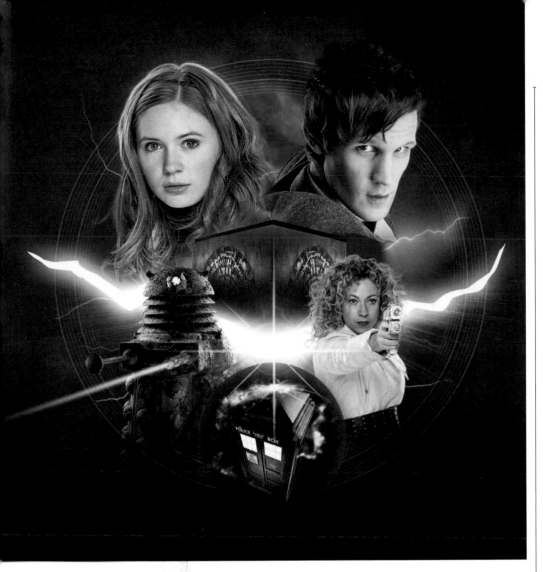

BEHIND THE SCENES

STEVEN MOFFAT

Writer

Not many episodes of *Doctor Who* have ended with the creation of a whole new universe. Is it important to end each series with audacious stories like this?
No, it's not important, it's just fun to do. You could end a season of *Doctor Who* on saving a kitten, if you cared enough about the kitten. That's the beauty of this show. And keep a look out for *Mind That Kitten* next year...

The final episode still leaves some mysteries – chiefly, when will the silence fall, why, and who's behind it? Can we look forward to some answers in the future?
All the answers are coming, I promise – including the answers to questions people haven't even thought to ask yet. I mean, we know how Amy remembered the Doctor. But how did River...?

FANTASTIC FACTS

›› The date of the destruction of creation – as well as Amy's wedding day – is 26 June 2010. This was, of course, also the day this episode was broadcast. ›› Richard Dawkins is mentioned in connection with the crazy 'Star Cults', who believe that stars should exist in the sky. The famous scientist appeared in *Doctor Who* in a cameo role in *The Stolen Earth* (2008), and he's married to Lalla Ward, who played *Doctor Who* companion Romana (1979–1980). ›› When the two time-crossed sonic screwdrivers touch, there is a discharge of temporal energy. This is a symptom of the Blinovich Limitation Effect, as described in *Day of the Daleks* (1972) and *Mawdryn Undead* (1983). But there's no such crackle of energy when Amy pats her younger self on the head. This may seem odd, but it's also worth noting that there's no energy discharge when the Doctor makes physical contact with himself on the rare occasions that he crosses his own time stream (*The Five Doctors*, 1983, for example, not to mention this episode itself). Perhaps time travellers are personally immune to the effect? ›› On the Doctor's trip backwards through the events of this series, he first arrives in Colchester to see Amy leaving a message telling him Craig's address (so he can find his way there in *The Lodger*). Then, he arrives on the crashed *Byzantium* to tell Amy (whose eyes are shut tight) to 'remember what I told you when you were 7' – a scene first shown, effectively out of context, in *Flesh and Stone*. Finally, he arrives back at Amy's house, as seen in *The Eleventh Hour*, to tell 7-year-old Amelia a fairy tale about 'something old, something new, something borrowed and something blue'. (It's this story that he's encouraging her to remember when he speaks to Amy in *Flesh and Stone*; by doing so, he's planting a memory of himself in Amy's mind, so she can conjure him back into existence on her wedding day.) ›› In a scene cut from the wedding reception, Amy said that the dancing Doctor looked like 'a drunk giraffe'. Matt Smith earned this nickname on set, because of his clumsy habit of dropping, breaking, or knocking over props. See more on page 126...

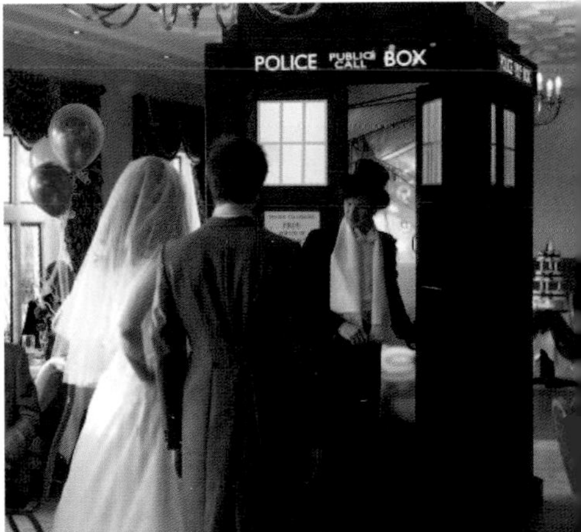

FAMILIAR FACES

CAITLIN BLACKWOOD

Amelia Pond

Caitlin – who also played the young Amelia in *The Eleventh Hour* – is the cousin of star Karen Gillan, who plays Amy.

FRAGILE
THIS WAY UP

THE CONSTANT WARRIOR

Although initially dismissed as nothing more than 'Britain's Bigfoot', the overwhelming evidence for the existence of the Constant Warrior has forced historians to reconsider their opinions. Although at its heart the concept of a lone Roman guarding the treasured Pandorica appears to be impossible, his repeated appearances in the chronicles of history over a period of nearly two thousand years have, at the very least, imbued the story with a cultural significance that defies rational explanation.

THE ROMAN OCCUPATION

The Legend of the Constant Warrior begins here, and this mosaic was discovered in the atrium of a large Roman villa belonging to one of the noblemen in the Roman town of Isca. Apparently the warrior attempted to pay a local farmer to transport the Pandorica to London in his cart.

The most fascinating aspect of this image is the fact that the Constant Warrior had painted a variety of messages across the six faces of the Pandorica in preparation for the journey. Unfortunately neither the innkeeper nor the artist who created this mosaic would have been able to understand them since they had been written in modern English. The legible phrases in this mosaic appear to say both 'FRAGILE' and 'THIS WAY UP', although a third, unreadable phrase had been painted lower down. Experts have speculated that this also says 'THIS WAY UP' but has subsequently been crossed out.

THE BAYEUX TAPESTRY

This famous embroidered cloth – not, in fact, a tapestry at all – which depicts the events leading up to the Norman conquest of England, is one of the best-known historical relics in the world. What is less known is that the Tapestry also seems to depict the Constant Warrior. His Roman armour instantly recognisable amongst the Saxon chainmail, the Warrior stands behind King Harold during the climactic Battle of Hastings – a position usually reserved for the king's favoured military general. The addition of crudely crafted 'goggles' to his outfit has not been mentioned either before or after this appearance, which has led some experts to doubt whether this figure is the Constant Warrior at all. The proof, for those who are less doubtful, appears to lie to the right of the embroidered figure, where a large box, strongly resembling the Pandorica itself, can clearly be seen.

SAMUEL PEPYS'S DIARY

It has been well established that the Constant Warrior was a good friend of Samuel Pepys, and the numerous references to him in the MP's diary are testament to the strength of the bond that the two shared. The following two extracts are of particular note as they once again imply that, though apparently human, the Constant Warrior was privy to a degree of foreknowledge that has yet to be explained. They may offer clues as to the nature of his seeming immortality.

'... As September draws near, the Warrior's nerves have seemed increasingly on edge and he has taken to pacing to and fro across the living room in a most unsettling manner, whilst on more than one occasion the cook has spotted him taking great quantities of cheese from the pantry to bury in the back garden. Upon confronting the young man about such matters he merely gesticulates wildly and his usually polite manner gives way to such bouts of anguish as I have never seen.

'He speaks about events to which I must not be made privy and has proposed, at great length, fictional scenarios in which I might alter events that have previously happened but would choose not to for fear of altering the present in such a way that my wife and children would no longer exist. I find these discourses most intriguing and it is with great reluctance that I remind him of the hours that have passed and the need for me to partake in sleep of even the briefest kind before my morning appointments.'

'The fire was most terrifying up close and the heat seemed to draw the breath from my body as I waited for the Warrior to emerge. When he did, it was to much applause from both my family and household staff which rose even further when the man drew back his cloak to revealed the baker's infant daughter asleep in his arms. He handed the child to my wife before declaring that he must take leave of our company for good,for he still had business in the city. I was most distressed at this announcement and struggled to hide the heaviness of my heart as he took little heed of my warnings and shook my hand firmly in farewell. Whether it were a trick of the light or the heat of the flames I shall never be sure, but when I looked into his face during that parting moment, his skin displayed the most curious of textures that reminded me greatly of a softened wax and his grip was unnaturally smooth in my grasp.

'I have vowed to seek him upon my return to London, but I fear that tonight's encounter shall be the last.'

VICTORIAN CARTOONS

During the late 19th century, the Constant Warrior was a source of great inspiration for the political cartoonists of the time and his Roman armour was seen to represent a damning indictment of British colonialism. In this image from an unknown publication, the Constant Warrior protects Queen Victoria from the natives of various provinces whilst she sits astride the Pandorica, seen here to represent the stolen wealth of the protectorates.

DON'T LISTEN TO HITLER.

HE'S

THE LAST PIECE OF RECORDED EVIDENCE

During the summer of 1934, residents of central London were inundated with a constant stream of leaflets adorned with the warriors face, and a curiously prescient message. Less than a fortnight after this spontaneous one-man campaign took place, Adolf Hitler awarded himself the title Head of State, and the Third Reich was formed. It is an unfortunate irony that the Constant Warrior was apparently destroyed by the enemy he had predicted and, after his apparent death during the height of the London Blitz, this cultural icon faded into legend. Only one final image survives, and its veracity is questionable, but it appears to show the Warrior sacrificing himself to protect his prize from the burning skeleton of the warehouse in which the Pandorica was contained.

THE HISTORY OF THE STONE TOTEMS

THE EXQUISITE PIECES you see here are over 4,000 years old. Rarely have items passed between so many different hands through the ages. Handed from generation to generation, tribe to tribe, they are arguably the National Museum's most significant finds.

'The Stone Totems', as they have become known, are thought to have come into existence after a mishap during the Druids' epic construction of Stonehenge. While one huge block of stone was being lifted into place, it fell from a great height and broke in two. The Druids transformed both halves into the intriguing shapes you see today. Legend has it that the Totems remained hidden beneath Stonehenge for two millennia – though such a chamber has never been discovered since. In 102AD, a group of Roman soldiers were sent to Stonehenge in search of a missing party of their own men. They failed to find them, but unearthed the Totems.

As the following centuries would demonstrate, the 48 curved structures on each of the Totems' lower halves are very much open to interpretation.

The Roman Empire worshipped the Totems as physical manifestations of their solar deity Sol Invictus. They thought the spheres represented our universe's one heavenly body, the sun.

By the Middle Ages, the Totems were deemed cursed as those same half-spheres were thought to symbolise pestilent boils caused by the Plague. As a result, the Totems were often attacked by angry mobs, which must account for many of their cracks and abrasions.

During the Stuarts' reign, King James VI of Scotland believed the Totems' lower sections to be kilts, insisting that everyone in his service wore stone replicas. He then reportedly became frustrated when his staff went about their business very slowly.

So who was correct in their take on the spheres? Conceivably, nobody. It could be that the Stone Totems' curves each represent the Earth – a defiant celebration of our world's lonely position on a black canvas.

Perhaps the most plausible theory of all is that the Stone Totems are merely pieces of abstract – if undeniably beautiful and arresting – Druidic art.

THE NATIONAL MUSEUM

THE WEDDING OF
Amelia Jessica Pond
AND
Rory Williams

DOCTOR WHO ART DEPARTMENT

THE DALEKS

WHEN *Doctor Who* returned to UK screens in 2005, it reintroduced the Doctor's oldest and most popular enemies, the Daleks. The team's art department, led by production designer Edward Thomas, gave them a new look, turning them into deadly bronze beasts.

Come 2010, David Tennant passed his sonic screwdriver baton to the incoming Matt Smith and the previous production team gave way to a new one. Because everything was changing, it made sense that the Daleks should follow suit, making a startling 'reboot' appearance in the TV story *Victory of the Daleks*.

Peter McKinstry was the art department whizz tasked with redesigning one of *Doctor Who*'s most iconic images last year. He had prior Dalek form, having designed the Dalek Supreme for 2008's *The Stolen Earth/Journey's End*.

'Series 5 was all about the new look,' he says. 'New logo, new TARDIS, new sonic screwdriver, new companion, new Doctor – a new era under new producers! And as great as the Daleks were, they had become over familiar.'

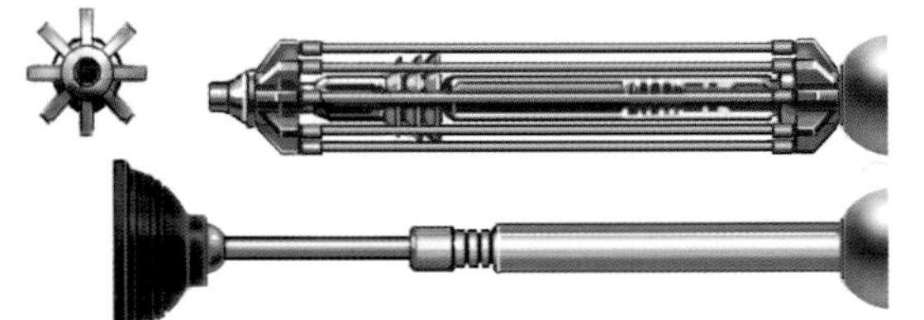

The redesign was not a job that Peter took lightly. '*Doctor Who* had been one of the reasons I started to draw as a child. At a young age, the imagination of that show was almost intoxicating. I had the knitted scarf, the cricket pullover – I even had an old-fashioned school desk in my room which I carved the TARDIS controls onto with a compass! The large dining room table became my drawing board, where I would make huge illustrations – usually of spaceships, monsters and adventurers – on any paper I could find. So to end up designing everything from *Doctor Who* spaceships, to laser screwdrivers, to the planet Gallifrey, and now Daleks, is going to be hard to beat for wish fulfilment!'

Peter joined *Doctor Who*'s art department in 2005, after initially filling in for Matthew Savage, the man who'd designed the new 'bronze' Daleks.

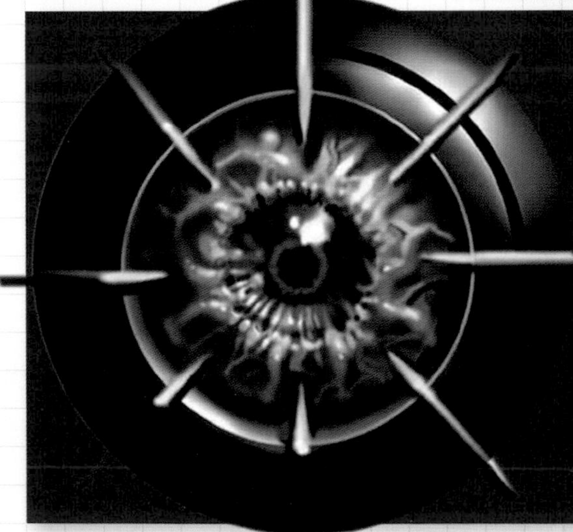

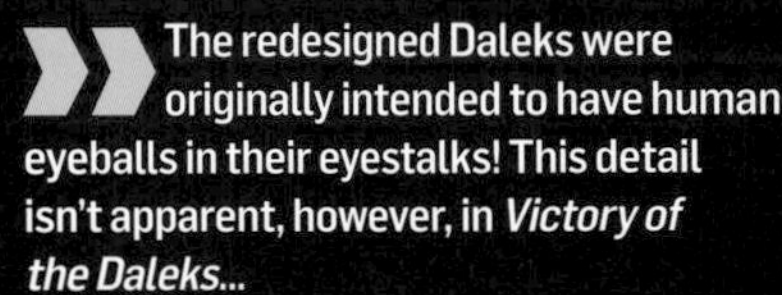

UNSEEN CONCEPTS

The redesigned Daleks were originally intended to have human eyeballs in their eyestalks! This detail isn't apparent, however, in *Victory of the Daleks*...

'The idea for an actual fleshy eyeball in the eyestalk came directly from Steven Moffat,' says Dalek redesigner Peter McKinstry. 'It came at a part of the redesign process which saw us looking for something unique to this form of Dalek, in order to set it apart. There were quite a few variations suggested along the way – some of which I think are being kept locked up for possible future use! One of the ideas which did make it was the spine'section at the back, providing an aperture which could open up and reveal new weapons. In terms of that eyeball, though, I think that the version in the concept was ultimately classed as being too gruesome to transmit at 6pm on a Saturday night! So it was altered slightly during the building process...'

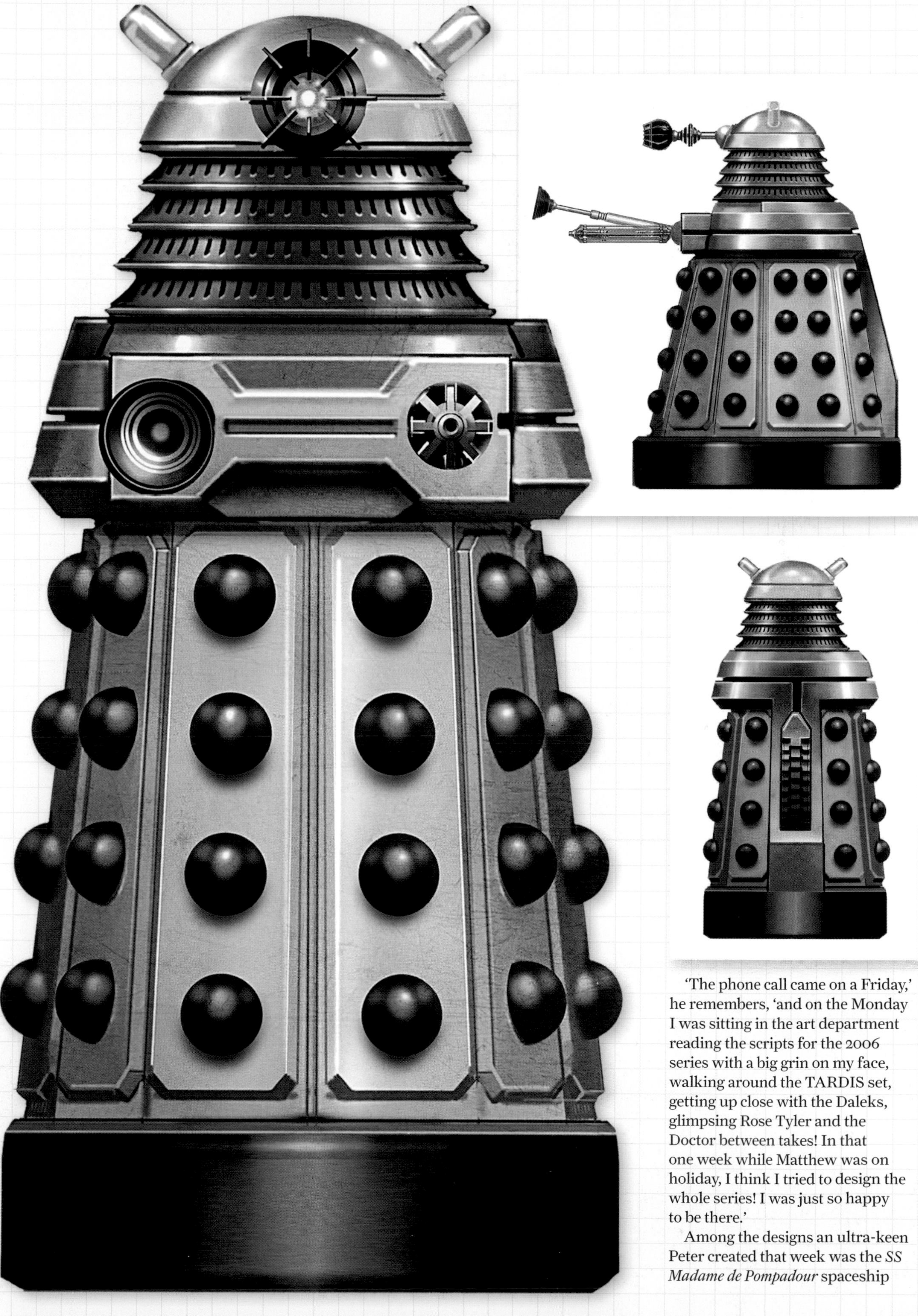

'The phone call came on a Friday,' he remembers, 'and on the Monday I was sitting in the art department reading the scripts for the 2006 series with a big grin on my face, walking around the TARDIS set, getting up close with the Daleks, glimpsing Rose Tyler and the Doctor between takes! In that one week while Matthew was on holiday, I think I tried to design the whole series! I was just so happy to be there.'

Among the designs an ultra-keen Peter created that week was the *SS Madame de Pompadour* spaceship

BUILDING THE NEW DALEKS

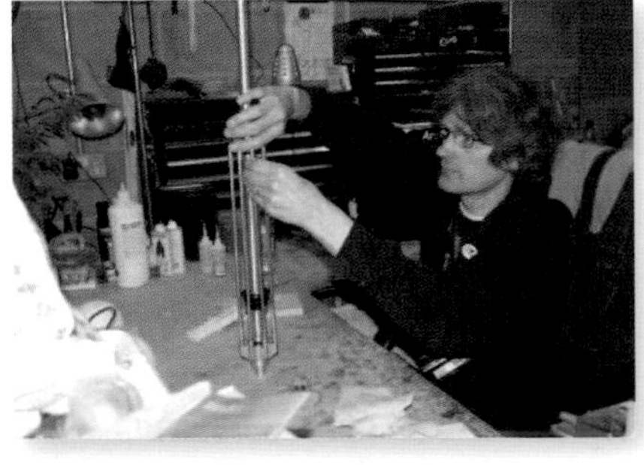

Say hello to **Barry Jones**, *Doctor Who*'s prop fabrication manager. He's the fellow who supervised the redesigned Daleks' construction...

Hello Barry! To what extent is building a Dalek fun? Or is it just a very daunting task, having to live up to previous Dalek builds?
As with all *Doctor Who* props, building Daleks is a lot of fun! However the time constraints set by the shooting deadlines are very demanding. The new Daleks were built to a higher spec than before. They are bigger and have more engineered component parts, such as the eystalk, gun and sucker arm. We followed Peter McKinstry's design brief very closely. We also had to make sure they were strong but light for the operators inside them.

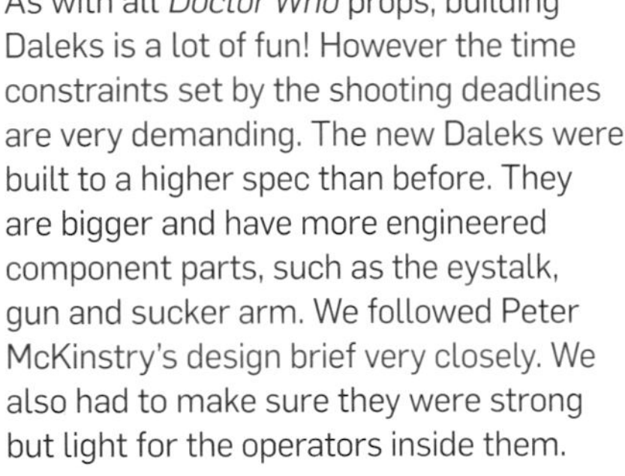

What are the main pitfalls in building a Dalek?
The only pitfall was making sure they were ready in time – it's not all that easy building a Dalek! At times, the team worked all hours and seven days a week to ensure they were finished. We also had to deal with days of heavy rain and high winds.

Describe the Dalek build process.
First, we scaled Peter's design up to size – a size which was set by the height of Matt Smith. His eye level had to meet the Daleks' eyestalks! The process was pretty much the same as the old ones: a lot of fibreglass and moulding. The pattern was built from timber and MDF – this is then moulded in fibreglass. Repeat Daleks are then pulled from that. The head rings, guns, arm and eyestalk were all machined in the workshop. They are then sprayed. Finally, they can be assembled and tested for meanness!

How many did you make? Was each Dalek 100 per cent identical, apart from their colour?
We made five, all the same apart from colour, but the white and the blue are fitted with animatronics. The project went remarkably well considering the tight deadline. I put this down to the skill of the team. Everyone, although totally exhausted in the end, had a great time!

from 2006's *The Girl in the Fireplace* ('I would go back to the hotel and keep sketching till the early hours!'). At the end of his temporary stint, he fully expected that to be all he'd ever do for *Doctor Who*.

'To my genuine surprise, Ed Thomas said, "Lets go for a walk". We went down to the TARDIS set and he offered me a permanent job! That's something that I'll never forget, that moment.'

WHILE the task of providing a facelift for a classic design might initially seem fantastic, it can also be something of a poisoned chalice. What if you mess it up and the world bays for your blood?

'The job of redesigning the Daleks – to alter them more than had ever been done before in the whole history of the show – was just very, very exciting,' says Peter. 'Rather than countless people throwing their oar in with scribbled little Dalek doodles muddying the water, I was left to work from the design brief without any interference. The Daleks have been part an iconic part of British TV and British life since they first appeared, so it's a really big deal. It was clear the impact of having new Daleks as well as new everything else would be massive. There was about a month spent on the redesign, submitting one version, getting feedback, tweaking it, looking at the scale, to arrive at something that everyone was very enthusiastic and excited about.'

One of Peter's priorities was to reassert the Daleks' onscreen impact. 'The previous Daleks had been created to be the size they were, to be eye to eye with Rose in the episode *Dalek*,' he says, 'whereas these new versions are eye-to-eye with Matt Smith's Doctor! The intention was that they have a really dramatic entrance in *Victory*: a really powerful 'reveal' moment when they appeared on screen for the first time. I ended up broadening out the shoulder section, so that along with the added height, the new Daleks tower over the previous version and have a more muscular, intimidating presence. The new colours were mentioned in the script, but my concern was the overall look of them: the five final colours were eventually chosen, I think, with a lot of to-ing and fro-ing with Steven Moffat and the producers to get just the right mix.'

Would Peter have liked to have gone even further with the redesign?

'We went about as far as it's possible to go,' he judges. 'Any further and it may have become unrecognisable as a Dalek! Overall the effect might look quite subtle to some – and more obvious to others – but in fact every part of the Dalek has been altered in some way. Budget and time constraints are always an issue on *Who*: the pace of work is very fast. You might be working on designs for more than one script at a time, awaiting approval by directors and producers.'

All that hard work certainly paid off, and the new Daleks made a considerable impact when they emerged from the Progenitor and blasted their 'inferior' predecessors into oblivion. A resounding Victory!

STONE COLD KILLERS

'To create the stone Daleks needed for episode 13,' says prop fabricator Barry Jones, 'we chose two of our five redesigned Daleks – the blue and the orange. The blue Dalek has an animatronic head,' he points out, 'so this was to become our main stone Dalek. We didn't want to trash either of these Daleks that we'd laboured so hard to make, so we removed the blue Dalek's skirt, kept it safe and made a whole new fibreglass, cracked-up stone one. We also replaced the eye and sucker with modelled stony ones.

'As the orange Dalek could be more in the background of shots, we totally covered it in clingfilm, then textured it with the same spray foam that was used on the TARDIS interior's walls. Then we added textured paint, for a lovely stone finish!

'All this was removed with ease when shooting had finished,' he reports, 'and the two Daleks were returned to their original state. No Daleks were hurt during the making of *The Big Bang*!'

Do the Drunk

It is a well established fact that the Doctor dances like an old man in a young man's body – especially at weddings (and most especially his own). Here, for the first time, we reveal the moves that will, like the Doctor, make people want to impress you...

Important note: Please do not confuse the dance pictured here with the physical movements seen during times of intense mental or physical trauma such as possession or foot-based radiation expulsion.

1 THE STARTING POSITION
Put your feet together and bow your knees. Then, whilst at all times keeping your arms firmly in line with your sides, begin to sway forwards and backwards on your heels.

Arms still firmly by your sides

2 A SURPRISING RUN
It's time to put your audience on the back foot as, with seemingly no warning, you run forward precisely seven steps until you are face to face with your dancing partner (or a random passer-by).

5 A HOP, STEP AND JUMP
It's now time to absent-mindedly abandon your partner until further notice. Whilst keeping your fists in front of your chest, do a quick 180-degree hop, then step and jump back to your original starting position.

Side to side.
(one, two)
Up and down.
(three, four)

6 SCAN FOR ALIEN TECH
Just because you're dancing doesn't mean you have to let your guard down, and now is the perfect time to take some readings of your surroundings. Whip out your sonic screwdriver from an inside pocket and point it at something, anything, or maybe even the air. Then one, two, three, let's scan!

Giraffe

You may wish to accompany Step 3 with a series of questions to which your partner has no answer.

3 RUBBERNECKING

Keep your body swaying and feet together as per Step 1, but this time thrust your head forward into your partner's and start to waggle it around whilst maintaining eye contact at all times.

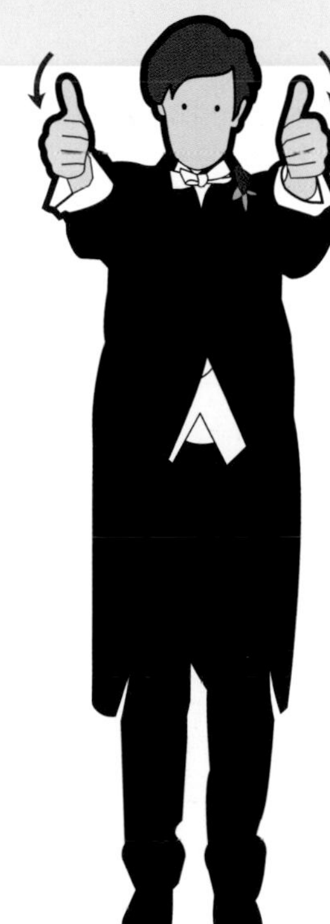

4 THE BICYCLE

Examination complete, raise your arms in front of you and bunch them into fists. To avoid making this gesture look overly threatening, be sure to rub your thumbs animatedly over your fingers whilst moving your fists around in mini-circles.

7 THE FLICK'N'CHECK

Time to check those readings now, so flourish the screwdriver and snap it open whilst pointing it straight up. All good? Great! Now close the device and throw it between your hands four times before pocketing it.

If the readings aren't good, it is recommended that the performer completes the dance before announcing this fact to the audience.

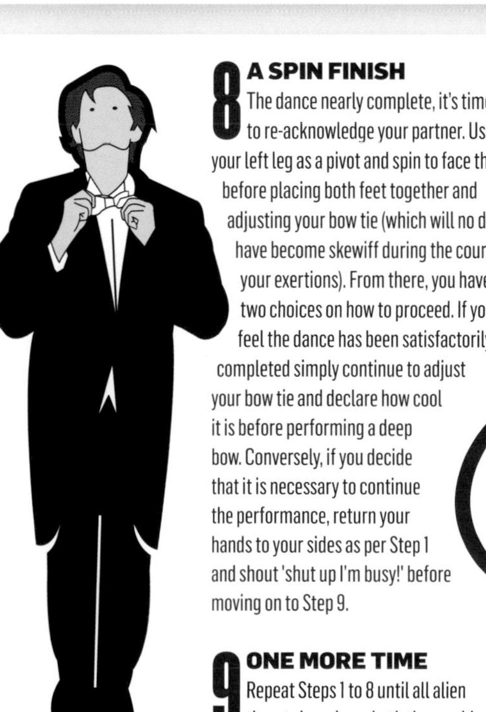

8 A SPIN FINISH

The dance nearly complete, it's time to re-acknowledge your partner. Use your left leg as a pivot and spin to face them, before placing both feet together and adjusting your bow tie (which will no doubt have become skewiff during the course of your exertions). From there, you have two choices on how to proceed. If you feel the dance has been satisfactorily completed simply continue to adjust your bow tie and declare how cool it is before performing a deep bow. Conversely, if you decide that it is necessary to continue the performance, return your hands to your sides as per Step 1 and shout 'shut up I'm busy!' before moving on to Step 9.

9 ONE MORE TIME

Repeat Steps 1 to 8 until all alien threats have been both thoroughly investigated and resolved.

Absolutely everything we learned

The Eleventh Hour There's a crack in Amy's wall, and everywhere in time and space. » The TARDIS has a swimming pool and a library, sometimes combined. » The Doctor loves apples, and has never had a craving for food before now. » Yoghurt is just stuff with bits in. » The Doctor invented fish custard. » Leadworth is in England. » Amelia Pond doesn't have a mum and dad, just an aunt. » Amelia's mum scored faces onto apples. » Prisoner Zero has escaped. » Everything's going to be fine. » The psychic paper can receive messages. » The cloister bell rings when the TARDIS's engines are phasing. » There are four or five rooms on the first floor of Amy's house. » There's a perception filter around the door to the fifth room. » A perception filter stops you noticing a thing. » Stay away from the door to the fifth room. » Do not touch the door to the fifth room. » Do not open the door to the fifth room. » Prisoner Zero is an inter-dimensional multiform, which can disguise itself as more than one creature at a time. » Amy Pond is a kissogram; her outfits include policewoman, French maid, nurse and nun. » When a TARDIS is rebuilding, it locks out its occupants. » Twelve years passed between Amy's first and second meetings with the Doctor. In that time, she visited (and bit) four psychiatrists. » The Doctor is worse than everybody's aunt. » The Atraxi are able to hijack the broadcast signals of an entire planet. » Leadworth does not have an airport or a nuclear power station, nor does it have ducks in its duck pond. It's half an hour's drive from Gloucester. » The Atraxi seal a planet with a forcefield before incinerating it with a 40% fission blast. » Multiforms need to study a living subject with a dormant mind. Forging a psychic link with the subject's dream world enables the multi-form to take its shape. » Earth is a level 5 civilisation. » The Atraxi are a level 20 civilisation. » Multiforms can dissolve their form to slide through small spaces. » Multiforms can live for thousands of years. » Patrick Moore is a devil. » Fermat was killed in a duel before he could reveal the real proof to his famous theorem. » The universe has cracked. The Pandorica will open. Silence will fall. » The Doctor will never say 'Who da man!?' again. » The first time the Doctor sees his new face, it's actually Prisoner Zero that he's looking at. » Article 57 of the Shadow Proclamation protects low-level civilisations from damage by more advanced cultures. » The TARDIS key is able to signal important events by heating up to extreme temperatures. » Fourteen years passed between Amy's first and third meetings with the Doctor. » The TARDIS wardrobe contains plenty of clothes, of all sizes and fashions. » The TARDIS is able to construct sonic screwdrivers. » The Doctor is a madman with a box. » Bow ties are cool. **The Beast Below** Amy was due to marry Rory the day after she left Leadworth with the Doctor. » In Starship UK's schools, if a pupil gets a score of zero in a test, they are unable to use a Vator and must walk home. » Vator Verse is sponsored by McLintock's Candy Burgers. » Humankind abandons Earth in the 29th century, when the planet is engulfed by solar flares. » Each nation builds and launches its own starship. » The only rule the Doctor has is that he must never interfere. » Unless there are children crying. » People use bicycles to travel around Starship UK, and the streets are lit by wind-up lamps. » Amy never could resist a 'Keep Out' sign. » Scotland constructed their own starship to escape from Earth. » Every five years, all citizens of Starship UK over the age of 16 must enter voting booths, where they learn the truth behind 'the Beast Below'. » In the booths, they must decide whether to Protest or Forget. » If only 1% of the population of Starship UK choose to Protest, the truth will be revealed to all and the carefully constructed society will be dismantled – whatever the consequences. » Amy's middle name is Jessica. » There is no power being fed to the engines of Starship UK; this is why there are no vibrations in any glasses of water aboard the ship. » The Doctor is the last of the Time Lords. » If a voter chooses to Protest, the floor of the voting booth slides away and they are plunged into a blood-red abyss. » This abyss is actually the mouth of a Star Whale, an unimaginably huge creature kept hidden beneath the streets of Starship UK. » Vibrating the chemoreceptors of a giant Star Whale will force the creature to vomit. » Escape from the mouth of a Star Whale via such means isn't big on dignity. » Upon escape, the voter has one option: a locked door will release only when the voter hits a Forget button. » The Smilers – the android policemen of Starship UK – will help to ensure the voter's agreement in this matter. » Liz 10 is the current queen of Starship UK. » Liz was told stories of the Doctor that had been passed down through the Royal Family for centuries. » According to these stories, the Doctor has met King Henry XII, Queen Victoria, and Queen Elizabeth I. »The Star Whale is armed with a multitude of stings, which look like the tails of scorpions. » These stings occasionally break through to the streets above. » Liz 10 claims to be 48, her body clock having been slowed down by her government. » She wears an air-balanced porcelain mask in public, so her subjects do not realise that she has not aged. » Although they appear human, the Winders are actually all half-Smiler. » The Star Whale is fed Protesters and other civilians of limited value – but it will not eat children. » The pain centre of the Star Whale's brain is stimulated by the Winders, forcing the creature to provide propulsion for Starship UK. » The Star Whale is constantly screaming, but the sound is outside the range of human hearing. » Liz's porcelain mask is over 200 years old – and Liz herself is nearer 300. » Liz thinks she has been on the throne for ten years, but she too has been constantly Forgetting the plight of the Star Whale for the good of her people. » The Star Whale beneath Starship UK is the last of its kind. » Britain lacked the resources to escape from the inferno-threatened Earth, so instead they captured the creature, built Starship UK around it, and abused its powers of space flight to escape from the solar flares. » If Liz 10 were to Abdicate instead of Forget, the Star Whale would be released, the ship would disintegrate, and the population of the UK would die in the cold emptiness of space. » Amy doesn't ever decide what the Doctor needs to know. » The Star Whale had heard the terrified cries of Britain's children, and was actually coming to the rescue of the humans when they decided to capture and torture it instead. » The Star Whale volunteered. » When released from its agonising torture, the Star Whale is able to increase the speed of Starship UK to levels the occupants had never seen before. » Amy is running away from something. » The TARDIS has a working telephone on the console. » Wartime British Prime Minister Winston Churchill has the TARDIS's telephone number. » Churchill is in a tricky situation. **Victory of the Daleks** Churchill has a secret weapon with which to combat the Nazis in the Second World War. » His secret weapon is the Daleks. » The Doctor is good friends with Churchill: they had a fist-fight during his military service in the Sudan, he stood with him during the Blitz, and finally visited his memorial service in 1965. › Churchill has met more than one incarnation of the Doctor. » From his point of view, Churchill's phone call to the Doctor was a month ago. » The Doctor's TARDIS is a Type 40. » Professor Bracewell is the head of the Ironsides Project. » The Ironsides are Daleks. » The Daleks are your soldiers. » Bracewell appeared a few months ago, with the blueprints for the Ironsides in hand. » Amy cannot remember the audacious Dalek attack that transported the whole Earth across the universe to become a vital component in their Reality Bomb. » If Hitler invaded Hell, Churchill would give a favourable reference to the Devil. » Bracewell has dreamt up many incredible scientific advances over recent weeks, including hypersonic flight and gravity bubbles for protection in space. » The Doctor is the Doctor, the Oncoming Storm, and the Daleks are the Daleks. » The Daleks created Bracewell, who is in fact an android duplicate. » The TARDIS self-destruct button is, in fact, a Jammie Dodger. » Following the destruction of the Reality Bomb, a single Dalek ship survived, falling back through time where they found a Progenitor Device with which they plan to rebuild their race. » The Progenitor wouldn't recognise these surviving Daleks as 'pure' members of the race; it would therefore not activate unless the Daleks could prove they really were Daleks. » With the Doctor's testimony, the Daleks can now activate the Progenitor. » The original Daleks are judged inferior to the new ones created by the Progenitor, and are exterminated. » The new race of Daleks has five different strands: Scientist, Strategist, Warrior, Eternal, and Supreme. They call this their new paradigm, a model for the rebirth of their whole race. » Dalek ships are able to take control of planets' power grids, activating or deactivating any technology they want. » The Daleks have time corridor technology, and they measure time in rels. » Although Bracewell is an artificial life form, he has all the memories of a real man. » Using Bracewell's futuristic inventions, Churchill is able to send Spitfires into space to engage with the Dalek battleship. » The Bracewell android is powered by an Oblivion Continuum, a contained wormhole which can provide endless energy. » The Oblivion Continuum can be detonated, creating an explosion big enough to smash a hole in reality. » Bracewell has memories of his family's Post Office, the death of his parents, and the First World War. » Bracewell once fancied someone he knew he shouldn't: a woman called Dorabella, with eyes so blue they were almost violet. » By summoning up a Dalek replica's most moving memories, it is possible to convince them that they're a true human being. » Free of the Dalek's conditioning, Bracewell escapes to live a real life of his own. » Amy's enemy is the woman outside Budgens with the mental Jack Russell. » The Doctor is always worried about the Daleks. **The Time of Angels** Hallucinogenic lipstick can be used to incapacitate security guards with a kiss. » The Delirium Archive is the biggest museum ever. It is also the final resting place of the Headless Monks. » The Doctor uses museums as a way of 'keeping score', checking them for evidence of his previous adventures. » Category 4 starliners were fitted with Home Boxes, a data recorder which, in the event of a crash, flies back to the ship's point of origin. » Old High Gallifreyan is the lost language of the Time Lords. » This language could be used to manipulate universal forces, destroying stars and altering the time lines. » These powerful words include one which translates as 'sweetie'. » The *Byzantium* will never reach its destination. » A starliner's engines won't normally go into phase-shift, except in the case of sabotage. » Doctor River Song is not a professor yet. » The Doctor will always be there to catch River every time she feels like jumping out of a spaceship. » There's a thing in the belly of the *Byzantium* that can never die. » This episode takes place prior to the Doctor's adventures in the Bone Meadows. » In the 51st century, a military version of the church has developed, in which bishops command sqaudrons of clerics. » Time can be rewritten. » The Doctor never normally lets people call him 'sir'. » The Weeping Angel in the *Byzantium*'s vault was taken from the ruins of Razbahan at the end of the 50th century. » River ripped three seconds of footage from the security cameras in the *Byzantium*'s vault, showing the dormant Angel in captivity. » There's a difference between dormant and patient. » The Doctor will not confirm that River is his wife. » Weeping Angels exist in a quantum-locked state, only able to move when they are unobserved. » Angels can feed on loose energy, such as that leaking from the damaged engines of the *Byzantium*. » The Aplans, the indigenous lifeform of the planet on which the *Byzantium* has crashed, died out four hundred years earlier. » Humans colonised the planet two hundred years after that, and the population of the planet now numbers six billion. » The Doctor will never get done saving humanity. » The *Byzantium* crashed into an Aplan Mortarium: a 'maze of the dead' built to honour departed members of their race. » Only one book on the Angels has ever been written, and it was penned by a madman. » But the book is wrong. » The book doesn't have any pictures. » That which holds the image of an Angel becomes itself an Angel. » Any recording of an Angel is able to 'come alive', stepping out of the monitor on which it is displayed. » When faced with a Weeping Angel, don't even blink. » Furthermore, do not look into an Angel's eyes. » The eyes are not the windows of the soul, they are the doors. Beware what may enter there. » The *Byzantium*'s three-second footage features a 'blip' where the loop winds back to start again. » Pausing such footage during this 'blip' can incapacitate the Angel. » There is something in Amy's eye. » Human expeditions often use Gravity Globes – free-floating, brightly lit spheres – to illuminate their surroundings. » Aplan Mortariums are filled with miles of corridors lined with stone statues. » The walls of these corridors contain the buried remains of the dead. » A human's metabolism can be protected against the effects of radiation by an injection of viro-stabiliser. » River will not confirm that she is the Doctor's wife. » The clerics are given Sacred Names in the service of their church. » Such Sacred Names can include Octavian, Angelo, Christian, Crispin, Marco, Pedro, Phillip and Bob. » Scared keeps you fast. » The Aplans were humanoid beings with two heads. » The Doctor once had dinner with their chief architect. » The Doctor is on Virginia Woolf's bowling team. » The Aplans were a happy race, even though it took them a long time to develop the wheel. » It was acceptable for the two heads of an Aplan to kiss, although their society eventually developed laws against self-marriage. » Although the Aplans had two heads, the statues in the maze of the dead only have one head each. » A low-level perception filter can hide such discrepancies from onlookers. » So can being thick. » Every statue in the Aplain Mortarium is actually a Weeping Angel. » These Angels were the cause of the Aplans' extinction. » Ever since the Aplans died, the Angels have waited, hungering for new prey. » The leaking energy from the *Byzantium*'s shattered drives is enough to revive the army of Angels within the Mortarium. » The crash of the *Byzantium* wasn't an accident; it was a rescue mission. » Weeping Angels kill by displacing people in time. » Angels do not usually snap the necks of their victims, unless they need the bodies for something. » Clerics of the church carry data packs which can display their vital signs. » Weeping Angels have no voice. » Angels can strip the cerebral cortex from a dead body,

from *Doctor Who* this series...

reanimate a version of its consciousness, and use its voice to communicate. » Only a fully restored Angel is powerful enough to do this. » When a person looks into the eyes of an Angel, the Angel is able to play tricks on its victim's mind. » Such tricks include making them believe their limbs have turned to stone, or that ground stone is pouring from their eye. » Amy Pond is magnificent. » The Doctor is sorry. » Angels are able to drain any power in their immediate environment, including light sources. » There's one thing you should never, ever put in a trap: the Doctor. » The Doctor knows what he's doing. **Flesh and Stone** Destroying a Gravity Globe can create a gravitational 'updraught', enabling a person to jump many times higher than normal. » As they absorb more energy, weakened Weeping Angels start to take on their more recognisable form. » A starliner's artificial gravity always orientates to the floor. » Isolating a single power grid can protect it from absorption by Angels. » There isn't a manual for being attacked by statues in a crashed spaceship. » River will not confirm that the Doctor isn't some kind of madman. » A starliner's interior doors can be strengthened by the use of magnetic clamps. » Weeping Angels are strong enough to open even magnetised doors. » Category 4 starliners are *galaxy-class* ships, capable of spending years in space without having to stop at a planet. » Such ships contain forests on board, which are used to provide oxygen for the crew and passengers. » The trees in these forests are technological hybrids: they are fused with cables that lead to hull-mounted sensors, through which the trees absorb light from the stars. » There is an exit to a starliner's Primary Flight Deck at one end of the forest, opposite the entrance to the Secondary Flight Deck. » Starliners are equipped with comfy chairs. » The Weeping Angels plan to consume all the worlds in the universe, gaining dominion over all time and space. » The Weeping Angels have no need of comfy chairs. » The Angels are in Amy's eye. » Amy is five. » She means 'fine'. » The Angels' laughter is a horrifying sound. » The Doctor in the TARDIS hasn't noticed. » The crack from Amy's bedroom wall is somehow also on the wall of the *Byzantium*'s Secondary Flight Deck. » It is the energy contained in this crack that the Angels want. » The crack contains the fire at the end of the universe, an explosion so big that it is sending shockwaves backwards and forwards into every moment in history. » Never let the Doctor talk. » Clerics of the church carry med-scanners, with which they can diagnose a range of sicknesses and injuries. » When the Doctor is in the room, the mission is to keep him alive long enough to get everyone else home. » It's not easy. » The Angels are in the forest. » Amy is not fine, she is dying. » The Angels are able to create new versions of themselves inside the visual centres of a victim's mind. » Once this new Angel is formed, it is able to kill the victim as it emerges. » Rendering the victim unconscious merely makes the Angel's job easier. » The only way to delay the victim's death is for the victim to close his or her eyes, shutting down the visual centres of the brain. Denying the Angel this stimulus cuts off the source of its power. » Even in doing this, the victim will still carry the dormant image on an Angel in his or her mind. » Category 4 starliners are fitted with compressors to extinguish any accidental fires. » The Doctor doesn't know if he has a plan until he's finished talking. › Always respect the thing in progress. » Where Doctor Song goes, Father Octavian goes. » The Doctor always says that he'll come back for a person as soon as he can. » The Doctor always comes back. » At some point in the future, there will be an explosion large enough to crack every moment in history. » The date of this explosion is 26 June 2010. » The Doctor is able to calculate data written in the base code of the universe. » River Song is a sucker for a man in uniform. » River was released from the Stormcage Containment Facility four days prior to the crash of the *Byzantium*; she now resides in Father Octavian's custody. » The Primary Flight Deck of a Category 4 starliner can be entered via a service hatch. » The trees are going out. » Once it has opened, a crack in time takes on the form of a shimmering curtain of energy. » An open crack is enough to frighten Weeping Angels. » The crack is following Amy. » Anyone or anything that falls into the crack is wiped out of existence, as if they had never been born. » Time can be unwritten. » No one now recalls the march of the CyberKing through Victorian London. » River was in the Stormcage because she killed a man who was a hero to many people. » The Doctor knew Father Octavian at his best. » The Primary Flight Deck of a Category 4 starliner is equipped with a teleportation device. » The cleric's communicators can be reprogrammed to act as proximity detectors. They will beep repeatedly if something is in the holder's way. » When distracted, a Weeping Angel can be fooled into believing it is observed, even when the observer's eyes are actually closed. » The only way to seal a crack in time is to feed it a complicated space-time event. » The Doctor is one such event. » River is not as complex as the Doctor. » But the Weeping Angels from the Aplan Mortarium are. » When a starliner's artificial gravity fails, the space inside the ship takes on the ambient gravity of the world around it. » Time travellers, with their own complicated histories, are generally immune from the secondary effects of the cracks in time: they are able to recall the existence of anything that fell through a crack, because they exist outside the normal stream of events. » Even when a crack is sealed, the explosion that caused it continues to happen. » The man River killed was the best she had ever known. » River will see the Doctor again when the Pandorica opens. » The Doctor thinks the Pandorica is a fairy tale. » The Doctor is 907 years old. » The date of Amy and Rory's wedding is 26 June 2010. **The Vampires of Venice** Guido is a boat builder, and his daughter Isabella has no prospects. » Isabella is Guido's world. » Rosanna Calvierri will take Guido's world. » The Doctor bursts out of the right cake. » Lucy is a lovely girl and diabetic. » The Doctor wants to send Rory and Amy on an amazing date. » Rory has been reading up on scientific theories, and knows that the inside of the TARDIS is in another dimension than the outside. » The Doctor likes the bit where someone says, 'It's bigger on the inside!' » The Doctor decides to take the TARDIS to Venice in 1580. » Venice was founded by refugees running from Attila the Hun. » Signora Calvierri has warned the Venetians that the plague is rife in the world outside the city, and so inspectors are posted at every gate to keep out potential carriers. » The Doctor uses the psychic paper to pose as the Pope of the Roman Catholic church; Amy is passed off as a viscountess, and Rory as her eunuch. » The Calvierri girls always cause a stir. » The Calvierri girls don't like sunlight, and they have fangs. » Something happens to the girls in the Calvierri school. » It is important that Rosanna regularly hydrates. » Rosanna doesn't think she has converted enough Venetian girls, though Francesco is keen to introduce them to his brothers soon. » Amy thinks Rory's stepmother is a monster. » Francesco really is a monster. » The Calvierri girls cast no reflections in mirrors. » Houdini is shorter than the Calvierri girls. » The Doctor hasn't updated his library card since his first incarnation. » The Calvierri girls won't tell the Doctor the whole plan. » There is a secret tunnel into the House of Calvierri. » Guido works at the Arsenale, where he helps to build warships for the navy. » The Doctor is too young to be Amy's father. » Vampires are just humans that have been transformed, with human thought processes and logic. » Rory uses the psychic paper to prove that he and Amy have references from the King of Sweden. » Amy only kissed the Doctor because he was there. » Rosanna is immune to the psychic paper. » The Doctor carries an ultraviolet torch, which gives out light of a similar wavelength to sunlight. » Amy is not from OFSTED. » The Calvierri vampires drain their victims' bodies of all their moisture, not simply their blood. » What's dangerous about the Doctor is that he makes people want to impress him. » Rosanna converts humans by drinking their moisture, then replacing their blood with that of her family. » There are ten thousand husbands waiting in the water. » Rosanna Calvierri is not a vampire. » Rosanna wears a perception filter to hide her true, alien form. » All Venetians can swim. » Rosanna is actually a Sister of the Water from the planet Saturnyne. » The perception filter clouds the human mind so much that the wearer has no reflection when seen in a mirror. » A human's instinct for self-preservation is so strong, however, that it overrides the perception filter in cases of extreme danger – which is why the Calvierri girls' fangs are sometimes visible. » The Doctor should be in a museum, or a mausoleum. » The Saturnyne refugees ran from the silence, and from the cracks in the universe. » They were drawn to Earth because of its vast oceans. » Rosanna plans to turn Earth into a new home for her race. » Isabella has been executed. » The Doctor let his own people die. » Rosanna will bend the heavens to save her race, while the Doctor philosophises. » The Doctor will tear down the House of Calvierri stone by stone, because Rosanna didn't know Isabella's name. » Rosanna's perception filter was seriously damaged by Amy, and it has become unreliable. » The actions of a time traveller in his or her past can change the future, making their home time unrecognisable. » Rosanna plans to flood Venice in an enormous storm, then breed a new Saturnyne race from her converted girls and the many sons she has waiting in the waters. » The Calvierri girls are now fully converted into Saturnyne creatures. » The Doctor tells you to do something, and you do it. » Francesco stinks of fish, not cheese and biscuits. » He is extremely sensitive to comments about his mother. » Rory is a dab-hand with a broom. » Rory's getting reviewed now. » Extreme manipulation of the Earth's weather systems can trigger earthquakes. » Rosanna's throne is the hub of the weather-control mechanism. » The secondary hub is also linked to the mechanism's generator. » The Doctor turned the mechanism off, basically. » One city to save an entire species was too much to ask. » Remember the Saturnyne race. Dream of the Saturnyne race. » The TARDIS contains enough space and suitable equipment to carry thousands of aquatic lifeforms. » Amy wants Rory to stay. » The Doctor and Rory are Amy's boys. » There isn't anything underneath the sounds of the city; just the silence. **Amy's Choice** Five years in the future, Amy is pregnant, married to Rory and living back in Leadworth. » Leadworth is not a busy town. » Leadworth is restful and healthy; its residents live long lives. » The Doctor, Amy and Rory didn't get a lot of time to listen to birdsong in the TARDIS days. » The Doctor, Amy and Rory all had the same dream. » Red flashing lights on the TARDIS console mean something. » The Doctor, Amy and Rory's psychic episodes are triggered by the sound of birdsong. » Trust nothing you see, hear or feel. » Never use force on the TARDIS console – unless you're feeling cross, then always use force. » The Doctor threw the TARDIS manual into a supernova because he didn't agree with it. » If you suspect you're in a computer simulation, look for signs of motion blur and pixellation. » Rory is a doctor now. » Stiff hip joints can be soothed by a treatment including a topical application of D96 compound. » Mrs Poggit used to babysit Rory. » The Doctor is the same size as Mrs Poggit's grandson. » The Doctor always puts on a jumper when it's cold. » The Dream Lord creates dreams, delusions and cheap tricks. » If anyone's the gooseberry, it's the Doctor. » Amy has to choose. » If the Doctor had any more tawdry quirks, he could open a Tawdry Quirk Shop. » The Doctor must work out which is real, and which is a dream: Leadworth in the future, or the powerless, drfting TARDIS. » If you die in the dream, you wake up in reality. » If you die in reality, you never wake up again. » The Dream Lord has no physical form. » In conventional dreams, time spent asleep does not match time in the real world. » Bow ties are cool. » Rory would be happy to settle down and have a baby with Amy. » Amy wonders why anyone would give up a life with the Doctor. » It's the night before Rory and Amy's wedding for as long as they want. » The Doctor doesn't know if a star can burn cold. » The Doctor knows who the Dream Lord is. » There's only one person in the universe who hates the Doctor as much as the Dream Lord does. » Mr Nainby ran Leadworth's sweet shop. » The Eknodines were driven from their homeworld by upstart neighbours; ever since, they have been inhabiting the bodies of Leadworth's senior citizens. » The Eknodine inside can extend an eye and a small number of tendrils out through its host's mouth. » Eknodines can fire off a spray of green venom that reduces their victims' bodies to dust. » Eknodines are able to imbue their human hosts with supernatural strength and resilience. » Ponchos are the biggest crime against fashion since lederhosen. » Saving people is what the Doctor does. » If a world without Rory is real life, Amy doesn't want it. » The Dream Lord has no power over the real world. » A speck of psychic pollen from the candle meadows of Karassdon Slava is a powerful thing. » Psychic pollen is a mind parasite, which feeds on all the dark thoughts and feelings of its host. » It chooses its victims carefully, picking those with the darkest thoughts. » Amy didn't know that she wouldn't die. **The Hungry Earth** Elliot is dyslexic. » No one loves Elliot more than his father does. » 21km is further than anyone has ever drilled into the Earth before. » Homo Reptilian transport discs disrupt telecommunications signals when in operation. » Cwmtaff is not Rio. » Ten years in the future, Amy and Rory decide to revisit sites of their past adventures. » Amy's engagement ring cost a lot of money. » Cwmtaff is a former mining town but, since the mines shut down, most people have moved on. » The ground under Cwmtaff doesn't feel like it should. » Sherlock Holmes famously said that when you've eliminated the impossible, whatever remains, however improbable, must be the truth. » Homo Reptilia has used bio-programming to alter the internal molecular structure of the earth above them, to use it as a weapon against the humans. » Bio-programming is mainly used in engineering and construction, often on jungle planets, in the far future. » Cwmtaff is dotted with patches of blue grass, which contain trace minerals unseen in the UK for nearly 20 million years. » Homo Reptilia is able to erect energy barricades, used to trap their victims or to defend their settlements. » The energy patterns of these barricades cause interference to a TARDIS's circuits. » The minute you pick up a gun, you've lost the argument. » Artist Leonardo da Vinci and scientist Albert Einstein were both dyslexic. » A pulse from the sonic screwdriver, when channelled through a network of communications devices, is enough to incapacitate most things in the universe. » The energy barricades can also block out light. » The sonic screwdriver doesn't do wood. » Homo Reptilia has a deadly venom, which they deliver to their prey via glands in their long, forked tongues. » These venom glands take 24 hours to recharge. » Homo Reptilia are cold blooded. » Homo Reptilia transport discs ride on geothermal currents rising from deep beneath the Earth. » Homo Reptilian systems interpreted the drilling project as an attack on the oxygen pockets above their settlement; the systems revived the hibernating warrior class to defend the settlement. » Homo Reptilia inhabited the Earth before humans evolved. » Any humans brought into the Homo Reptilian settlement are decontaminated, removing any bacteria and viruses which could be harmful. **Cold Blood** Amy is a nifty pickpocket. » Homo Reptilian cities contain their own internal eco-system, able to process carbon dioxide and provide food for their residents. » Homo Reptilian weapons can be set to release a gas that knocks targets unconscious. » Homo Reptilian venom poisons the victim's blood. » The leaders of each class within the Homo Reptilian tribes are considered of equal rank. » Restac is the leader of the military class, Malokeh the leader of the scientific class. » The Doctor has two hearts, and the human bacteria in his system help to keep him alive and healthy. » Hibernating Homo Reptilia are kept in pods lining the city's corridors, and also in vast caverns, where greater numbers can be housed. » Homo Reptilia entered hibernation when their astronomers predicted that a huge astral body was going to crash into the Earth; in reality, this was simply the Moon moving into its orbit. » The Doctor met another tribe of Homo Reptilia in his past; the humans wiped them out. » Restac is authorised to protect the security of her species while they are in hibernation. » Homo Reptilia is able to send communication signals through more primitive technology. » Rory is so clingy. » Homo Reptilia is led by tribal elder Eldane. » Homo Reptilians used to hunt apes for sport. » The Homo Reptilian transport discs are protected by gravity bubbles when in motion. » Both humans and Homo Reptilia have a genuine claim to Earth. » There are fixed points in time where things must always stay the way they are. » This is not one of them. » Malokeh took specimens of the young of various Earth creatures and slowed down their rate of ageing to study how they grew and what they needed to survive on the surface. » Malokeh has been carrying out this work for 300 years. » The Doctor rather loves Malokeh. » Homo Reptilian technology is far in advance of humanity's: they have alternative sources of energy, advanced methods of water supply, and advanced medical and construction techniques. » As well as tranquillising gas, Homo Reptilian weapons can also emit powerful death rays. » The sonic screwdriver can incapacitate weaponry by overloading its circuits. » The venom in Tony's blood is mutating him into something new. » The Cwmtaff drill can be destroyed by an energy pulse sent up from the Homo Reptilian settlement via their travel tunnels. » The Homo Reptilian city has a toxic fumigation failsafe in case of biological infection; a warning signal is issued, and all Homo Reptilians must seek shelter in their cryochambers before the settlement is flooded with toxic gas. » After the fumigation, the city enters hibernation for 100,000 years. » The Doctor can reset this timer to 1,000 years; humanity has that long to prepare for a peaceful coexistence between their race and Homo Reptilia. » Homo Reptilian technology is operated by fluid controls. » The TARDIS sickbay can be found by following the stairs up from the control room, turning left, then left again. » Everybody knows what caused the cracks in the universe – but not the Doctor. » Where there's an explosion, there's shrapnel. » Rory is dead. » If Amy forgets Rory, she'll lose him for ever. » Although time travellers usually retain memories of things wiped from time, if the thing is from the time traveller's own history, they can still forget it. » Ten years in the future, Amy decides to revisit sites of her past adventures. » The TARDIS was involved in the explosion that caused the cracks in the universe. **Vincent and the Doctor** In his lifetime, Vincent van Gogh was a commercial disaster. » His paintings are now worth tens of millions of pounds. » The Doctor is being nice to Amy. » Amy has visited Arcadia and the Trojan Gardens with the Doctor. » Vincent was cared for by Doctor Gachet during his mental illness. » Vincent's painting of the church at Auvers shows a sinister face at the window. » He painted the picture at some time between 1 and 3 June 1890. » He took his own life less than 12 months later. » Bow ties are cool. » Vincent spends his evenings at the Café Terrasse. » Vincent pays for his own drinks. » No one ever buys any of Vincent's paintings. » Amy's cute, but the Doctor should keep his big nose out of other people's business. » Vincent is from Holland. » Through the TARDIS's telepathic filter, Dutch accents sound Scottish, and Provençal accents sound like English West Country. » Amy's hair is orange; so is Vincent's. » The monster from the church window is invisible to everyone but Vincent. » The Doctor's visual recognition system was a gift from his two-headed godmother. »Sunflowers are not Vincent's favourite flowers. » The invisible monster is a Krafayis, and he has been separated from his pack of travelling scavengers. » If Vincent is killed by the monster, half the pictures on the wall of the Musée d'Orsay will suddenly disappear. » The Doctor has met Michelangelo ('what a whinger!') and Pablo Picasso ('a ghastly old goat'). » Amy can't breathe any quieter. » The Krafayis is blind. » Vincent doesn't see the night sky quite like anyone else sees it. » The TARDIS console is fitted with dispensers for ketchup and mustard. » Amy's not really the marrying kind. » Every life is a pile of good things and bad things; the good things can't always soften the bad, and the bad things don't necessarily spoil the good. » The Doctor and Amy added to Vincent's pile of good things. **The Lodger** Craig lives at 79A Aickman Road, Colchester, Essex. » Colchester has a Ryman's. » The fifth moon of Sinda Callista does not. » The man who lives at 79B needs help. » There's a patch of rot on the living room ceiling in Craig's flat. » Craig has put an advert in the paper shop window, looking for a new lodger. » Melina is prone to crises. » Craig loves Sophie. » The Doctor is Craig's new lodger. » Craig didn't put his address on the advert. » The Doctor likes sweets. » The Doctor doesn't know why people call him the Doctor. » He also doesn't know why he calls himself the Doctor. » The Doctor is not to be called the Rotmeister. » Craig's friend Mark inherited a ton of money from an uncle he never knew he had. » The psychic paper shows fake NI and NHS numbers for the Doctor, along with a reference from the Archbishop of Canterbury. » Craig and Sophie both work at a call centre. » People never stop blurting out their plans when the Doctor is around. » The Doctor learnt to cook in Paris in the 18th century. » Craig can't see the point of Paris. » The TARDIS is locked in a materialisation loop. » Something at 79B Aickman Road is stopping the ship from landing. » The thing at 79B can detect the use of advanced technology. » The Doctor communicates with Amy via an earpiece which scrambles their conversation, making the technology itself undetectable. » To anyone listening in, the Doctor's conversation sounds like gibberish. » Bow ties are cool. » Ordinary blokes play football, watch telly and go down the pub. » Whatever's happening at 79B causes time distortions, which endanger the TARDIS further. » The thing at 79B doesn't need Craig's help. » The Doctor is good at football, he thinks. » Sophie isn't Craig's mascot. » Nor is she his date. » Sophie has two sets of keys to Craig's flat. » The Doctor is good at football. » The team from the King's Arms is going to annihilate the team from the Crown and Anchor. » Earth screwdrivers have no on switch. » Sophie really wants to work with animals, perhaps at an orang-utan sanctuary. » Craig was offered a job in London, for better pay, but he didn't take it. » Craig can't see the point of London. » Sophie can do anything she wants. » The rot in Craig's living room is poisonous. » The enzyme decay caused by this poison can be reversed with the excitement of tannin molecules, such as you might find in strong tea. » Craig is important. » Mr Lang was one of Craig's best clients. » Craig's boss Michael loves the Doctor. » Sophie has applied to be a volunteer at a wildlife charity. » The Doctor can communicate with cats. » No one ever comes back out of 79B Aickman Road. » The last three days have been the weirdest three days of Craig's life. » The Doctor can share information telepathically by slamming his forehead against another person's. » The Doctor has used non-technological technology of Lammasteen to build a scanner to investigate 79B Aickman Road. » There is a time engine in 79B; the thing in 79B has been luring in innocent people in an attempt to launch the engine, but they have been killed by the process. » There is no upstairs at 79 Aickman Road. » The time engine exists behind a perception filter which gives the impression of a second storey. » The control panel of the time engine is protected by a deadlock seal. » The thing in 79B is actually the holographic emergency crash program; it has been seeking a new pilot. » Human brains aren't strong enough to survive the interface with the engine. » The Doctor's brain is strong enough. » The emergency crash program didn't want Sophie before today, when she finally decided to leave Colchester. » The time engine needs to leave, so it only targets people who also want to leave. » Craig doesn't want to leave Colchester because Sophie is there. » Craig loves Sophie. » Sophie loves Craig, too. » When a time engine enters emergency shutdown, it implodes. » Craig and Sophie have spoiled their friendship, and intend to destroy it completely. » The Doctor will never return to 79 Aickman Road. » The Doctor rocks. » The crack in Amy's wall has followed her to Aickman Road. » The Doctor is a right little matchmaker. » He carries an engagement ring in his jacket pocket. **The Pandorica Opens** River Song is held in Cell 426 of the Stormcage Containment Facility. » The TARDIS can reroute calls through the time vortex. » Time Agents use vortex manipulators to travel through time. » A Calisto Pulse can disarm micro-explosives from up to 20 feet. » Planet One is the oldest planet in the universe; on a diamond cliff-face on the planet, there is written a fifty-foot high message that no one has ever translated. » The message says: 'HELLO SWEETIE', along with a string of coordinates in Old High Gallifreyan. » The coordinates are for Salisbury Plain, England in AD102. » The Roman invasion of Britain was Amy's favourite topic at school. » *The Pandorica Opens* is an unknown painting by Vincent van Gogh, depicting the TARDIS exploding. » The Pandorica is a prison, built to contain the most feared creature in all the universe. » It is also a fairy tale. » Stonehenge was built thousands of years before the Roman invasion. » Discharge from energy weapons leaves traces of fry particles in the air. » There is an underhenge beneath Stonehenge. » The Pandorica is more than a fairy tale. » The separate parts of a Cyberman can operate without being connected to a whole body. » The story of Pandora's Box was Amy's favourite book when she was a child. » Anyone can break into a prison. » Something is unlocking the Pandorica from the inside. » The Pandorica is kept sealed with many security systems, including deadlocks, time-stops and matter-lines. » Stonehenge is actually a transmitter, built to send a warning signal through all time and space: the Pandorica is opening. » The alien races converging on Stonehenge include the Daleks, the Cybermen, the Sontarans, the Terileptils, the Slitheen, the Chelonians, the Nestene, the Drahvins, the Sycorax, the Haemo-Goths, the Zygons, the Atraxi and the Draconians. » Whoever takes the Pandorica takes the universe. » The Romans are the greatest military machine in the history of the universe. » The Pandorica also contains force-field technology. » There are fruitflies on Hoppledom 6 who live for 20 minutes. » They don't even mate for life. » Amy feels something when she holds the engagement ring. » Nothing is ever forgotten, not completely. » And if something can be remembered, it can come back. » The Doctor asked Amy to travel with him for a reason. » Amy's house is too big, with too many empty rooms. » Amy's life doesn't make sense. » The Cybermen have weapons built into their arms. » The separate parts of a Cyberman can seek out new organic beings for harvesting. » The heads of Cybermen are fitted with anaesthetic darts. » Rory was erased from time, but he's better now. » After he fell through the crack in the Homo Reptilian city, Rory awoke as a Roman, with all the memories of a Roman. » Structures hold psychic residue; this residue is sometimes interpreted as ghosts. » The TARDIS exploding is what causes the cracks in the universe. » If there is no one inside the TARDIS, the ship's engines shut down automatically. » The Romans are actually plastic duplicates, controlled by the Nestene Consciousness. » The Pandorica is ready. » It is known the Doctor cannot die. » The Doctor is the greatest warrior of all. » The Pandorica is a trap for the Doctor. » In the event of a Total Event Collapse, all the stars in the universe will go supernova throughout every moment in time. » The Universe has ended. **The Big Bang** There's a crack in Amy's wall, and everywhere in time and space. » The stars have gone. » Richard Dawkins is involved with the Star Cults. » The Anomaly Exhibition at the Natural History Museum features Nile Penguins, stone Daleks and the Pandorica. » Amelia never could resist a 'Keep Out' sign. » When the same item from two different points in its time stream touches itself, there is a massive discharge of temporal energy. » The whole history of the universe was unwritten in the Total Event Collapse. » Rory isn't Rory, he's a Nestene duplicate programmed to believe he's Rory. » The Doctor can leave telepathic messages in an unconscious person's brain. » The Pandorica won't let its occupant die, holding them in a stasis-lock. » It can restore its occupant to full health if it receives a scan of the correct, living DNA. » During its lifetime, the Pandorica was removed from the underhenge, taken to Rome, stolen by the Goths, sold by Marco Polo and found at the bottom of the Aegean Sea. » Vortex manipulators are a rubbish way to time travel. » Plastic Rory does not age. » Nestene plastic can be damaged by heat and radio signals. » Rory guarded the Pandorica for 2,000 years, meeting the Roman Emperor Hadrian twice, and befriending Isaac Newton and Samuel Pepys. The last recording sighting of Rory was during the London blitz in 1941. » Stone Daleks are cool. » You can do loads in 12 minutes, such as sucking a mint or buying a sledge. » An exploding TARDIS looks like a sun. » River Song once dated a Nestene duplicate. » Fezzes are cool. » The light inside the Pandorica is actually a restoration field, able to 'repair' anything it shines upon. » In theory, you could extrapolate the entire universe from the information contained in a single atom. » The Pandorica contains a memory of the universe, and the restoration field transmits that memory. » The universe can be rebuilt from the atoms caught within the Pandorica, but it will require a source of infinite energy to do so. » An Alpha-Mezon burst through the eyestalk of a weakened Dalek is enough to destroy it. » The exploding TARDIS contains enough energy to kick-start the rebuilding of the universe; the explosion also reaches through all of time and space, and so is able to transmit the memory of the universe to every corner of existence. » The Doctor must fly the Pandorica to the heart of the explosion. » If the Doctor is aboard the Pandorica when the cracks in time are sealed, he will be lost for ever. » Nothing is ever forgotten. » The Doctor and Amy visited Space Florida. » When she was 7, the Doctor told the sleeping Amelia a fairy tale about himself and Amy. » Amy's mother is called Tabetha, and her father is Augustus. » Augustus will be the death of Tabetha – unless she strikes pre-emptively. » There's someone missing. » Amy remembers the Doctor. » The TARDIS is old, new, borrowed and blue. » Rory's not Mr Pond. » Except he is. » Bow ties are cool. » The Doctor is going to find out who River is very soon – and that's when everything will change. » Space and time isn't safe yet. » The Silence is still out there. » An Egyptian goddess has broken free of the Seventh Obelisk and is now loose on the Orient Express. In Space. » This is goodbye.

THE BRILLIANT BOOK 2011

WAS EDITED BY **CLAYTON HICKMAN** AND DESIGNED BY **PAUL LANG**

IT WAS WRITTEN BY **BRIAN ALDISS**, **JASON ARNOPP**, **DAVID BAILEY**, **BENJAMIN COOK**, **MARK GATISS**, **MURRAY GOLD**, **CLAYTON HICKMAN**, **DAVID LLEWELLYN**, **STEVEN MOFFAT**, **NICHOLAS PEGG**, **GARETH ROBERTS**, **DARREN SCOTT** AND **OLI SMITH**

AND WAS ILLUSTRATED BY **LEE BINDING**, **ANTHONY DRY**, **MARTIN GERAGHTY**, **LEE JOHNSON**, **BEN MORRIS** AND **BEN WILLSHER**

THIS BOOK WOULD NOT HAVE BEEN POSSIBLE WITHOUT THE HELP OF **CHRIS CHIBNALL**, **RICHARD CURTIS**, **ARTHUR DARVILL**, **KAREN GILLAN**, **NEILL GORTON**, **BARRY JONES**, **DAVY JONES**, **DAVID JØRGENSEN**, **ALEX KINGSTON**, **PETER McKINSTRY**, **STEVEN MOFFAT**, **KERRY MONIGHAN**, **LUKE MORRISON**, **SIMON NYE**, **GARY RUSSELL**, **MATT SMITH**, **JUSTIN RICHARDS**, **EDWARD RUSSELL**, **TOM SPILSBURY**, **EDWARD THOMAS**, **ALEX THOMPSON**, **STEVE TRIBE**, **DAVE TURBITT**, **KATE WALSH**, **ASHLEY WAY**, **PIERS WENGER**, **TOBY WHITHOUSE** AND **BETH WILLIS**

1 3 5 7 9 10 8 6 4 2

Published in 2010 by BBC Books, an imprint of Ebury Publishing.
A Random House Group Company

Doctor Who is a BBC Wales production for BBC One
Executive producers: Steven Moffat, Piers Wenger and Beth Willis

Daleks created by Terry Nation. Cybermen created by Kit Pedler and Gerry Davis. Silurians created by Malcolm Hulke. Sontarans created by Robert Holmes.

The Random House Group Limited Reg. No. 954009

Addresses for companies within the Random House group can be found at *www.randomhouse.co.uk*

A CIP catalogue record for this book is available from the British Library.

ISBN 978 1 846 07991 7

To buy books by your favourite authors and register for offers, visit *www.rbooks.co.uk*

Commissioning editor: Albert DePetrillo
Project editor: Steve Tribe
Production: Phil Spencer
Editorial Manager: Nicholas Payne

Printed and bound in Germany by Mohn Media GmbH

BBC Books would like to thank the following for providing photographs and for permission to reproduce copyright material. While every effort has been made to trace and acknowledge all copyright holders, we would like to apologise should there have been any errors or omissions.

All images copyright © BBC, except:
pages 38-39 courtesy Murray Gold and David Bailey
page 50 (top right) © Joey Boylan/istockphoto.com
page 51 (right) courtesy Oli Smith
page 90-91 (background) © Nic Taylor/istockphoto.com
pages 92-95 courtesy Clayton Hickman and Rex Duis
pages 96-97 courtesy Clayton Hickman, Tom McMillen, Paul Metcalfe, Dylan Keightley, Melina Pena, Emma Price and Chris Gould
page 118 (top) © Hulton Archive/istockphoto.com
pages 84, 85, 87 courtesy Millennium FX
page 86 courtesy Davy Jones

Doctor Who series photography by Adrian Rogers.

All production designs reproduced courtesy of the *Doctor Who* Art Department.

Thanks to *Doctor Who Magazine* and *Doctor Who Adventures* for additional images and artwork.

Original illustrations:
cover and pages 15, 23, 31, 45, 53, 61, 73, 79, 89, 97, 109, 115 – Lee Johnson
pages 17, 24-25, 50-51, 116, 126-127 – Ben Morris
pages 32-34, 117 – Lee Binding
page 35 – Peter McKinstry
pages 41, 42, 100, 102 – Martin Geraghty
pages 80-81 – Anthony Dry
pages 118-119 – Ben Willsher